John Hope

Thoughts

In Prose and Verse

John Hope

Thoughts
In Prose and Verse

ISBN/EAN: 9783744689427

Printed in Europe, USA, Canada, Australia, Japan

Cover: Foto ©Thomas Meinert / pixelio.de

More available books at **www.hansebooks.com**

In PROSE and VERSE,

STARTED,

IN HIS WALKS,

BY

JOHN HOPE.

Together let us beat this ample Field,
Try what the Open, what the Covert yield;
The latent Tracts, the giddy Heights, explore,
Of all who blindly creep, or sightless soar;
Eye Nature's Walks, shoot Folly as it flies,
And catch the Manners, living, as they rise.
     POPE's Essay on Man.

STOCKTON:

Printed by R. CHRISTOPHER: And sold at LONDON by W. Goldsmith, Pater-noster-row; Richardson and Urquhart, Royal Exchange; John Donaldson, No. 188, Strand; and T. Durham, Charing Cross. 1780.

To the OFFICERS of the Northamptonshire Militia.

My Lords and Gentlemen,

I HAVE received infinite pleasure in your company, without making any Return for it. I have frequently enjoy'd your Discourse, without contributing one word to the conversation.---- To many friends, indeed, my natural taciturnity lays me under equal obligation; but, if there be any entertainment in this Book, it ought particularly to be presented to You; for the Thoughts,
contained

contained in it, were mostly started in my agreeable Walks in your County.---Where the Game is sprung, some acknowledgment is due to the Lord of the Manour.

I am, with sincerity,

My Lords and Gentlemen,

Your much obliged and

most affectionate Wellwisher,

JOHN HOPE.

The PREFACE.

WHEN we recollect the number of distinguished Persons, of both Sexes, who have, within these few years, published their names with their Writings;—and when we call to mind the many Societies lately instituted for our improvement in eloquence;—we may safely pronounce, this is particularly the Age, in which "our Pride in Reasoning, not in Acting, lies," and that Timidity cannot be termed one of our most fashionable Defects. Be That as it may, the character of an Author has certainly gained a consideration, of late, that makes one no longer ashamed of it. There was formerly connected with it an idea of Poverty, of which it seems now to be stript.—But though a man may not be ashamed of being called a *good* Author, he would not, unnecessarily, hazard the acquiring the reputation of a bad one. I must therefore declare, that I did not determine to put my name to this Book, until I read in the Parliamentary Debates, that, of the thirty-three Scotch Members, who were present in the House of Commons, when Mr. Dunning's motion was put to the Vote, "that the Influence of the Crown has encreased, is encreasing, and ought to be diminished,"—twenty eight of them voted against it. As one who had once the honour of sitting in that House,

House, I now willingly risk the acquiring the name of a bad Author, that I may encrease the small number of constitutional Scotsmen.

I am aware that, by so doing, I shall have a charge of *Imprudence* fully exhibited against me; but this is no time when any friend to freedom should be hid. The Voice of no one Individual can save the State; but the collective body is composed of Individuals; and the People, at this conjuncture, should know on whom they may safely depend.——Respecting what I have said of the twenty-eight Gentlemen mentioned above, I mean not either to depreciate their private characters, or to arrogate any praise to myself. I firmly believe, that our difference, in political Sentiments, proceeds entirely from the different educations we have received in our youth. I was early used to the Customs of a Republic, and I have since looked a little into the Laws of England, to which I give the preference, in many respects. They, on the contrary, have chiefly studied the imperial Law, and have been educated in a country, where it is regarded as a kind of Treason to speak of the measures of Government with the smallest contempt. I know, too, it is the opinion of many well-meaning men, that, as the people have lost their virtue, the hands of Government must be strengthened, to preserve peace and order in the State. But, unfortunately, some of these men have seen little but the Luxury and Dissipation of a metropolis; nor do they seem to know more of the morals of their Countrymen, than what they may have learnt at St. James's, or the Court of King's-Bench. The late Petitions, however, should teach them, that much virtue still remains with the People, though it be not so common within the precincts of a Court.——There is another argument

argument commonly used with Gentlemen in Parliament, to prevail on them to give their friends, at any time, a Vote:—" Can your *single* Vote, it is said, be of any benefit to your Country?—Or, if it be in danger, can it save the sinking State? Why, then, hurt yourself and your family, by incurring the displeasure of Government, in opposing the Motion that is made?"—This may indeed, quiet the conscience of some Casuist? but will it exculpate him before his God? or even in any criminal Court?—I would ask the Lord Chief Justice of England himself, (for the Case cannot be brought into the *Chancellor's* Court,) whether, if a Person were found murdered by a gang of Ruffians, his Lordship would not pronounce every man to be *guilty*, who had given the Deceased but a single Stab?—Or would his Lordship humanely recommend it to the Jury, to bring in their Verdict *Chance-medley;* because, forsooth! it could not be proved against any one particular man, that he gave a *mortal* wound, and the Deceased died only from a Loss of Blood.

But let the Influence of the Crown prevail in Parliament; let King, Lords, and Commons against the People unite; let the Machinations of the Cabinet be never so tyrannical,—Despotism will prove impotent, without Instruments wherewith to execute its Plans. Now, these (as the American War has shewn us) cannot, among Britons, very easily, be found. The Promoters of that War, among other things, certainly forgot, that all generosity and love of freedom must be banished the breast of a British Soldier, before he will oppress his fellow-citizen. They forgot, too, that War has now lost, among Christians, the barbarity and fierceness formerly inspired by bigotry and fanaticism. An Army used formerly to

A   subdue

conquer a whole Country and keep it in Subjection by the terrors of fire and sword. The Inhabitants, left behind it in its march, were intimidated from revolting, by the frequent exemplary Massacres that were made. But, now, no country can be effectually subdued, unless you can garrison it; for the Conquered are ever ready to rise again in the absence of their Oppressors, while military executions against Insurgents are no longer practised;—the Spirit of freedom, among the people, has encreased, in proportion as cruelty and rapine have been discountenanced in the art of war. Though the Americans were every where hostile, some of our bravest Generals, *Howe*, *Grey* and *Erskine* disdained to injure any, but them who had arms in their hands. General Burgoyne too declares, that, by the violent Proclamation which he published, he meaned only to intimidate; and that he never had an idea of putting the unarm'd to the Sword, or of setting fire to the Houses of the helpless Inhabitants.—That Humanity can dwell in the breast of a Soldier, will hardly be credited by barbarous and tyrannical Statesmen; yet, more humane is even the Executioner, than the *Judge* by whom the *Innocent* are, coolly, condemned.

At this place, I thought to have finished my politics; but, in the parliamentary Phrase, now that I am upon my Legs, (and some of my Readers will think them sufficiently long) I cannot help taking notice of two opposite extremes, into which my Countrymen have frequently run.—When once we are engaged in a War, nothing is thought of but War, as if we should never have Peace again. On the contrary, when we are at Peace, our Seamen are dismissed, and our Ships are left to rot in the Harbours, as if we never more should have an enemy on the

the ocean. The French and Spaniards have acted in a far different manner; and if example cannot teach us wisdom, Adversity surely can. Let us, therefore, in future, keep our Fleet in repair, and be careful to support a stronger standing body of Seamen. All the Powers of Europe, now, perceive the utility of preserving the balance of Power in the empire of the Sea, as well as in the Dominions on land. For that purpose, a confederacy seems to be forming, if we may judge from the Memorial lately presented from the Empress of Russia to the States-General of the United Provinces; and the meaning of it, in plain English, is, that they all intend to come in for a share of the North-American Trade, even against our Will.—As then, "Le Jeu ne vaut plus la Chandelle," let us, in God's name, leave the Americans to act for themselves.—Our sly neighbours the Dutch, have, in this business, imitated the sagacity of the little Terrier-Dog, mentioned in page 47 of my Thoughts. Our surly English Bull-Dog fell on them, last year, in a manner which they could not then properly resent;—" maar ik zal het U wel betaalen;" but I will be revenged on you, says Pug; then, away he trots to the great Russian Bear, and entreats of him to take up the quarrel for him, and make a common Cause of it.—The Bear, again, improves upon my Staffordshire Mastiff, and brings along with him two or three little vindictive Curs;—so that, among them all, our noble British Bull-Dog runs the risk of being worried, if he should only happen to growl.—We venture, however, to publish a *growling* Proclamation. " Ay! but, says the Dutch Pug, I am a match for you now, my Lad. I have got two or three good friends, here, at my back; and as you dare not *bite*, you may shew me your blunted teeth, you surly Dog, as much as you will. I shall gain as much, by the American Beaver, in one year, as ever I got by you in my whole life; so that, I value your friendship not a single pin."—'Tis a melancholy consideration, when we *seriously* reflect, how we are fallen from that glorious State, in which the British Navy, last War, was able to have stood against all the Fleets of Europe combined.—But as the present first Lord of the Admiralty is confessedly a man of business, we can impute to *him* no farther blame, than as he may prove himself to be one of an infatuated, unfortunate, and dim-sighted *Cabal*.

Although I cannot clear myself of the charge of Imprudence, in putting my name here to several political Truths; nor yet of Self-importance, in supposing the example can be of any use; my Readers will find, (in pages 7, 187 and 188,) that I have entered my protest against the imputation of Vanity and Self-conceit.—Some apology, too, should be made for the desultory manner in which I commonly write. My health not permitting me to sit, for any long continuance, with my breast at the desk, I can never undertake, in prose, any thing of a regular Dissertation; and as to my Rhimes, (or, as my Printer has been pleased to call them, my miscellaneous Poetry,) I could never sit down, with the Pen in my hand, to compose one Couplet; they are all the productions of my solitary Walks.—My Readers will soon perceive, my Language is not studied, and that I deal not in sesquipedalian words. I hope too, that, in my Expressions, I have seldom occasion to explain myself. I recollect but one Couplet, in my Rhimes, where I am apprehensive of being misunderstood:

"But

"But still a *murmur*, from the neighb'ring Shore,
Disturb'd the Ear with harsh resounding *Roar*."
(Page 276.)

sounds a little uncouth; for a *Murmur* cannot, at the same time, be termed a *Roar;* unless it be granted me, that the noise of the Sea, on the subsiding of a Storm, may be *comparatively* called *a murmur of the Sea;* although, when conveyed to the Ear, it may still be denominated *a Roar*. Contrariwise, I conceive that the roaring of the Sea, at a great distance, may be called only a murmur to the Ear; on the propriety of which the Critics will best decide.—— I have, however, the opinion of one good Writer on my side; I mean, of William Falconer, Author of the *Shipwreck*. He even commended my Pastoral so far, as to say, there were some Lines in it, (where the Sound is intended to be expressive of the Sense,) which he wished he had composed himself. His friendship may have made him *partial* to *me*, but he had a spirit above *flattering* any man. He wrote part of his Poem under my roof; and, to comprehend his Virtues in a few Words, I knew him to be " an *honest Man*, the noblest Work of God!"—His excellence as a Poet is sufficiently known; but I can attest what may not be so certain to every one, (altho' he alludes to it in the exordium of his Shipwreck,) that he had received but a short grammar-school Education, and that his Youth had been passed in a sea-faring life. Yet, the Enthusiasm of the Bard, which he fully possessed, surmounted every obstacle to writing, and produced us a Poem by few modern Poems surpassed. He took his Passage, a few years ago, for the East-Indies, on board of the *Aurora* Frigate, in which, it is believed, he suffered a *real*
Shipwreck;

Shipwreck;—*fatal* too, 'tis feared:—for he has not been heard of more!—So much, at least, is due to the memory of a departed Friend!

If my Book should not meet with a ready Sale, I have, to those of the Critics, two reasons to add, which will save my Vanity some little pain. The *first* is, that my Printer could not provide me with as good paper as I wished for, without my waiting a longer time, for it, than I meaned to remain at Stockton. The *second* deserves to be generally known:—there is in London a certain combination of Booksellers who discourage every thing that comes from a *country* Press, and would willingly make a monopoly of their Own. But though I would always shew a proper respect to *polite* company, by introducing myself to them in my *best Suit*, I am never displeased at obtruding myself on a parcel of purse-proud Fellows, with my *rusty Coat* on.

I have, in my Preface, made use of the freedom, with which an Author is commonly indulged, of saying a great deal concerning myself, and my Writings. I must, however, beg pardon of the Public; for being so much of the egotist in the body of my Book. My Readers, *unknown*, will be so kind as to suppose, that it is the *Leveller, An Advocate in the Cause of the People*, or any *other* person than myself, who is writing; for most of these Miscellanies have already been well received, under such fictitious Names. And my Readers, who know me, are desired to figure to themselves, their old acquaintance seated beside them, in his easy Chair, and thence familiarly relating what he thought of in the Fields.

April 24*th*, 1780.

CONTENTS

CONTENTS.

The Leveller's Cursory Thoughts   page   1
The Leveller, No. I. His Introductory Paper   49
———— No. II. On Pride, with rules for polite behaviour ———— 53
———— No. III. On Patriotism ———— 62
———— No. IV. On Horsemanship ———— 65
———— No. V. On Painting ———— 70
———— No. VI. On Architecture ———— 79
———— No. VII. On the same ———— 85
———— No. VIII. On Love ———— 90
———— No. IX. On the same ———— 100
———— No. X. His Defence of Laughter, against Lord Chesterfield's unwarrantable attack   105
———— No. XI. An Essay on the Nature and Mutability of Stilts   115
———— No. XII. Another Essay on the same   124
———— No. XIII. A short Dissertation on Masks   134
———— No. XIV. Another Dissertation on Masks   144
———— No. XV. His Answer to Scrutator's Remarks on his last Leveller ———— 151
———— No. XVI. Some Thoughts on Music and Dancing ———— 161
———— No. XVII. Addressed to the Officers of the Militia, on that part of our national defence   168
———— No. XVIII. His Salutiferous Creed   179
———— No. XIX. Continuation of it   187
———— No. XX. Conclusion of it ———— 196
———— No. XXI. His Speech to the Benches in both Houses of Parliament ———— 205
Letters on Credit ———— ———— page 214
Supplement to the Leveller's Cursory Thoughts   311
Letters on the Custom of impressing Seamen, with *Junius*'s Letter to the Author on the same Subject ———— 317

Three Letters from a Merchant in London to his Friend at Amsterdam; containing a Sketch of British Politics in the year 1779 — — — 336

MISCELLANEOUS POETRY.

An Epistle to Dr. ******, on his changing the Fashion of his Wig — — — 247
An Epistle concerning Tatlers;—especially those in a country Town — — — 250
The Disconsolate Widow — — 253
A Broil, between some Men offended, That was *begun*, but never *ended* — 258
The Provoked Steed — — 263
Lines with the Present of a Nosegay — 266
Lines with the Present of a Pocket-book, &c. 267
Lines written on the Canvas of a half-finish'd Portrait of Mrs. Crewe — — — 267
An Answer to Eliza's Choice of a Husband, &c. 268
Maria's Epitaph — — 270
Elegy on the Death of a Turtle-dove — 271
A Consolatory Elegy on the Death of another 272
Verses sent to a Lady with the Present of a Landskip-drawing 274
A Northern Pastoral, on the Death of the Earl and Countess of Sutherland — — 275
An Epitaph for Michael Uttely of Enfield — 282
On the Death of Mr. Sterne — — 282
Epitaph for an old Servant at Hopetoun-house 283
In Memory of Robert Cox, Town-crier of Northampton 283
An Occasional Prologue, spoken at the Opening of a country Theatre — — — 285
A Prologue, spoken at the Rehearsal of some favourite Passages from our most celebrated English Authors 286
An Occasional Prologue to the Mourning Bride 288
The Sailors and the Stone Images; a Parable — 289
Contentment within the common Reach — 290
The New Brighthelmstone Directory — 293

THE

THE LEVELLER's CURSORY THOUGHTS.

THE man who speaks to a private company, has considerably the advantage of the Author who addresses the Public in writing. The former has it generally in his option to fit his discourse to the temper, capacity, age, profession, and sex of his hearers; but the *latter* must deliver his sentiments to readers in very different predicaments; many of whom will be too dull to comprehend him, and many, though sensible, will dissent from his opinions. In the reception of any *humorous* story, the *Author's* success is particularly doubtful. A merry tale, that would convulse the Physician with laughter, will perhaps cause the Divine to bless himself at the Writer's nonsense; a jest for which the Merchant would give one credit, will make the Lawyer gravely demur at the first reading; what would pass for a damn'd good joke in the Camp, would be sunk to perdition in the Navy; and a
smart

smart thing pointed at a Young Lady, would be accounted both stale and infipid in a Circle of Old Tabbies.——But the moſt difficult thing which an Author has to encounter is, the *accidental humour* of his Readers: for, as *Sterne* obſerves, a man, to be able to reliſh a merry ſtory, muſt bring half the entertainment along with him.

STERNE's maxim, That a man muſt bring half the entertainment along with him, is applicable to *every* amuſement. There are times of low ſpirits, when the beſt poetry and the beſt muſic are thrown away upon me. In ſuch moods, I frequent neither Concert, Ball, Opera, nor Play; but I take a ramble in the fields, or ſtay at home, and ſhew my dull face to nobody. The ſhunning one's acquaintances, in ſuch fits of deſpondency, ought not too haſtily to be attributed either to Pride or Diſaffection; for when one cannot reliſh the mirth of his friends, 'tis but civil not to ſpoil it with his gravity.

I WOULD not condemn any man's underſtanding, either by the teſtimony of defects in his writings, or a default and heſitation in his ſpeech. If I ſaw an incorrect, immethodical compoſition, I ſhould wiſh to know, before I paſſed ſentence on the author, whether his ideas did not crowd ſo faſt upon him, that it was with the greateſt difficulty he could arrange his thoughts. If I heard another man make a confuſed, incoherent ſpeech, I ſhould alſo like to know, before I pronounced him wrong-headed, whether

ther he cannot make himself, in writing, be perfectly well understood. One whose invention is dull, who is slow in recollection, or at a loss for words, may write sensibly enough, although, from all, or any of these causes, he should cut a despicable figure in discourse; for, while he is writing one sentence, the next will occur to him; or, if he should find himself reduced to hum and ha, and scratch his pate, he may sit at his leisure till a thought starts, or till he has recollected some word that he is in want of. There being no witnesses to his distress, he can boldly write that, which, from the want of a facility in expression, he would never have dared to speak. Mr. Addison's difficulty of utterance is known to every one who has read his life; and whoever has been in company with the late David Hume, will grant it me, that he was not very fluent in his speech; yet no writers were more ready at their pen, or shewed, in their productions, a greater command of words. To them we may add Mr. Soame Jenyns, an excellent writer! but one who is not much given to speak.—I remember being in company with Dr. Robertson, when it was known that he was employed in writing his History of Charles the Fifth. One of his friends took the liberty of asking him when it would be published. "I really cannot tell you, said the Doctor; but if (added he, with all the modesty of good sense) I were as quick at my pen as my friend David Hume is, I could be able to promise when my book would be ready for the press. For David can sit down to write, at stated hours of the day, as regularly as a merchant's clerk; and he is so correct in his language, and so methodical in the arrangement of his thoughts, that the fifth and sixth volumes of his History of England, which are no way inferior to the rest, went to the press in the original and only copy of them which he wrote."—Dr. Robertson, however, is one of those few people who can, with equal facility and correctness, either write or speak; and besides him I recollect none other, who have lately distinguished themselves as public writers, excepting my Lord Chesterfield, the late Lord Lyttelton, and Mr. Edmund Burke. Innumerable are the Orators, both in the Senate and at the Bar, who are known to make but contemptible scribes. When, therefore, I hear of any one that speaks much, it is no proof with me that he has more sense or learning than the silent man; but only that his imagination is more lively, and that he has a greater command of words. Nor would I be willing to pronounce a man void of understanding, even tho' he could not, either by speaking or writing, perfectly express his thoughts; for, though Mr. Locke somewhere says, that a man cannot think without thinking in words, I am sensible I can have an idea, and at the same time be at a loss for a word by which to express myself. If, then, *that* can happen at all to me, why may it not frequently happen to any body else? Or, shall we say, that a child has no ideas till he acquire his speech; and that a man, who has been deaf and dumb from his birth, has no reflections of his own for want of words?——Charles the Twelfth of Sweden, was a monarch so little endowed with speech, that he was accounted almost an idiot before he commenced the great actions of his life. Cromwell, too, was most incoherent in the delivery of his words; nor have we ever heard, that what he wrote was either elegant or correct. Yet every one will allow, that both these great men shewed, on many occasions, an uncommon presence of mind, and a surprising depth of thought.

SINCE,

SINCE, with man, the want of words, nor even the total deprivation of speech, does not imply a default of sense, why should we deny all reason to the dumb brutes? We are certain that the understanding of many of them can be improved, though they cannot go beyond the limits by nature prescribed; but to alledge, that, because they cannot go beyond that pitch, they have no reason at all, is as much as to say, every man is an ideot, whose judgment is not as perfect as that of a Mansfield, a Camden, or a Burke. And if the gift of speech is to be the test of reason, and my poor dog is to be allowed no reflections of his own, until he shall have the talent of communicating his ideas in words; then must his master be reckoned a fool, until he be as great an Orator as any of the great men mentioned above; which is not yet demonstrated, and which I am very unwilling to grant.—A friend of mine has two dogs; the one named *Toby*, the other *Omiah*. The *first*, I sometimes figure to myself to be an Englishman; the *last*, a native of Otaheite. They have no common language by which they can make themselves to each other understood; but they have *signs* and *looks*, which, as they reciprocally give, they seemingly comprehend; and which, by custom, I can very well understand myself. They also improve by *imitation*. If they are not capable of greater improvement, it is because they have not the faculty of speech. Heaven, by denying them that, hath placed them far beneath mankind; yet are they much above others in the scale of created beings upon earth.

NOTHING

NOTHING is more common in mixed companies, than to see men of a ready utterance, gain the afcendant over thofe of better underftanding, though of few words; and, with puns, quibbles, and fatirical ftrokes, pafs among the fhallow thinkers for men of real wit.—It happens in converfation, as in the tranfactions of a bufy life: as a man of cunning, who regards neither juftice nor honefty, will, in many cafes, outwit the man of wifdom, whofe principles allow him not to deviate from the rule of right; fo will a wag, who pays no attention to the laws of good-nature, frequently outfhine the confiderate wit, who will fupprefs many a good thought, through fear of hurting or giving his neighbour offence. But the firft will cut and thruft at friend or foe, wherever he fees an opening; and provided he can fhew his dexterity, will give little heed what object he happens to hit. The beft method of dealing with thefe practitioners in the cut-and-thruft, is, to keep yourfelf entirely on the defenfive, till, by fome unlucky ftroke, they throw themfelves off their guard; if you will then aim a blow at them that perhaps will lay the fcull open, and expofe its contents; or if you will make a thruft, which, if they are not callous, will pierce them to the heart, they will fall moft abject at your feet, and will feldom have the courage to renew the attack upon fuch a dangerous foe. Such wits I look upon as far inferior to a thrumber of wire, or a fcraper of catgut, who can tickle my ear without doing mifchief to any one. But when I meet with a man of learning and underftanding that is communicative, I court his friendfhip; and I liften to him to him with so much the more pleasure, as I can acquire knowledge from him, without impairing my sight by the reading of books.

I AM no enemy to a Pun, provided it have some pretensions to Wit, and be not a mere Play upon Words.—A Gentleman of some Consequence in *Canada*, did me once the honour of a visit of Congé, on his return to that Country.—He observed a *Pitchfork*, as I call it, (which Mrs. H. made use of to tune her Mandoline) lying on the parlour-table. It was then a new invention; and, on enquiring the use of it, he could not help expressing a desire to have one to carry with him to Canada. Mrs. H. immediately desired he would accept of *that*, and keep it in remembrance of her. He received it with a respectful bow, and gallantly exclaimed: "Madame va donner le *Ton* à l'Amerique."

THE timidity which men often shew in delivering their sentiments in speaking, and the repugnance which some authors feel to submit their writings to a public perusal, proceed not always from modesty, nor from a diffidence of their own judgment. With an inward conviction of his own merit, a man may dread censure; though seemingly humble, he may, in fact, through vanity, tremble under the apprehension of losing applause. This remark I once made, when I had not leisure to inlarge upon it. But now, to pursue the thought a little farther:—I honestly confess, that I make no scruple of shewing
my

my insignificant productions to any of my old acquaintances; nor do I in the least hesitate in delivering my opinion in private to them; because I imagine they must already have fathomed my capacity, and found whether it was extensive or narrow. But I never could get over that tremor, which affects me on making any public oration; because I am unwilling to discover my ignorance to strangers, nor do I like to expose my folly unnecessarily among people, who, if I had remained silent, might have mistaken me for a man of a better understanding. As little should I choose to put my name, without necessity, to any Literary Publication; because *that* would also subject me to the censure of strangers; and it would have the appearance, too, of my being perfectly well pleased with my own compositions. This is far from being the case, however; for, though I would never put pen to paper, if I did not amuse myself by my writings, I have seldom been satisfied, but rather wished to express myself in a better manner. At the same time that I am so bashful, with regard to the public exhibition of any thing that hazards the exposing of my understanding, I have not the least dread on me in performing any of the exercises which I learnt at the Academy. I can dance a minuet with the utmost unconcern, before the most genteel assembly; I can scrape a fiddle, with perfect facility, before the most numerous audience, provided always they be previously acquainted that I am no professed musician; I have rode in the manège, and practised in the fencing-school, without any tremor upon me, before the most beautiful female spectators; and I never made a difficulty of shewing, to any body, the wretched productions of my pencil. All this I do, because I dare. I consider it as a matter of indifference, tended, whether I excel or not in any of these exercises. They are not *mental* accomplishments. They are things which a gentleman may learn for their private utility, or merely for his own amusement. Whether he knows them or not, I esteem him neither the better nor the worse man for it. If, on the contrary, he learns them with a view of *shining* in public, it will cost him infinite labour to arrive at the requisite perfection; and, after all his trouble, the anxiety about gaining applause will not, perhaps, allow him to perform with that ease which is necessary in a graceful execution.

IT is astonishing to me, how many sensible Readers suffer their opinion of books to be guided by the judgment of others. I have known several learned men who never dared acknowledge they were pleased with a new publication, till they had first seen the sentence passed on it by the Gentlemen Reviewers. So far as *their censure* goes, it must be allowed they acquit themselves in a most masterly and judicious manner; but their *praises*, at other times, are so partially good-natured, that I would not always bestow my money at their friendly recommendation. —'Tis easy to find defects in the best compositions; and a defect being once exposed (unless some beauties of the same book be also given) it may damn the author of it as a bad writer for ever. It cannot, on the other hand, be an execrable performance in which nothing is found that is worthy of commendation. If, then, we get but one good extract from it, the Gentlemen Reviewers, by suppressing the rest, and giving a doubtful opinion on the subject, may easily

favour

favour their friend the publisher. I do not, therefore, trust to them entirely.—Concerning books of great value, I wait for the opinion of the public; and in small-priced publications, I sometimes venture to purchase, even contrary to the verdict of a critical Jury. If there is any thing *good* in a book, I am, like *Moliere*'s Housekeeper, struck with it immediately. Heaven has given me a taste and feelings, to which I owe great enjoyment in the reading of Poetry, and particularly of dramatic pieces.—I was once, in a special manner, diverted with a friend of mine, who had read to me Mr. Goldsmith's Comedy, *She Stoops to Conquer*, when it was first published. He was highly delighted with it, and laughed at the reading of it as heartily as I did; but unluckily, within a few days after the perusal, a tolerable author and a great dramatic critic, of his acquaintance, happened to pay him a visit, and deliver his opinion of this new Comedy. I then heard my friend every where running it down as a mere Farce, replete with improbabilities, extravagance, and buffoonery; and when I took the occasion to remind him of the entertainment it afforded us both, when he was so kind as to read it to me:—True, said he, I was certainly diverted, but it was at the *extravagance* of the Author I laughed, not at his wit nor his humour. Come, come, my friend, said I, confess that you was highly entertained with this same *Comedie outree;* and that you never found those faults with it, till you heard the opinion of your friend the Ranter. I have read it twice over, since I saw you, and I can boldly say, it left nothing with *me* in the reading. There are many strokes of genuine humour in it; the incidents are truly comical; there is not a character in it but what I have known in real life; there

is

is not one circumstance beyond probability, excepting that of Tony Lumpkin's carrying his mother rather too long a journey, in bad roads, for the time allowed him to perform it in; and as for the mistaking a gentleman's house for an inn, the thing might happen to any man who had ever travelled the Bath-road, or who, in his rambles, had never been off the post-roads of England.

THE *Republic of Letters* is a common phrase; but, from what I have observed above, there appears to be as much a *Tyranny* of Letters as a *Republic*. Let some great critic send forth his learned edict, and all opinion is borne down before it. To dissent from it, as often implies folly and ignorance, as it is accounted treason to rebel against the King, or heresy at Rome to differ with the Holy Pontiff.

ONE day, as I sat resting myself on a stile, with a field of ripe wheat before me, I imagined a man could not take a better pattern for a genteel bow and a handsome recovery, than from one of the stalks as it bent beneath the breeze that blew upon it. The stalk, or body, first inclined, and the ear, or head, next followed its slow motion. The stalk then gently rose again, and the ear recovered in succession. I sat like a King upon his throne, and I could not help fancying, I saw so many of my loving subjects bowing, with Addresses, before me. When my Readers recollect, that the great Homer himself compares the spears of an army to a field of corn, no less than

C 2 three

three different times in his first Book of the Iliad, they will readily forgive me for one poor simile which I made on the standing corn, although reeds have more frequently been used in the like comparisons. But reeds being a little stiff in the back, represent not so properly the easy graceful motions of a Courtier's body. To *that* of the bending corn, I will oppose another simile of the stubborn oak; and both may be applied to the addressors and non-addressors at some future meeting of Parliament.

When Nobles bow, and bring, in humble tone,
An abject vote before the Monarch's Throne,
They yield to breaths of indolence and ease,
And bend, like corn, beneath the fragrant breeze.
Not so, the sturdy oak withstands the blast
Of foulest storm;—'tis stubborn to the last:
Yet, Tree of Freedom! O majestic head!
Thy leaves oft wither—while thy branches spread.

ALL poetry, and indeed all literary compositions whatsoever, must be allowed to be proportionably distant from perfection, as they stand in need of additional notes and explanations to enable their readers to comprehend them. For, in other words of my own;

" A well-written book ('tis a rule that some quote)
" Should be understood without comment or note."

'Tis therefore, with all due submission, I stand corrected, for not making myself sufficiently understood in the allusion of the last line in the following stanza:———— .

" Not

" Not so, the sturdy oak withstands the blast
" Of foulest storm;—'tis stubborn to the last:
" Yet, Tree of Freedom! O majestic head!
" Thy leaves oft wither—while thy branches spread."

That is to say, in Mr. Bayes's stile,—altho' individuals may suffer in their lives or fortunes, by withstanding the foulest blast of corruption, yet the public will reap the benefit of a formidable resistance;—their rights will, in consequence of it, be extended; the Tree of Liberty will flourish and spread in a future more luxuriant verdure. Though a Russel and a Sidney fell, and many leaves of the tree dropt off in the last century, yet the branches suffered neither fracture nor amputation; the majestic head enlarged, and this generation enjoy its protection.—To push the allegory no farther, I cannot but acknowledge that my lines stood much more in need of an explanation than many of Pope's plain passages, on which dull notes are written by some of his learned Commentators.

I WOULD not have it understood, that I regard the genteel exercises learnt at the Academy, as tending solely to the *amusement* of a gentleman. They are often of singular use to him. *Music* indeed may lead a man into low company; but then, as the mind must sometimes be unbent, after any necessary application to business, it is a great happiness for him to have some musical instrument to apply to, instead of hazarding his purse at the gaming-table, or impairing his constitution in the debaucheries of a tavern.—*Painting* and *Drawing* may be learnt by gentlemen

tlemen of independent fortunes, for the same good purpose of relaxation. But they may be hurtful, rather than of service, to people whose necessary occupations are of a sedentary kind.——*Fencing* may prove of infinite use to a gentleman, on some unfortunate occasions; and the more any humane, considerate man knows of that science, the more cautiously will he avoid a quarrel; for, though he might have the advantage of an unskilful adversary, and might with perfect facility run him through the body, yet he would not willingly put a man to death for a trifle; or if, to save his own life, he saw it absolutely necessary to disable his adversary, he would find it a very difficult matter, without imminent danger to himself, to make a home thrust at a man of courage, who found a sword in his hand, and was determined, at all hazards, to advance upon him. The affair of Lord Byron and Mr. Chaworth is a case in point, which I cannot help mentioning: The *latter* was an excellent swordsman; and seemed to have presumed too much on his dexterity; the *former*, being acquainted with his antagonist's superiority, was the more precipitate in disabling him for ever, as the surest method of preserving his own existence.—As quarrels, however, cannot always be avoided, it is of great importance to a man to be able to *parry*, and (if necessary to terminate the difference) to be able to draw blood at no very dangerous part of the body.—To attend the *riding-school* is also of great advantage to a gentleman; for, besides the acquiring, by it, a graceful seat on horseback, it may also save him many a dislocated joint, or many a fractured member. The riding a race, or a fox-chase, is the least part of the art. A boy will do *that* with almost as little practice as reflection; but a gentleman ought to

know

know how to manage any vicious horse he may be accidentally mounted upon; for want of which knowledge, I have seen even Officers of Dragoons, who were the boldest fox-hunters, make no figure at all with their regiments.—*Dancing* is certainly of service to form the limbs, and to make a man genteel and active in walking; but most exercises within doors being relaxing to the body, I recommend it for its *utility* only to the Gentlemen of the Army. In what shape it is *useful to them*, in particular, may require some explanation. I would not be thought to mention it ludicrously, but I will venture to affirm, that no expert figure-dancer would be at a loss in learning any of the evolutions of the army; for nothing teaches a man to keep his mouth shut, and his eyes and ears open, more readily than dancing: now these are qualifications of acknowledged importance in a soldier upon duty; and though an Officer has a greater privilege in using his tongue, the less he opens his mouth unnecessarily, the more he will be attended to on necessary occasions.——For the same reason of accustoming the eyes and ears to be attentive, the practice of *music* is of advantage to an Officer; for, while he is reading and playing his own part, he must also listen to the instruments of the other performers.—*Landship-drawing* is of acknowledged use to an *Engineer;* and by exercising the eye, is worthy of the notice of all Officers. *Riding*, as I above hinted, is an exercise to be recommended particularly to the Gentlemen of the Army.—*Fencing*, and the use of the broad-sword, is of singular utility in exercising the attention of the eye, and improving the activity of the body: but the knowledge of them, excepting to the Horse and Dragoon Officers, is not so requisite as it used to be, when man was frequently

quently opposed to man in battle; for now that cannon, and the as-merciful firelocks, have put close fighting out of fashion, the rifle-gun is the chief weapon for practice.—— Since I have been drawn into the subject of amusements that are attended with utility to the Gentlemen of the Army, I must not omit mentioning my favourite *Game of Chess*. Whoever can with a glance of the eye command every move that can be played on the Chess-board, might, with equal facility, discern the whole disposition of an army, and be prepared for every attack which an enemy could make upon him. *Hunting* and *Shooting* are also amusements of acknowledged utility to an Officer; by improving the quickness of his eye, they give him a readiness in perceiving every inch of ground around him; and he acquires, in time, a tolerable certainty in guessing at the face of the adjoining country, from the appearance of the field immediately within his prospect.

NOTWITHSTANDING these thoughts are written in a most stormy night, I will venture the communicating an observation on the weather, which may give some comfort to the under-writers in London, and for which I shall expect their acknowledgements, accompanied with a handsome *premium*.—— I have heard it once observed, as I have found it by experience, for these three last years, to be a *just* observation, that, as the weather rules for about a week before, and after the equinoxial day, it will, in general, be the same kind of weather for three or four months next ensuing: That is to say, if the fortnight above named should be stormy weather, the long
months

months after will, for the most part, be stormy too; but if that fortnight should prove fine, mild weather, (as it lately did) we may expect a continuance of the same for the greater part of the four months to come.

MAN was certainly formed for exercise and laborious employment; and unnatural to him must be the occupations of a sedentary life. I cannot therefore but think, it will turn out greatly to the advantage of the male sex, the women having taken so much to reading and writing of late. The honest profession of a taylor, so generally derided for its effeminacy, could not, with propriety, have been committed to the trust of a *female* hand; for it would be indecent in a woman to be constantly fumbling about a man's breeches, and to be necessarily feeling his ribs, or tickling his sides, while she was taking his measure for a suit of clothes.——But various are the other employments, which the learned part of the fair-sex can now take off our hands! By changing the custom of flogging the posteriors, to the flagellating some other part of as exquisite feeling, the Ladies may teach our youth the *ancient* and *modern* languages as properly as the men can. For the *first*, the women have generally most excellent memories, capable of retaining the minutest and most particular circumstance or event; for the *last*, it will be readily allowed, that their tongues are sufficiently pliant and voluble to acquire the most difficult twists. The Spanish, German, and Dutch gutturals, indeed, would not be so easily managed, unless the fair teachers were Northumberland or Scotch.—In the *Senate*, and at the *Bar*, the loquacity of the women would be of extraordinary use. And, in the *Pulpit*, how would their sweet persuasion, and their winning looks make converts to the truth!—As to *trade* and *manufactures*, 'tis very well known, that a widow in Holland and Flanders continues her traffic, with little inconvenience, after her husband's death; and I trust that our English widows are clever enough to do the same with us. In the practice of *Physic*, I doubt not but the Ladies would be very expert. The sight, I grant, of a beautiful woman might sometimes disorder a man's pulse, and the feel of her delicate hand would naturally accelerate the course of his blood; but then, how many patients would revive at the mere sight of their doctor! or be restored to all their pristine vigour, at her very magical touch! As custom reconciles us to every thing, old King David's method of prolonging his days might come again into vogue:—a man might have a handsome female doctor on each side of him all night, and dismiss them in the morning (with their guinea a-piece), without his giving the world the least scandal or offence —— *Certain disorders* would be difficult to treat, without putting the *surgeon* to the blush. But, in these cases, I think the Ladies might easily get over their delicacy; for, considering the liberties which the *men-midwives* have already taken with the fair sex, I see no harm in the women using the same freedoms with us. If any there be, the *examiner* and *examined* sharing the reproach, there is but half the immodesty in it.—I will tell it in *Italian;* for my Latin I have partly forgot, plain English would be vulgar, and almost as well understood would be the original French:— *Un servitiale mollificante, per rinfrescar le Viscere del Signor,* would give infinite relief, when administered by the hands of a pretty female *apothecary;* whereas,

in

in the present way, by being frequently left to the care of an old nurse, it is not so likely to have all its proper and benign effects.

THERE is a rule to be observed in conversation, that a man ought to consider, whether his companions shew a willingness to listen to *his* discourse, or would like better that he should hear *them* speak. And, similar to *that*, is a maxim in politics, to which every wise Statesman attends: To avoid, as much as possible, the making any innovations in the laws of a nation; but such as the people are already predisposed to receive. I think, therefore, that our Legislature might take into serious consideration the hint I have offered above. The Ladies having already met us half way, Government would not find it difficult to enforce the observance of any law which the *omnipotence* of Parliament (a phrase, however, which Heaven seems to resent) should think proper, for the wise purposes hereafter named, to enact, viz. to oblige the women in general to attend our grammar-schools and academies; and to finish their studies at our two universities of Oxford and Cambridge. Those intended for physic, should have liberty to resort to Edinburgh. I am certain that the Ladies would swallow such a law more readily, than the Americans ever will do those Acts and Resolutions which we are endeavouring to cram down their throats. My reason for proposing such a law is evidently this: That men being so much wanted for our warlike operations abroad, they ought by no means to be encouraged in the occupations of a sedentary life.—I cannot bear to think seriously of the blood

blood that has been shed; and I am extremely afraid that many more lives will be lost before there is an end to this strife. For supposing that General Howe should force the lines at New-York, it is a doubt if he will be able to leave his ships, and march up the country, to meet the little army coming from the Lakes above. My private intelligence of 23d June, 1776, from Montreal, said, that our troops in Canada had then no vessels ready to carry them across the Lakes. And, perhaps, it was lucky they had not; unless the Grand Army under General Howe could have marched up the country to meet them, they would probably have been cut off by a much superior force. All which makes it appear to me that affairs will not, by the *sword*, be settled this campaign; that more men will be wanted for recruits; and that four shillings in the pound Land-tax will be again requested of the landed Gentry, who have been so greedily strangling their hen with her golden eggs. If I saw my brother in a quarrel, in which I thought him to blame, I would certainly not assist him in his injustice; yet I could not wish him to be beat. In no other sentiments do I find myself with regard to this American dispute.

WHATEVER happens in the affairs of this world, we must acknowledge to be permitted by the will of God. We cannot pretend to account for the expediency of every event we are witnesses of. If, however, we examine the Records of History, we shall find, that though many bloody battles have been fought, which, for unknown purposes, have swept whole millions off the face of the earth, Providence

vidence has seldom permitted the entire conquest of a nation, but for its punishment under vice and corruption, or for its civilization and improvement from a barbarous State. The Americans being equally virtuous, and equally civilized with us; I cannot perfuade myself that our coercive measures against them will ever succeed.

OUR passions and judgment being equally the gifts of God, I cannot but think it borders on impiety to treat the impetuosity of Man's passions, or the defect of his judgment, with ridicule or contempt:—it is sneering at God's Providence for the unequal distribution he has made. Yet, when a man is at no pains to controul his passions, or to improve his understanding, ridicule may be permitted, when it is employed with the well-meaning intent of shaming a person into a reformation of life. I hope never to use it in any other thought. Perfectly sensible of my own defects, I shall never speak contemptuously of other's faults, nor arrogantly attempt to write a satire on the human race. The humiliating idiotism of the once-humourous Dean Swift should serve as an awful example, to deter all presumers to wit from wantonly ridiculing the wonderful works of that Deity, whose designs are unaccountable to us.

I HAVE met with some lines in the Whitehall Evening-post, addressed to a Gentleman who happened always to vote on the *Ministerial* side in Parliament; and which finished with this stanza:

" Yet

" Yet *passing wise* the men may be,
" With whom you ever did agree,
   " With whom you e'er did vote;
" Or else this inference I draw:
" You neither *heard*, nor ever *saw*,
   " But held by *Cooper*'s coat."

I hope there are not many *such* in the House of Commons, who suffer themselves to be led by the Treasurer, or his Secretary, like blind beggars following their Dogs: yet, (if such there are) I think an apology might be penned for them, which few of them would be bold enough to make: " You, Gentlemen, who style yourselves Patriots, you obstruct the wheels of Government by opposing the Minister in *every* thing; and you justify this opposition by saying, you are persuaded he is an enemy to the constitution, and that our ancient rights are in danger, till you have turned him out of place.—Now, We of the Majority, having a confidence in the integrity and abilities of this same Minister, think it incumbent upon us to keep him *in;* for which reason, and to counteract *your* scheme, we give him our constant support."— The argument is of equal weight for every one who chooses to go through the *dirty* work of either side. The man, however, who supports the *Premier* in every thing, will oftener be in the right, than he who thwarts every measure of government, merely to turn a bad Minister out.

OF all the superstitious tenets of the Church of Rome, the Belief of the Infallibility of the Pope is one of the most ridiculous; yet, from the King to the

Cobler, there is not a Protestant among us, who does not, at times, believe himself to be infallible. This conceit of our own infallibility is, perhaps a greater cause of strife among mankind, than any thing else we can imagine; for, rather than we will allow, in some favourite opinions, the possibility of our judgment being erroneous, we positively pronounce our opponents to be ignorant; or, guided by self-interest, to be utterly insincere in their professions.——Hence it is, that we so often conceive a hatred or dislike of them who differ from us in sentiment. The King's servants brand, with the opprobrious name of a seditious and *detestable* opposition, every party of men who dissent from their opinions; whilst, on the other hand, the Gentlemen in opposition imagine, that no man can be honest in his principles who can give his support to certain measures of Government, which unfortunately incur their displeasure.—In like manner, we may see our Counties, Towns, and Villages torn with dissentions, or divided by party and faction, where almost every man expects that you shall side with him, and quarrel with his neighbour; because only they have happened to differ in opinion, and each would have you believe him to be a man of an infallible judgment.

THERE are two things in life, which I frequently meet with, and which, as often as they happen to me, give me inexpressible pain. The first is, when I see a poor drudge of a waiter made the sport of a company at a tavern, and obliged to submit to the arrogance of every haughty or unthinking fellow, who assumes the authority to abuse him on any little, trifling

trifling concern. The next is, when Gentlemen take upon them to scold and reprimand their servants before any company of visitors whom they entertain. In both these cases, I bring the condition of the waiter and the servant home to myself, and, by my feelings, I find, I could never be able to endure the ill-usage they must so often sustain. To the proud and haughty, whatever I could say on the subject would be of little avail. But I must beg leave to remind the giddy part of men, (who, from wantonness or thoughtlessness, sometimes act against the known humanity of their own minds) that nothing is so mean as to give ill language to any man, whose condition in life renders it unsafe for him to return the abuse; and that nothing can be more ill-mannered to a company, than to address one's wit to a waiter, when there are gentlemen to converse with in the room. Nor, at one's own table, can any thing be more ill-mannered to guests, than to give vent to one's anger or ill-humour before them; because it must proportionably spoil their entertainment, as they partake of their Envitor's concern.

MUCH has been written for and against the inclosing the open fields in England; but one plain observation must strike any man of reflection, in the county where I reside:—That if the fields, which lie fallow for a whole summer, were inclosed, they would certainly produce something more profitable than the scanty pittance of food which the sheep that browse on them at present receive.—When, from an eminence, one beholds the third part of the land covered, in the midst of the summer, with the winter's russet

russet brown, it immediately occurs to his mind, that a very small portion of that same land, if laid down in grass, would serve as pasture for its usual stock of sheep; and that the rest of the produce of these fallow fields, when cultivated every year, would be so much of public advantage gained. A large crop, indeed, may be expected from a field that has lain fallow for a whole summer; but the farmer, by changing every year the seed that is sown in the same soil, or by manuring it well, makes the inclosed land yield an additional produce, for which he is ever ready to give an advanced rent. Whenever a country can be brought to yield an additional produce, the inhabitants must, in general, be benefited by it. It is not, therefore, by the *act* of inclosing, but by the *manner* of it, that we see so many individuals suffer in the case. If the small tenants were not turned a-drift on the world by some of their avaricious landlords; if the value and extent of a farm were to be fixed by Act of Parliament; and if an adequate compensation were always given to the poor, who have a right of common on the open fields—then would the vallies smile, and every one would rejoice at the daily improvements that are made. But as matters now stand, though the Public reap advantage by an increase of produce, individuals are frequently oppressed, and must too often curse that power that deprived them of their bread.——One national benefit, however, arising from large farms, must be candidly confessed. They serve the purposes of public granaries; for when a year of scarcity arrives, the great farmer has generally a store in reserve, which supplies the deficiency of a bad crop; and though the hoarding of his corn may sometimes make it high priced, we shall not, as formerly, experience those sad times of famine and general distress.

THERE is a well-known story of a sailor, who, coming off a cruize with his pocket full of prize-money, admired the Admiral's velvet waistcoat so much, that nothing could satisfy him, till he had one made for himself of the very same stuff. He accordingly inquired for the Admiral's taylor, of whom he went to bespeak his vest. The taylor, after having taken his measure, asked him what he should make the back of. "Why, of the same stuff, to be sure!" quoth Jack. "'Tis not usual, said the taylor, to make the back of those rich waistcoats of the same stuff with the front; the Admiral had the back of *his* made of common cloth."——" No matter for that, quoth Jack; make *mine* ALL velvet; I'll have no sham about me, by G—!" Soon after, when Jack had got his waistcoat on, he met the Admiral in the street; but instead of taking off his hat (for which he felt himself too great), he held his coat-lappets up with one hand, and with the other he clapped his back—" No sham *here*, Admiral! no sham about *me*; 'tis *all* velvet, by G—!"——No less absurd is the modern taste of some of our Nobility and Gentry in the building of their country-seats. It seems to be a prevailing fashion among them, to build the front of a house towards a place whence it cannot be seen, unless one is at the pains to ride some miles round it; which is just as troublesome a manœuvre as that of Jack's pulling up the lappets of his coat to shew us his velvet back. A man may furnish

the

the *inside* of his house to please himself and his friends who visit him, and he may place the windows of the principal rooms towards the most beautiful prospect; but, surely, if I were to bestow any money on the ornamenting the *outside* of my house, I would choose to have it as conspicuous as possible; otherwise the expence of the fine front might as well have been saved to my purse. I have often seen an honest, plain Citizen with a gold-laced waistcoat, which he endeavoured, by buttoning his coat, to keep carefully hid; yet, by a bit of the binding peeping out, I could discover the finery he was ashamed of. I should have made this comparison at the first; but I had many doubts whether I could lay to the account of a bashful modesty in our great folks, their late custom of concealing their ornamented fronts. I need not bar a pun here, for my Readers will perceive there is not affinity enough.—This custom, I take it, has arisen from an observation on the proximity of Citizens' boxes to the dust and noise of a London road; and so, to avoid the inconveniences attending such a situation, or the indignity of having a noble mansion compared to a Citizen's box, our gentry have run into the other extreme, and will not have their houses seen at all, unless it be at the distance of a mile and a half.———I leave it to any architect to judge, what a grand figure his works will cut, when viewed in the diminutive scale which such a prospect would make. There is a certain point of view, beyond which all grandeur, as well as richness, is lost: as the minute ornaments will not be *seen* at too great a distance, so the building itself will be *diminished* too much.—If a house be so near a road that passengers may look into it, I would certainly shut it up on that quarter, and turn my front to some other place. But if it be far enough not to be overlooked, nor to be incommoded by the noise and dust of a high-road, I would prefer to run my front parallel with the principal road, from whence it will oftenest be viewed.— A house ought also to humour the ground on which it is placed. It ought to square with the slope of the lawn, and not diagonally to run it across.

I LATELY remarked on the sulky custom among our Gentry of concealing their houses from the notice of travellers; but I must here animadvert a little on their sullen manner of keeping *themselves* too closely shut up from the knowledge of strangers.——I am confident that no mortal would suffer less by having a window in his breast, than an Englishman; and yet a stranger would seldom be able to prevail on him to sit with his blinds open. His window-shutters would be eternally barred and bolted against every unknown comer that approached him, as if he must certainly be a thief or a pickpocket. Such a cautious conduct in *business* is prudent and commendable; for the surest method of preventing all consequent misunderstanding, is, to transact every affair of interest, even with one's own brother, as if one was guarding against the tricks of a sharper. But, in the common intercourse of life, Christian charity should teach us to suppose every man honest, till we shall have received a contrary information. Instead of this charitable behaviour, nothing is more common than to see two well dressed people sit the whole evening next each other, at the Opera or the Playhouse, without so much as exchanging one civil word about the beauties or the defects of the performance. This
shyness,

shyness, I am perfuaded, proceeds from a certain inbred haughtiness of spirit, that hinders each party from condescending to make the first advances. 'Tis partly from my own experience I say it;—for having spent seven years of my youth in a foreign country, I was, on my return to Britain, as totally unacquainted with its customs as if I had never seen it; I had no conception of any shyness between one genteel person and another; so that, wherever I seated myself at a public entertainment, I never failed to say some civil thing between the Acts, to my next neighbours, and to shew them my willingness to begin a conversation. As it is a compliment due to every company where one is not intimately acquainted, to put on a better dress than ordinary, in which to appear before them, and as I always made a point of complying with that rule of politeness, I never ventured into public (after the manner of some of our English Bucks) in a dress that would make a stranger ashamed of my acquaintance. I have, accordingly never found, that either the Gentlemen or the Ladies were offended at my speaking to them; but, on the contrary, my civility has frequently recommended me to the friendship of people, whom, unknown, I had sociably accosted, and to whom I had afterwards the opportunity of a formal introduction.

BESIDES the reserved behaviour above mentioned, to strangers, I have often heard my countrymen reproached for their ingratitude to foreigners. An Englishman, after receiving many civilities from a Gentleman abroad, will frequently shew but little attention to him in London. This I can account for no otherwise, than from the multiplicity of engagements which people generally have who come to reside only a few weeks in London; and from our Nobility and Gentry not looking upon themselves as *at home* in Town, but rather as temporary residents, as well as the foreign travellers. This behaviour, which is sometimes imputed to political dissensions, may pass among ourselves; and I can the more readily forgive it, as I have myself experienced the greatest civilities in many parts of England, from Gentlemen, whose Parliamentary business, or family engagements, would scarcely allow them time to accept of the least return from me in London. Yet I could wish my countrymen would sacrifice a little more of their own convenience to the hospitable reception of foreigners; because their ingratitude to them is really become a national reproach.

THERE is no greater obstacle to the introduction into *good* company, than a non conformity with the custom of card-playing. From what we can learn in the annals of the Polite World, this fashion has prevailed in *London*, with little variation, for a whole century; but, within my own memory (and I am not a very old fellow), it has gained such considerable ground in the *country*, that it has intirely banished bowls, cricket, and other manly games, with which the Gentlemen used to amuse themselves in the summer-evenings. Nay, there is not so much as a butt to shoot an arrow at, in any of the gardens, in Scotland; and the *goff* club and ball are never used now, but in a tedious morning. From one end of the Island to the other you will find, that when

neighbouring

neighbouring families are met together in the country, they will be sitting at cards during the most delightful hours of the day, totally unmindful of the rural beauties around them. 'Tis absolutely murdering one's time thus to confine one's self to the house, in a fine summer-evening; but to fill up conversation with cards, in a winter's night, may prevent a great deal of ill-natured discourse, and a great deal of scandal.—Divines are too severe in their censure of this custom. As the best things may be perverted in their use, so is the playing at cards attended with its evils. The trifling too much of our time away in *any* amusement, is undoubtedly sinful; and if a man who has any necessary vocation in life, should dedicate too many hours of the day to cards, he is doubly censurable. But people of independent fortunes, who cannot all find employment in the service of the State, may be allowed to entertain themselves at cards (as we give toys to children), to keep them out of mischief. Of necessary evils we must choose the least; 'tis therefore better, that a man should throw his time and money away at cards, than that he should employ them in disturbing the public peace, or in ruining his constitution in all kinds of excess. I appeal to History for the truth of this: Since play has been in fashion, civil broils, rapine, murder, and drunkenness, among our gentry, have visibly decreased.—For several reasons, I seldom play at cards myself: the games do not interest me sufficiently to fix my attention for any length of time; I do not like to part with my money, where no pleasure to myself, nor good to others, is purchased by it; and if I were to win any considerable sum, it would give me no satisfaction, as I imagine that my friend, or neighbour, would choose to lose as little

as

as I do.—But though I do not relish cards myself, I am far from being of the opinion of some of our moralists, who say, that the love of them proceeds from a principle of avarice, or an unbounded desire of gain; for I am acquainted with so many people of most generous sentiments, who are fond of play, that I am convinced they are inticed to cards by nothing but a certain keenness of temper, and restlessness of spirit, which would take a more useful turn, if they had something of more importance to work upon.—I once knew an extraordinary instance of this in two very sensible men of my acquaintance, who happened to be wind-bound at Helvoetsluys, in Holland. They fell in there with two other gentlemen, with whom they played at Whist from breakfast to dinner, from dinner to supper, and from supper to bed-time, for three days successively, for nothing but *honour*. From my own feelings, I can readily conceive *another* more pleasing temptation to play. I never won a game at cards without feeling a kind of complacency of mind, a sort of flattering approbation of my own judgment; when, perhaps, I owed my success intirely to chance, and nothing to my own skill or understanding. If I lose, however, as I never play high, it gives me no manner of concern; and I would advise no man (for his own happiness) to play at cards, who cannot meet his ill-luck with the same philosophical temper.

"NOW, the Devil confound those Ancients"— (said an honest Irishman, as he was reading one of their Writings) "Now, the Devil confound those Ancients, for they have stolen all my good thoughts from me!"—A man, who has read little and thought much, ought indeed to be very cautious how he lays claim to originality; for (excepting in the Arts and Sciences) it is difficult to strike out a thought, but what one may find already expressed in some ancient Author, and with fewer words than it can be conveyed in by any Modern.—What brings the Irishman's speech into my head at present, is the sight of Sir John Hawkins's Advertisement of a speedy Publication of Five Quarto Volumes on the subject of Music. I have some thoughts of my own on the same subject, which I am resolved to put soon into some kind of order; lest, peradventure, they should be too late in their publication, and I should find that Sir John "had stolen some of my good Thoughts from me."

I HAVE seldom met with a native of any foreign country, I am acquainted with, who had never travelled till he had attained the age of manhood, but I could tell the nation he belonged to, by the cadence, or accent, in which he spoke the English language. Let his pronunciation be never so perfect, he will still retain something of the same cadence in which he was accustomed to speak in his youth, and of which, in his riper years, it will be impossible for him, by any delicacy of ear, or pliability of tongue, to become totally divested.—The reason of it I take to be this:—The voice having been long exerted in speaking in the same *national* cadence, some particular parts which form the voice, and whose function it immediately is to found that cadence, become thereby more strengthened than others; and this may occasion, for ever, a cadence in speaking as involuntary,

tary, as are the various natural notes in the convulsion of laughter. Anatomists may give a better account of it; although to me it appears, that it is neither the *Larynx*, nor any one single part, that forms the voice, but the combined powers of *three;* and these are, the throat, the breast, and the lungs. The *last*, like the bellows of an organ, are the *sine qua non;* without which there would be no sound. The other *two* serve to *modify* the voice; that is, to give it the *manner* of its existence. The throat seems to preside over the function of modulation in singing; and to the breast is specially assigned the power of giving the emphasis in speaking. Accordingly, we find many accomplished singers, who have no command of their voice in speaking; and, on the other hand, many great orators and theatrical speakers, who can scarcely sound a note of music with their voice; though they may perhaps shew us their musical capacity, by whistling any tune that has been sung to them.

IT is by some maintained, that the music of each country bears an affinity to the cadence of its language. However that may be, this at least is certain,—that as, by custom, we can be brought to admire the rant of the Stage at Paris or at London (a rant, which, at first hearing, appears unnatural to us), so we become enamoured of any strain of music we have been long used to, and give it the preference to every other kind of composition. An untravelled, uninstructed Frenchman imagines, there is no music comparable to the Airs of his country. An untaught North-Briton will have a similar prepossession in favour

vour of the Scotch tunes. But any one, who has practised music from his youth, and who has not always resided in his native country, will give the preference to the Italian music, on account of its variety; although he will, at the same time, learn to relish what is agreeable in the music of every nation. Thus will he increase his taste and enjoyment of music, by an unprejudiced practice of every kind of composition, in the same manner as a man may get rid of all cadence in speaking, by an *early* intercourse with the natives of many different countries.—When I first learned the violin and violoncello, I played, for several years, nothing but Italian composition. I then met with some French Airs, and their words and tunes together gave me infinite pleasure. I next heard Handel's Oratorios; some pieces of which, when I knew the words they meant to express, charmed me beyond any thing of the Italian. Mr. Robert Bremner's Collection of Scotch Songs came last in my way; and though he has given me no directions how the tunes are to be played, I think I have guessed both the taste and the time of the music, by the strain of the words for which it is composed. ——The following is my manner of playing some of them; and if I have not hit on their true meaning, I hope Mr. Bremner, in the next impression of his book, will be so obliging as to correct me.

Mournful and *tender*. *Adagio*.
Gilderoy.
An' thou wert my ain thing.
The Bush aboon Traquair.
The Broom of Cowdenknows.
I'll never leave thee.
Peggie, I must love thee.
Woe's my heart that we should sunder.

Plaintive

Plaintive and *tender.* *Largo.*
Katherine Ogie.
The laft time I came o'er the Moor.
She rofe and let me in.
For the lack of gold fhe left me.
My Apron dearie.
Sae merry as we twa hae been.

Graceful and *tender.* *Andante.*
The Birks of Invermay.
The Lafs of Patie's Mill.
Low down in the Broom.
Nancy's to the Greenwood gane.
Tweed Side.
Corn Riggs are bonny.
The Yellow-hair'd Laddie.

Chearful and *tender.* *Andantino.*
Beffy Bell and Mary Grey.
Fee him, Father, fee him.
The Boatman.
There's my thumb, I'll ne'er beguile thee.

Chearful. *Allegretto.*
The Blathric o't.
Hooly and fairly.

How expreffive of rapture are the notes to the line, "Then I would clafp thee in my arms," in the Song of *An' thou wert my ain thing!*—How plaintive the notes to "A Lafs that was laden with care," in the Song of *Sae merry as we twa hae been!*—How mournful the notes to "Hear me, ye Nymphs, and every Swain!" in *the Bufh aboon Traquair!*—How mournful, too, the notes to "As from a rock, paft all relief," with the whole firft ftanza in *Peggie, I muft love thee!*—And how expreffive the fall in "He's low down in the Broom!"——But my limits will not
allow

allow me to quote every favourite paſſage in theſe ſongs, which, I think, equal in expreſſion the moſt admired compoſitions of the Italian maſters.

To Antiquarians I ſhall leave it to determine, which particular Scotch tunes were compoſed by *David Rizzio*, or which are the productions of the country. Among thoſe above mentioned, I am willing to relinquiſh *Tweed Side*, and the *Yellow-hair'd Laddie*, which have much of the Italian Air in them. I would alſo give up the *Laſs of Patie's Mill*, unleſs it has the original words to it; for, in that caſe, it cannot be above a century and a half old; " *Hopetoun's* high mountains," which the ſong mentions, having not been much longer in the poſſeſſion of that family; and *then* I ſuppoſe the poſſeſſor to be called by the name of his eſtate (after the Scotch manner), as the Peerage of that name is no older than from the beginning of this century.———I can ſcarcely pick out another tune in the book before me, but muſt either be originally Scotch, or purpoſely compoſed by *Rizzio* after the Scotch manner. They could not otherwiſe have been introduced among the vulgar, by whom they have been chiefly tranſmitted (as from them they have been generally collected); for, let the beſt modern ſinger, at this day, execute any favourite Italian Air to the common people in Scotland, it would be loſt upon them intirely; or they would ſtill give the preference to that ſtrain of muſic which they have ever been uſed to.—I cannot conclude without obſerving, that, as many of the Scotch tunes run the notes almoſt to two *Octaves*, it muſt require a greater compaſs of voice to ſing them, than we generally expect to find among the inhabitants of theſe northern countries.

AT

AT the battle of Lafelt, when the 37th regiment of foot had been thrice broken and rallied again, and when, at the fourth attack, they were totally defeated, *Dijan*, a French refugee Officer, who stood among the last in that regiment, found himself at the side of one Kerr, a bold, intrepid grenadier, whom rejoicing to meet, he instantly accosted in these words, " Bee garre! me be very glad to see you, Kerr; I know you vill follow me." " That I will, said Kerr, I will follow your honour to the bottom of Hell."— "Hold, hold, Kerr, not so far, eider; me vill only lead you to de gate, and dere me be obliged to leave you."—So, away they both went over a hedge and ditch, and continued the battle at the side of a Hanoverian regiment.———Though I would wish to banish, as much as possible, from the mind of the soldier, the recollection of his own danger, the want of reflection I would desire in him, is not of that dissolute, abandoned kind which the Grenadier above mentioned shewed in his answer. I would have no man, in a good cause, forget, that he fights in the presence of his Creator; for History shews us, that no armies have been more successful than those who fought under a religious inspiration; nor have any men been possessed of greater bravery in combat than those who had the fear of God constantly before them. We see, indeed, that a want of all Religion has often the same effect of rendering men fearless of danger; yet is the thoughtless, mechanical courage of the wicked not always to be relied on; for, if a temporary ray of reason should strike them, they will shudder at death, and the approach of a future retribution. A remarkable instance of this I can give, in another

another story that at present occurs to me. An English gentleman-traveller happened to be dining at a *Table d'Hote*, at the Hague, in company with some others, who had been concerned in the last Rebellion. In his discourse at table, he used great freedom with the Christian Religion, and went so far as to utter blasphemy against his Almighty God. He next attacked the character of the Pretender, and at last became so scurrilous on the subject, that one of the company, no longer able to contain himself, desired him to walk into the garden.—"Now, Sir, said the challenger, your blasphemy against my God, I leave *him* to punish, for He was present, and did certainly hear you. But for your scurrilous abuse of my Prince, who is absent, and cannot resent it, I demand instant satisfaction. Draw, Sir, or you shall ask his pardon."—These words were delivered in such a determined manner, that the offending gentleman imagined he heard the voice of an avenging Angel, sent from Heaven to punish him for all his wicked actions. Though as an officer in the army he had often distinguished himself in battle; though he had as often proved his courage in single combat; and though he now drew his sword with apparent resolution, yet his heart failed him on this occasion; and, after a few thrusts, his antagonist disarmed him, and obliged him to beg his pardon.

THERE is an expression in General Howe's letter of 30th November, that would be very characteristic of the cool courage of the German soldiers, had we not been previously informed, that four British regiments had scrambled up the hill like cats, and effectually

tually cleared the way for them:——" The Heffian grenadiers also coming up, and paffing the Brunx, afcended the height with the greateft alacrity, and in the beft order."—I can, however, conceive all this to be very true, without derogating in the leaft from the bravery of the Heffians.—A German and a Dutchman are naturally flow in their motions; and, in the face of danger, within the reach of a cannon or a mufket, it would be unreafonable to expect them to be uncommonly active in marching. Let us figure to ourfelves a man with head erect, fhoulders forced back, cheft pufhed out, his back ftreight, and his knees ftiff.—This man knows no other method of walking up a hill, and 'tis with difficulty he can perform it.—If, again, he attempts to go down the hill, 'tis ten to one but he will fall on his back; as may be tried any day on a flope, with our own foldiers in drilling. Commend me, then to the natural loofe walk, and the acquired agility of a South or North Briton; for, a man, to be an active foldier, ought to be able to walk on all-four when there is occafion for it.

Reading, in an old Newfpaper, a paragraph about fome depredations which Mr. Wildman's Bees had made in a Confectioner's Shop, it recalled to my mind an affair that happened fome years ago at Enfield, and that was equitably fettled by Mr. Smart, an honeft Attorney of that place. In what manner it was fettled by him, I fhall leave it to my Readers to guefs. But the fubject occafioning no little mirth in the neighbourhood, a club of friends, who fat as judge and jury, defired me to perfonate Mr.

Mr. *Doublefee*, and to plead before them on both sides of the case. The following, as far as I can recollect, were the chief points on which I enlarged.

COUNSEL *for the* PLAINTIFF.

My Lord, and Gentlemen of the Jury,

I AM Counsel, in this cause, for William Whitebread, the Plaintiff.——As my brief states the case, John Fenton, in the parish of Enfield, Middlesex county, is the proprietor of an orchard, lying and being in the foresaid parish of Enfield, the fruit of which orchard he let, for the term of one year, to Benjamin Blossom, the Defendant, and the pasture he reserved for his own use. The Plaintiff was the owner of a sow and nine pigs; which sow and nine pigs being one morning, as it was their natural custom, in quest of the acorns, crab-apples, hips, haws, and nuts, that are usually to be found under the trees and hedges of an inclosed country, arrived at the fence which inclosed the foresaid orchard, belonging to the foresaid John Fenton. In the said fence, which consisted of a quickset hedge, the foresaid nine pigs found a little hole, or aperture, through which, in search of food, they crept; and, notwithstanding the sage admonition of the old sow, their mother, who prudently remained on the public highway, they, thoughtless, strayed into the orchard. Far had the pigs not wandered, ere they beheld a windfall of tempting apples, which a late storm had scattered upon John Fenton's herbage. Of these apples, as it was natural for pigs to do, they did most plentifully eat; till the Defendant accidentally arriving, forthwith hurried them from off the orchard, and shut them up in the open pound. The Defendant demanding damages beyond all reason, and to which he had no manner of right, the Plaintiff *replevied;* but on the redelivery of the pigs into the poffeffion of the Plaintiff, the faid pigs were found to be *dead;—ergo,* not in the fame condition in which they were by the Defendant impounded. The Plaintiff demands the full value of his pigs to be paid to him, and that for fundry good reafons, which we mean to give. Firft, My Lord, and Gentlemen of the Jury, it can no ways be proved that the Plaintiff's pigs were guilty of any trefpafs on the Defendant's property. The clofe or orchard was the property of Mr. John Fenton. The pigs made no unwarrantable entry on the defendant's foil, by "*breaking* his *Clofe,*" nor did they do him any damage by "treading down and bruifing *his* Herbage". Both thefe are neceffary to conftitute a trefpafs; and yet the fence and the herbage were neither of them the property of the Defendant. Nor can he fay that the pigs "fpoilt his trees", fuppofing them to be his property, which in reality they were not; he could not lawfully cut one twig of them; 'twas only the fruit of them which he could difpofe of for that feafon. I will now afk him one plain queftion: Did the pigs *climb* the trees? or did they break the branches, or did they fpoil the fruit?—No; the pigs found the apples fcattered, by the wind, on Mr. Fenton's herbage; and whoever had been at the pains to have gathered them, would, by his labour, have acquired the property of them;——having dropt off the trees, they were no longer *fruit growing* on thofe trees, and therefore no longer the property of the Defendant.— But fuppofing that the pigs had committed an act which the law did deem unjuftifiable, your Lordfhip and the Gentlemen of the Jury will be pleafed to confider, that thefe were pigs but of eight weeks old;

they

they were not Hogs, my Lord,—they were not arrived at the age of possible discretion, and could not discern between good and evil. Their *ætas infantiæ*, or, at the most, their *ætas infantiæ proxima*, exempted them from punishment for any crime or misdemeanor.—Had the old sow, their mother, entered the orchard, Mr. John Fenton (for *he* was the man against whom the trespass, if any, was committed) might, with greater plea of justice, have impounded *her*;—but no;—she stood on the outside of the fence, and grunted warning to the pigs to keep on the uncontrovertible highway.

My Lord, and Gentlemen of the Jury, I will be bold to say, there has been infinite malice in this affair. The Defendant, Benjamin Blossom, is suspected to be no believer of the Holy Catholic Faith; he was never known to have attended Divine Service at any *Christian* Church. Excepting, now and then, an Alderman of London, how seldom do we find a *Benjamin* that is not a *Jew! &c.* and the Defendant is known to have a mortal aversion to pork; accordingly he shut up these nine poor pigs in an open pound, and that in a cold, bleak night of the October month, when, by the inclemency of the weather, they came to a miserable and untimely end!——We therefore hope that you will, as in your judgments shall seem meet, decree us the value of our foresaid nine pigs, and our full costs of suit.

* * * * * * * *

COUNSEL *for the* DEFENDANT.
My Lord, and Gentlemen of the Jury,
I AM Counsel, in this cause, for Benjamin Blossom, the Defendant. The Plaintiff's Counsel having admitted,

admitted, that the nine pigs, lately belonging to William Whitebread, were detected in the fact of eating the Defendant's fruit, it only remains with us to prove, that the said Defendant was justified in distraining the said pigs *damage-feasant* on his property, as hath already been stated in the brief.—We admit that the *herbage* of the orchard belonged to John Fenton, but the trees, and the fruit of them, constituted part of the *vesture*, and were, for that year, the property of the Defendant. *Cujus est solum ejus est usque ad cœlum,* is a maxim of the law with regard to the *soil;* and so it is, I will venture to affirm, with regard to its *produce,* which the proprietor may have let to any other man. The apples, therefore, belonged to Benjamin Blossom, though the trees had reached the clouds, or their roots shot down to Hell. The Defendant not having relinquished his property in the apples when they lay upon the ground, the pigs had no manner of right to convert them to their own use, and to devour them as they did. John Fenton, indeed, might have gathered the apples; because, by damaging his herbage, they became a nuisance to him; or, if they had dropt over the wall, or fence, upon another man's ground, the proprietor thereof might have lawfully done the same. But the pigs could never have acquired a property in the apples, even though they had found them on the public highway; unless the owner of them had for ever remained unknown.—The Plaintiff seems to lay a great stress on the *infancy* of his pigs; but with how much reason, I shall leave it to your Lordship, and the Gentlemen of the Jury, to judge. It being held that the capacity of doing ill, or contracting guilt, is not so much measured by years and days, as by the Delinquent's understanding. (for,

Malitia

Malitia supplet Ætatem,) we can prove that the foresaid pigs manifested a consciousness of guilt, by precipitately running away, and endeavouring to hide themselves, immediately upon the Defendant's appearance in the close.—As for the old sow standing on the watch without, there was a very evident reason for that. There are *holes* of various sorts and sizes, as your Lordship and the Gentlemen of the Jury well know; and one hole might give an easy admission to a pig, that would be found, upon trial, to be too small to let in a beastly hog.—Now, the hole, or aperture, in the fence which inclosed the Defendant's fruit-trees, being but a small one, the great sow (however willing) could not possibly follow her diminutive pigs.—In regard to *malice* in this affair, I believe, my Lord, and Gentlemen of the Jury, we can prove a good deal of that on the Plaintiff's side. The said Plaintiff, William Whitebread, is by trade a Baker, and as apples are generally used in puddings and pies, which diminish considerably the consumption of bread, it was therefore undoubtedly for the Plaintiff's interest to let loose his pigs on the Defendant's apples, and to destroy as many of them as he possibly could.——The Plaintiff lastly says, that his pigs died by the inclemency of the weather. We shall leave it to the Gentlemen of the Jury to determine whether a pig could die by cold in a mild October night. No; the truth of the case is this: The apples were blown off the trees before they were ripe; the apples were a *sour* fruit; the pigs did eat most immoderately thereof; the pigs consequently died of the *gripes.*

MUCH

MUCH has been related of the sagacity of the brutes of antiquity, and especially of that Lion which used to be seen in the streets of Rome, accompanying the pardoned runaway slave. I have been witness to equal gratitude, in a Lion of modern date.—One day that I had the honour of dining with the Duchess of Hamilton, at the so-named palace of Hamilton in Scotland, her Grace asked the company, after dinner, if they had any curiosity to see her Lion; she would attend us, and order the keeper to feed him?—We gladly accepted the offer, and went down to the court, to see the Lion get his dinner.—While we stood at the cage, admiring the fierceness of his looks, and his terrible roar, each time we provoked him, with sticks, to fly at us, and abandon his prey, the porter came, and told the Duchess, that a serjeant, with some recruits, at the gate, begged leave to be admitted to see the Lion. Her Grace, with great condescension and good-nature, asked permission of the company to let the travellers come in, as they would then have the satisfaction of seeing the animal fed.——They were accordingly admitted, at the moment the Lion was growling over his prey. The serjeant advancing to the cage, called out, "Nero, Nero, poor Nero, don't you know me?" The animal instantly turned his head, and looked at him; then rose up, left his prey, and came, wagging his tail, to the side of the cage. The serjeant then put his hand upon him, and patted him; telling us, at the same time, that it was three years since they had seen each other; but that he had had the care of the Lion on his passage from Gibraltar, and he was happy to see the poor beast shew so much gratitude for his attention. The Lion, indeed, seemed to be perfectly pleased;

pleafed; he went to and fro, rubbing himfelf againft the place where his benefactor ftood, and licked his hand as the ferjeant held it to him, and fometimes put it in his mouth. The ferjeant, on his part, was fo confident of the honour and integrity of his friend, that he offered to go into the cage to him; but he was prudently with-held; the company not being fo thoroughly convinced of the fincerity or generofity of the brute creation. And herein my next ftory might juftify their fcruples; for we fhall learn, that brutes have alfo their vices, as well as their extraordinary virtues.

Mr. M. of Whitmore in Staffordfhire, ufed to come twice a-year to town, on fome family bufinefs; and being a gentleman fond of exercife, he commonly made the journey on horfeback, accompanied moft part of the way by a faithful little terrier-dog, which, for fear of lofing in town, he always left to the care of my kind, good-natured landlady, Mrs. Langford, at St. Alban's; and, on his return to the country, he was fure to find his little companion well taken care of, and perfectly recovered from the fatigues of his journey.—But Mr. M. calling for the dog one time as ufual, good Mrs. Langford appeared with a woeful countenance before him:—"Alas! Sir, your little Terrier is loft, and I have been fretting my heart out about him. Our great houfe-dog and he had a quarrel together, and the poor Terrier was fo worried and bit before we could part them, that I verily believed he would never have got the better of it. He made a fhift, however, to crawl out of the yard, and no mortal here fet eyes upon him for almoft a week after. He then returned, and (will you believe it, Sir?) he brought along with him another dog, bigger by far than our's, and they two

fell

fell upon our great houſe-dog, and bit him ſo unmercifully, that he has ſcarcely ſince been able to go about the yard, or eat his meat.——After that your little dog and his companion diſappeared, and they have never ſince been ſeen at St. Alban's."——Mr. M. heard the old lady's ſtory with no ſmall aſtoniſhment; but he bore his loſs with perfect reſignation. Heaven ſent a ſpeedy reward to his philoſophy.—On his arrival at Whitmore, he found his little Terrier was got ſafe home before him; and, on inquiring into circumſtances, he alſo found, that the Terrier had been down at Whitmore, and coaxed his great houſe-dog to follow him back to St. Alban's, where he was ſure of being revenged on his enemy.—Theſe facts have been well authenticated to me; and one of the parties concerned I have often ſeen—I mean the little, ſagacious, revengeful animal. But in what manner Brutes are endowed with ſo much reaſon, as in the inſtances related, and the power of combining their ideas, I ſhall not take upon me to determine.

THE

THE LEVELLER. N°. I.

MOST of our Writers of Periodical Essays have been particularly careful to choose for themselves such names only, as were, in their interpretation, inoffensive, or were likely to prepossess their Readers in their favour. There are, 'tis true, over-curious and impertinent *Spectators*, wicked *Guardians*, idle *Ramblers*, gambling *Adventurers*, and trifling *Connoisseurs;* but, 'till we experience the contrary, we are still inclined to believe the Gentlemen, under these denominations, to be *honest* and worthy *Spectators, Guardians, Ramblers, Adventurers,* and *Connoisseurs.* The *Tatlers*, indeed, are rather equivocal, and so is the *World:* it requires some acquaintance with the *first,* before we can entirely divest ourselves of our prejudice against them; and, as for the *World,* it is either a very good World, or a cursed bad one, accordingly as one is disposed to judge of it. Now, I am sensible that the name I have assumed is of the number of the last equivocal kind, and therefore requires some little explanation. The Word *Leveller* seems to convey the meaning of pulling

ling down, rather than of raising up; although the levelling any thing may be performed by elevating or erecting, as well as by debasing or pulling down.

I would not be understood to be of levelling principles in my Political Creed. I have, on the contrary, the greatest veneration for our happy constitution,—the limited monarchy of Great Britain. My attempts shall only be to level and lay low the stubborn excrescences of the Mind: Pride, Vanity, and towering Ambition, I shall endeavour to humble in the dust. I shall remind the so-named *Gentleman* or *Man of Honour*, that, in the eye of God, he is on a Level with the very *Scum of the Earth*: if the *One* merit distinction, 'tis but by his virtue and honourable deeds; in the *Other* exists no vileness, but thro' his Debauchery and Vice. It is my wish, therefore, to bring Mankind on a Level or equality of *Mind*, by persuading the *Great* to Tenderness, Humanity, and Meekness, qualities the most rare in the Man of High Life; and by inspiring the *Poor* with those virtues, (most chearing to the Common Man) Fortitude, Resignation to the Divine Will, and a becoming Consciousness of the Dignity of the Human Race.

There are three things which gain the possessors of them the consideration of the World: Honour, Riches, and Parts. I have placed them according to their established and accustomed rank; but in my own mind I should reverse their order, or should esteem them in proportion to their connection with Virtue and Worth.

To give an example of the first rank: The Emperor of Germany, for a Speech he made, was once very high in my esteem. A Friend of mine, who had been introduced to him at Florence, and to whom he shewed a particular regard, met with him

again

again at Naples, some months after their first acquaintance. "Well, Sir, said the Emperor, how do you like Italy? Has the country answered your expectations?" O, perfectly, Sir; no Country more agreeable; no journey more delightfully entertaining. "As for me, continued the Emperor, you see how I travel; with very few attendants; three or four Gentlemen, my intimate Friends. In the day-time we separate, to make our rounds of the Town, and at night we meet to communicate our intelligence and observations to each other. In this manner I have travelled through Italy; and, I may say, I have made a glorious campaign, without its having cost one drop of human blood." There was a Speech worthy of an Emperor indeed! But, mark his falling off:—he has joined in the plunder and partition of a Free State.

Having thus given an instance how a Person of the highest Elevation may, in my opinion, debase himself, I shall next relate in what manner two miserable Beings, of the lowest State, raised themselves to a Level with his Majesty King George the Third and his Royal Mate. One day, as I was coming home to dinner, I perceived a poor Man and Woman standing near my door, in earnest discourse together. They did not observe me; and while I was scraping the dirt off my shoes, I overheard the Man uttering these affectionate words: "Do eat it, my Dear" (she was pressing him to accept of a piece of bread, that she held out to him with both her hands).—"Do eat it yourself—indeed I will not take it—it will do more good to you, for I can fast."—Here my knocking at the door disturbed them, and they withdrew a few paces from me. I put my hand into my pocket to relieve their distress. "There, good people, said I, there is a shilling for you; you seem to be in want." They received it with blessings and thanks. When I went into the parlour, curiosity led me to the window, to see what was become of that miserable Pair. I then beheld the Man devouring the morsel of bread like a Wolf; like a Wolf, driven by cold and hunger from his forests, to prey on the flocks of the plain. No conjugal affection restrained him; no feelings for the distress of his Mate; she had now got wherewithal to purchase a dinner, and he could make his meal on the crust of bread. I called my Dear Friend (my *Wife*, I mean,) to the window; there, Mary, behold that sight. I told her the story, and the tears gushed from her eyes in a flood. The Scene being too affecting for her compassionate heart, I led her by the hand to the fireside.—" You see, My dear Mary, to what misery we mortals are at times reduced; you have been bred up in affluence and ease in your Father's house, and have seen nothing but plenty in the country around. The fields, at the worst, exhibited to you the Labourer, toiling to earn, with the sweat of his brow, his pittance of bread: but in the city you will behold *real* sorrow and distress. Were you, like me, to walk the streets of this metropolis at night, you would behold your fellow-creatures, Men, Women, and Children, formed by the same hand of God, destitute of every necessary of Life;—bereft of cloathing, wanting food, without a home in the cold and chilling frost, they are fain to take shelter under the porches of the Rich, and at the doors of their fellow-citizens to pass the bleakest nights.—Who knows but such may be the the lot, this very night, of that miserable Pair? And yet, by their wickedness, they cannot have deserved it; they have shewn me such greatness of

mind,

mind, such nobleness of sentiment, in that short debate about their only Crust of Bread, that I am certain their lives have not been governed by vice.—Perhaps bred up in a virtuous and affluent state, they are, for unknown purposes, by the hand of Heaven thus levelled with the Poor. But let us assist them as much as we can."——I ran to the door, to give them a guinea; but they were gone, and were lost in a croud of passengers in the street.

The LEVELLER. N°. II.

On PRIDE.

EVERY one, who has travelled this country, must have perceived, that at most of the great Mansion-houses he had visited, he was first admitted into a spacious hall, large enough for the drawing of a public *Lottery*, and sufficiently capacious to incarcerate therein the whole Commons of England; after which he was, perhaps, in due form, ushered into an adjoining apartment.——In the days of old English Hospitality, these Halls were of material service: they were intended to contain a numerous company, at any grand and extraordinary entertainment; to hold any necessary meeting of Vassals and Dependents; and to have in them hung up and displayed

played the whole shew of the Family Armour. But in these modern Times, when generous Hospitality, familiar Society, and free, convivial Good-humour, are giving place to a stiff ceremony, and a vain, yet parsimonious ostentation, I can discover no other use a Hall is of in any Mansion, but to serve as a convenient *Ventilator* to the rest of the building. It has, on the contrary, one great inconvenience, to which few people have paid any attention: the Hall is commonly so large and so lofty, that, compared to it, the grandest Rooms in the house appear like diminutive Closets. I should therefore prefer to enter a house at a handsome, neat vestibule, in order that, when I was shewn further into the building, I should find the apartments improve in their appearance, and, in elegance and size, rather exceed my expectations.—Now, this taste of mine with regard to the apartments of a House, I thought it prudent to keep in remembrance at my beginning these periodical Essays which I have undertaken. Had I, peradventure, set off with a long, elaborate, ornamented dissertation, I should have raised my Readers hopes of me far above my intention, and beyond the power of my ordinary abilities to answer. He would, in that case, have served my Compositions as many a Traveller does some of our Gothic Mansions; he thrusts his nose into a room or two, with the doors half open; takes a hasty peep at them; then, suddenly wheeling round to his companion, he whispers in his ear,—"There is nothing worth seeing, but the Hall and the rusty Armour."—My Readers will, in due time, discover whether this was a needless preamble.

Tho' the word *Pride* certainly conveys to us the idea of a *vicious* quality of the mind, yet there is a sort of Pride, or greatness of spirit, which, in some instances,

instances, appears to be commendable. The Pride I mean, is that which deters a man from committing a mean or dishonourable action, and prevents him from stooping unworthily, or unnecessarily, to men of a superior station. It is easy for a tall, lusty fellow, in a croud, to make a considerable stoop without any danger of falling; but if a little, insignificant figure of a man should debase himself one inch of his stature, the elbow of the tall varlet will instantly be upon him; he will inevitably be borne down; he will be contemptuously trod under foot; and the whole scoffing croud will pass over his belly *. Let every one, therefore, retain in his mind a just sense of the importance of a Man to himself, and of the dignity of Human Nature; but let him banish from his thoughts an ungovernable self-conceit, which would prompt him to *arrogate* the submission and extraordinary respect of his neighbours. As Lord Mansfield once publicly declared with regard to *popularity*, so ought a man to be satisfied with the *respect which follows him*, and not presumptuously to expect that which he *claims*, or with anxiety *runs after*. I venerate the Archbishop of York †, for his unaffected Piety, his Learning, his Judgment, his Affability, and Good-nature; but, with a mixture of pity and contempt, I listen to an austere, proud pedant of a Parson, who is ever stunning my ears with his cant, and his learned quotations. I respect and admire Mr. David Hume and Dr. Robertson as much for their modesty as for the excellency of their writings; while I cannot submit to flatter the vanity of some other Authors, who, on the success of a new Play,

or

---

* Tho' this is a *foreign* Phrase expressive of Contempt, I have ventured to use it in my own Language.
† Drummond.

or the Publication of some Pamphlet or Poem of their writing, will assume the airs and consequence of the greatest Wit that ever put pen to paper. In short, that kind of pride and self-conceit which prompts a man to claim respect, as it were a tribute, from his neighbours, will only procure him the outward shew of it from his dependents; the rest of the World will yield him but their civility and secret contempt. A Man possessed of the pride of not stooping unworthily to those above him, ought to be cautious to whom he lays himself under obligation; for he may happen to receive benefits of a person of whom he has been deceived in his opinion, and to whom he must afterwards pay deference and respect; or he must else appear, in the eyes of the world, to be unaccountably ungrateful and unfeeling.—Yet, to scorn receiving benefits from a person one esteems, is to have a spirit too haughty for the Society of Man. For my own part, I think *Gratitude*, next to *Love*, (of which, in fact, it is the most durable composition) is the most agreeable Sensation of the Heart; and far from being ashamed of the favours I have received from my friends, I feel a satisfaction in the thought, that, if I had not been in some degree worthy of esteem, I should never have received them. ——I do not know that the folly and ridiculousness of Pride is any where shewn in a stronger light than in Gulliver's Travels to *Brobdingnag*. But, instead of the gigantic Natives of that Country, I can figure to myself "millions of spiritual creatures that walk the earth unseen." millions of superior beings, with which God has peopled other more glorious parts of the Universe: I can figure to myself one of These talking of us insignificant Mortals on earth, in the words of the King of *Brobdingnag*:—" What a contemptible

temptible thing is Human Grandeur! These diminutive insects! these short-sighted, mortal creatures, that have but a few hours to live! give themselves titles and distinctions of honour; they contrive little nests and burrows, which they call Houses and Cities; they make a figure in dress and equipage; they love; they fight; they dispute; they cheat; they betray!"——But of all the people in the World whose vanity and self-conceit deserve reprehension, the idle Drones of Society are, in their assumed airs of importance, the most ridiculous and contemptible: I mean those of our Nobility and Gentry, who giving themselves no concern about the welfare of the Community in which they live, waste their days in idleness and ease, or in a criminal and ruinous dissipation. Who but must smile, when he beholds these useless beings giving themselves the airs of men of real consequence and worth, when they are solely indebted to Chance (not to puzzle them with Providence) for their large possessions, or for their superiority in rank above their fellow-creatures? Who but must smile to see them behaving with superlative insolence and contempt to every honest, useful Member of Society, whose circumstances cannot afford an equal shew of of Dress and Equipage with them? With the sensible part of mankind, indeed, Virtue and a Liberal Education will gain a man esteem, and make him be reckoned fit company for a Duke; but as our Public Meetings of Fashionable People are not entirely composed of Men of Sense and Discretion, I must here beg leave to offer my Readers a few Rules and Directions, by which any virtuous honest man may soon rival the politest people of the *Ton;* and in consequence and importance raise himself to a level with the proudest and most conceited.

I   Rules

Rules, *by which One may easily gain the outward Respect and Consideration of his Neighbours; or,* Directions *to all* Gentlemen *and* Ladies *how to make themselves most conspicuous and remarkable at the various* Places *of public* Amusement.

I. IF you should happen to be elected Master of the Ceremonies, at any Country Ball or Assembly, take no notice at all of Strangers, (not even of his Majesty's Officers) for they are people that *nobody knows*. Notwithstanding it is the custom in the polite Countries of Europe, to inquire for the Strangers at a Ball, and to pay them the Compliment of taking them out to dance the first Minuets, you are not bound by *foreign* Laws. Strangers can have neither votes nor interest in your Country, and it would therefore be highly absurd to give them the precedence of Gentlemen of Property in it.

II. If you are a Man of Quality, spend at least two-thirds of the year, and the best part of the income of your estate, in London. Your residence in the Country must only be a kind of *Cantonment*, to recruit as much as you possibly can for your next Campaign at Court;—for which purpose you must live quite retired and secluded from the Society of the neighbouring Gentlemen of the County; or, if you chuse to honour any of them with a sight of you, keep two or three *public Days*, and ape his Majesty at St. James's. You will by that means, (of feeing them all in a croud together) save yourself a world of trouble, and keep your neighbours in proper respect. They will know their due distance, when you never receive them but in form; and by not returning their visits till you are just going to Town, you are sure to see none of them above once at your House, in a Season.

III. If

III. If you happen to live near any large country-town, pay no attention to any of the inhabitants, left you should have the whole town come swarming about your house. Yet, before you leave the neighbourhood of those Cits, and return to your amusements in London, it may not be amiss, just to join them for once in a Ball or a Concert, in order to shew them your superiority in Dress, and to have a laugh at the Country Putts before you set off for London.

N. B. The above Three Rules I particularly recommend, at this time, to all who wish to be popular at the next General Election.

IV. It will, however, be impossible for you, sometimes to live entirely for *yourself*. Good-breeding requires you should pay some attention to any of his Majesty's Officers that are quartered in your neighbourhood, or to any Gentleman who has retired to the Country for the benefit of his health. You may, in that case, pay them one formal visit, if you please, and give them a general invitation to your house; but I would advise you not to fix a day for them to wait on you, if you want them to keep their proper distance, and not to become too intimately acquainted; and if they have any good-manners themselves, they will be sure never to come near you at dinner time, left you should happen to have your house full of company, or left you should have a particular desire to be alone; in either of which cases you would think them cursedly familiar, and wish them at the Devil for their pains.

V. On your arrival at any place of public entertainment, be sure to make acquaintance with the best company only; such as Peers, Peeresses, Stars, Garters, and the like. This will certainly gain you some

some consideration and respect, whether you are intitled to any or not.

VI. If you are a Person of Quality, it behoves you of all things to make a Party at Cards; for to be at an Assembly without playing at Cards, would be to declare that you could amuse yourself in rational conversation with any of the company; than which nothing can be accounted more impolite.

VII. When you have made your Party, you must observe to assemble together every night. The same persons seated exactly in the same corner of the room every evening, cannot fail to make you conspicuous; and after you have made yourself thus remarkable, you need give yourself no trouble to speak to the rest of the company. You will be sufficiently known without it; and all one desires, you see, is to be known; as little matters it whether for civility or incivility, as for virtue or vice.

VIII. Remember, on a Ball night, never to come to the rooms at the hour when the company usually meet. Come in after the Minuets are begun, and bustle thro' the company till you get at the top of the room. *That* cannot fail of attracting the eyes of every body upon you; especially if the top of the room should not be the place properly belonging to your rank. Observe the like Rule when you go to a Play. Never come into the House till the second or third Act is nearly over; and then the opening and shutting of the Box-doors, the flapping of the Benches, and the adjusting yourselves to the best advantage, cannot but draw the eyes of the Audience, and their most devout benedictions upon you.—You may also, in like manner, obtain the blessings of a whole pious congregation, if you take care never to go to Church till the Service is half over.

IX. If

IX. If you dance Country-dances, take care to push yourself in at the top of the Dance, whether you stood up in time or not; and when you have danced down the Dance, sit down with your Partner immediately; for nothing is so vulgar as to dance a Dance up again; few Gentlemen can submit to the drudgery of it; and really when one has danced it down with spirit with an agreeable Partner, there is no standing conveniently after it.

X. At the time of Tea-drinking, you must, by all means, endeavour to make up a snug party in a corner by yourselves; for you will never be looked upon as *any-body*, if you drink Tea at the Long-table with the Mob.—The same rule observe on the public tea-drinking Nights; with this addition, however, that you must not appear in the Rooms till the main Body of the Company have drank Tea, and are arisen from table. Nothing is then so glorious, so delightfully entertaining, as to form a Circle of select Friends, to serenade the company with bawling for Coffee, Tea, Cakes, and Bread-and-Butter, and to keep half a dozen Waiters employed in running through the rooms with kettles of boiling water! It gives prodigious life to the company, if any of them should be accidentally scalded; and adds infinite spirit to the conversation, should any of the Ladies get their gowns spoiled by the unlucky encounter of some Bread-and-Butter.

XI. Soon after your appearance in public, (suppose at Brighthelmstone, Scarborough, or Margate) pay your respects to the handsomest Woman in the Polite Circle; and be sure to remain constantly at her elbow during the whole time of your stay in the Country. This will often gain you the reputation of having an Intrigue, though, from your disability of intriguing, the Physicians may have ordered you to dip in the Salt-water.

XII. I address myself particularly to the Ladies. You must be careful to encourage the attendance of the men who conspicuously attach themselves to you; not only for the above-mentioned reason, of making the World believe you have an Intrigue, (than which nothing can make you more notorious and remarkable) but also to awaken your Husbands to a thorough sense of your extraordinary Perfections. But the greatest Purpose herein answered, is, to shew the World that you are above its censure.

The LEVELLER. N°. III.

On PATRIOTISM.

IN poring over the Records of *Antiquity*, nothing, among the *learned*, is more common, than to neglect the study of *Modern* History, and to contemn the knowledge of recent events.

Through a profound veneration for their ancient Heroes, or through ignorance of actions of latter date, they will extol the magnanimous feats of a Greek or a Roman above all that a Briton could effect; and will celebrate the vain atchievements of a

Heathen

Heathen Commander, as surpassing the courage, constancy, or virtue of any Christian Chief.

But, esteeming the merit of every action according to the motives which produced it, what, for the most part, were the *ancient heroisms* of which we have read? What, the *disinterested Patriotism* so much boasted of? *Decius* dastardly drowned (or properly *suffocated*) himself in a marsh, to escape the shame and infamy of being taken by the enemy; whereas, after having to the utmost done his duty, he ought, with patient fortitude, to have submitted to the will of God:—Mere pride and vanity were, therefore, the occasion of his death. Pride and vanity, too, (the love of glory taught them in their youth) actuated *Fabius* and *Camillus* in *their* heroic deeds. Could we have read *Brutus*'s heart, implacable revenge against *Tarquin* animated him, perhaps, as much against the favourers of that Tyrant, as any real concern for the liberties of *Rome*,—any ardent zeal for the prosperity of the Commonwealth. The jealousy of power, and the resentment of a brutal, proud, imperious parent, may have provoked *Brutus* to put his sons to death;—may have so much enraged the inhuman *Manlius* against a haughty and undutiful child, as to order *his* son to be decapitated. In short, where ambition, the love of fame, an ungovernable thirst after praise, or any other motive than a desire to please his Creator, excites a man to action, he may gain his *earthly* reward; but it is not *patriotism*, it is not *virtue*. *He* may, indeed, be *literally called* a Patriot, who professes, and even shews a regard for the interests of his country; but the constancy, sincerity, and disinterestedness of that patriotism, can never be depended upon, which proceeds not from a motive of religious duty.

Nor,

Nor, in the days of the primitive Romans, was the merit of difinterefted Patriotifm fo fuperlatively great. What inducements had a *Quintius Cincinnatus*, a *Marcus Curius*, the *Elder Cato*, *Scipio Africanus*,—what inducements had they, I fay, to plunder their country, or raife themfelves on the ruins of it, when they could happily amufe themfelves in labouring in a turnip-field, and place their chief enjoyment in a country retreat? But, as we proceed in our knowledge of the Ancients, and read of the growth of luxury among them, how few do we meet with, among the latter Romans, who would facrifice their lives, part with their properties, or relinquifh their pleafures, to fecure the lives, liberties, and properties of their fellow citizens? After the age of *Auguftus*, Patriotifm fled to the Weft; and I may venture to fay, that in Britain it has difplayed itfelf with far more luftre than ever it did in Rome.—Howmuchfoever fome fhewed themfelves, in the event, to be ruled by avarice, ambition, or pride, the Patriots of the laft century were furely difinterefted in their motives, when they hazarded their lives and eftates to oppofe the mandates of Government, and bring to reafon an arbitrary King.—But luxury has fince increafed, and, with it, the temptations to deviate from our duty to the State. By a bafe compliance with the dictates of felf-intereft, we obtain the means of indulging every appetite or vice. If, then, Patriotifm is more rare than it has been, we muft allow it to be more meritorious where it actually exifts. The beft may err; the beft may heedlefsly go aftray, and by impetuous paffions be hurried into guilt; but we muft acknowledge *that* Patriot to be fincere, who, in thefe times of luxury and diffipation, will not *deliberately* fin, and who can facrifice his own intereft for what he is

convinced

convinced would be for the public good. If, in such times, a man should be elected to represent a county in Parliament, by friends and relations who entertained an opinion of his worth; if, bred to a profession by which disinterestedness is a bar to success; if chiefly dependent on relations for his future advancement in life, he should nevertheless give a constitutional vote, by which he foresaw he should forfeit their friendship, and endanger his Seat; such a man must be a Patriot: he must be sincere in his Patriotism; for he could have acted with no selfish intent. Such a Patriot there has been; such a Patriot there still is; and such a Patriot, I trust, there will be, as long as e'er he lives.

The LEVELLER. N°. IV.

On HORSEMANSHIP.

OF all the Subjects treated of by our Writers of Essays, there is none left so open for discussion as that on *Taste*. The reason of it is plain: our greatest Authors have agreed, that there is no fixing the Principles of Taste; and that we may dispute about them to eternity, without being allowed to be in the right; for, after all the fine arguments we can produce on the subject, a stupid, unfeeling fellow shall

shall knock them on the head with saying—"But that is not *my* Taste."—The learned, and otherwise elaborate Mr. HUME, declining, therefore, a minute examination of the principles of Taste, abandoned a field where nothing was to be gained, but where every would-be Critic could oppose him. But it was, perhaps, more a want of Taste in that great Author himself, than any *real* difficulty in the subject, that made him abridge it. No man likes to sit down to make a meal of a dish for which he has no relish; and far less is he capable of dressing it for another, it he is ignorant of the proper ingredients of which it ought to be composed. Most people, however, pretend to some share of Taste; and I am of the number of those Pretenders. It shall, in due time, be judged whether my Pretensions are well grounded. I will submit to the Public a periodical Essay of my Taste, with the best reasons I can give to support it; and tho' I may sometimes go out of the common highroad, I trust to their merciful candour not to convict me of a *Trespass*.

But not to trespass on my Reader's time with farther Preface, let me seat him on horseback, and we will proceed on our periodical journey.

Now that you are mounted, my Friend, let us, in good humour, jog on together. Sit perfectly at your ease; be not afraid of having the eyes of a Man of Taste upon you. I would rather see you sit at your ease, in all the negligence of an old woman travelling to market, than I would see you sit according to the Rules of Horsemanship, if those Rules stiffen and constrain you. The attempt you just now made at a graceful seat, was exactly what I saw practised by some Light Dragoons, when they passed before the King, last summer, at Northaw Common. They were,

were, moſt of them, riding eaſy and graceful enough, till they came within a few paces of his Majeſty; they then forced back their heads, cock'd up their chins, and thruſt out their cheſts, ſo that each of them appeared, as he paſſed along, like a Cock drinking at a pond, or a roaſted Lobſter held up on a ſpit, and ready for diſhing.—Obſerve that man riding with his long ſtirrups, his ſtiffened knees; and his legs ſtuck out nine inches at leaſt from the horſe's belly! Look at him behind—what a figure he makes! He is, for all the world, like a pair of ruſty tongs hung upon our kitchen-poker!—But he had his inſtructions at the Riding-ſchool. So had that other Fellow, with his legs in the poſition of the wings of an Oſtrich when he is running; his knees a little bent; his feet ſtuck out behind; and his heels pointing to the horſe's buttocks.—The Firſt attempts at Grace alone; the Second aims both at Grace and Conveniency in riding; for, by having the ſpur ſo much nearer the horſe's ſide, he thinks he has ſo much the leſs neceſſity to move his leg, when he has occaſion to work him. Behold that other ride by with his arms pinioned to his ſides, like the wings of a truſſed Turkey! That man was told at the Manège to keep his arms cloſe to his ſides, and now he dares not uſe them.—Since thoſe riders offend me ſo much, you will forgive me for ſeating you after my own manner:——Keep yourſelf erect by the ſole movement of pulling up your neck, as if you would make yourſelf taller. Try this when you are naked, and you will perceive it anſwers both the purpoſe of puſhing out the cheſt, and keeping back the ſhoulders; and it leaves your head, at the ſame time, at perfect liberty to turn to every object. You may give yourſelf a little more grace by drawing back the Joints of the Shoulders,

—If

—If you attempt to keep yourself straight by holding back the head, and forcing out the chest, you will find that you will stiffen your neck and your backbone, and put yourself into a very uneasy posture. From the formation of the human body, it is impossible, without constraint, to keep your Arms so close to your Sides, as that one cannot see through them. The *upper* Ribs naturally prevent the Arms from touching the *lower*; and, when viewed behind, place them in a direction correspondent with that of the Thighs below them. The only care then with your Arms is to keep your Elbows down, and prevent them from shaking; and this is chiefly done by drawing back the Joints of the Shoulders.

Now, as to your Seat in the Saddle.——But you may trot on as you are, till we get to Charing-cross. Observe the Leg of that Rider! his Knee is quite stiff, and his Heel is forced down in a most constrained, ungraceful manner.—Do not follow that fashion, for it is both uneasy and unnatural: it is also unsafe; for the straightening your Knee stiffens the muscles of the inside of your Thighs, and makes them the more liable to slip off the saddle.—The forcing down the Heel adds to the action of raising you from your Seat in a hard trot, or when your Horse unexpectedly flings out or capers.——We'll proceed, if you please, to Leicester-fields.—There, now, is the Seat I would recommend to you! That Rider appears not to sit upon his Bottom, but to hang upon his Thighs! His knee is gently bent, so as to allow his Legs to hang perpendicularly, and the Stirrup-leathers to continue the Line of Direction of his Thigh-bones. His Stirrups support his Legs only, and bear nothing of the Weight of his Body.——That seat is the most graceful and proper for journey-riding;

but,

but, when you follow the Hounds, I would advise you to take up your Stirrups a few Holes, so as to make your Stirrup-leathers, when you walk your horse, hang perpendicularly; by which means, you can give yourself a spring into the Newmarket-trot, or aid yourself in leaping.—You must not, however, trust to your Stirrups in hunting; trust entirely to your Thighs, and the balance of your body.—The Riding-master and Jockey generally run into the extremes of two opposite customs: the first, on horseback, confides entirely to the balance of his body; the last trusts chiefly to his stirrups.—Balance your body by all means; but let it also have the support of the Thighs.—With long stirrups, your Thighs being almost perpendicular, and nearly on a line with your body downward, prevent you from falling off sideways, when your horse unexpectedly starts aside. With shorter stirrups you are, on the contrary, better guarded against a fall over the horse's neck, if he should kick up behind, or take a sudden leap; for the thighs being advanced a little before the body, will support it when in danger of losing its balance by a violent jerk. I must not omit mentioning the common rule to you, that the body to the Haunchbone, and the Legs from the Knees, ought to be perfectly free and easy, and as much at your command as if you were on foot. To attain this ease or freedom, the Gallop is more useful than the Trot; for the *first* motion gives play to all the muscles of the body, but the *last* acts chiefly on the joints.— You must, however, be careful, by drawing up your neck, to keep yourself straight; for, if you allow yourself to lean forward over the horse's neck in galloping, it will in time draw your shoulders together, and give you a natural stoop. The figures of most of our Jockies, contrasted with those of our Light Dragoons, prove the justness of this remark; and observe the aukward stiffness of most of our heavy Dragoons and Coachmen when they are on foot, and you must acknowledge, that the Trot of a Horse, and the similar motion of a Coach-box, though they settle the joints of a man's back and shoulders, must, by constant practice, render his back-bone stiff. I am the more particular on this head, because the intention of riding ought not only to be for your pleasure, and for the health and exercise of your body, but should also be conducive in giving you an easy and graceful carriage in walking.

The LEVELLER. N°. V.

On PAINTING.

Addressed to the PRESIDENT of the ROYAL ACADEMY of ARTS.

SIR,

THE very learned and facetious Dean Swift hath, (in the Introduction to that admirable Work of his, called a Tale of a Tub) enumerated to us *three* wooden machines, originally constructed for the use and convenience of those Orators, who are allowed the

the privilege of talking much without interruption; and these are, the *Pulpit*, the *Ladder*, and the *Mountebank Stage*. But there is a *fourth* oratorial machine, the invention of which the good Dean could not possibly foresee, and which is left for *me*, a feeble yet observing critic, to record.——This *fourth* machine, Sir, is your right worshipful, presidential Chair;—the *Chair of the President of the Royal Academy of Arts*; from which you have, for several years past, been indulged with the liberty of delivering an annual speech, without any one hitherto presuming to interrupt you, or make thereto the least reply.——The same indulgence, however, is not due to you from the Public, as is shewn you by your hearers in the Royal Academy; your orations are *printed* as well as spoken, and no law or custom has prohibited your Readers from printing their remarks and observations in reply to them.——Yet, I mean not to criticise on any of your orations; my intention is only, in return, to give you some occasional thoughts of mine, which may prove of academical use. To *you* I shall leave the honour of expatiating on *antient* Painters and Painting; *my* observations shall be confined to the works of *modern* Painters which *you* could not so well comment upon, without breach of friendship with your brothers of the Brush.

The perfection of Painting consists in deceiving the sight; in making an object on canvas appear to the eye as a reality and a substance, instead of being discerned to be nothing but the image of a thing described.——The nearer a resemblance of any thing in Painting approaches to that perfection, the more excellent, in my opinion, is the Painter's art.

I can conceive a face with a bad complexion; a robe that does not hang perfectly loose; an unbeco-
. ming

ming dress; a long nose; a wry mouth; hands and fingers out of all proportion, and other members equally out of size; for *such* Nature herself presents every day to my sight;—but I can never conceive an object on canvas to be natural, that is flat; it can never deceive my sight if it wants *Relief*.———Without *That*, though the colours of a Painting may be uncommonly beautiful, and it's Drawing most elegant and correct, it will not, in my estimation, be a *Picture*, but a *coloured Plan*.———In this art of giving a Relief, many of the modern Painters are very defective; and among These, I am sorry to say, Mr. —— is the chief. His portraits are, in general, unexceptionable, immediately as they come from his hand; they are elegantly drawn, great fancy is displayed in them, and the resemblances are strikingly like;—but their colours soon fade, and leave the Painting, to my eyes, as if I beheld it through a veil or a mist. As his defect, then, does not proceed from want of judgment, but from an imperfection in his colours, I hope he will not think it beneath him to learn the art of mixing them from Mr. Wright of Derby, Mr. West, Mr. Dance, Mr. Romney, or some of those masters who seem to have made it their particular study.———By experience I know, that he has sufficient good-sense and good-nature, not to take amiss any friendly advice that is given him. It is not many years ago, since I used the freedom to observe to him, that his portraits would receive additional beauty, if he would be at the trouble of shewing the eyes, and finishing them, instead of throwing a shade over them; which saved him, indeed, a great deal of Painting, but which rendered his Portraits dead and uninteresting. He accordingly took the hint; his Eyes have, ever since, been more in the light, which

has

has certainly given more life to his Painting. The reasons for my advising this alteration, you must allow, were well grounded. If the Eyes of a Portrait are painted as if looking at me, and if they are natural, finished in the light and highly executed, I overlook many defects in the rest of the figure, and almost forget that it is but an inanimate Picture; more especially so, if it should be the Portrait of a handsome woman; for, let my eyes wander ever so much over the rest of her beauties, they will ever return to meet her looks. In this particular, many of Vandyke's Portraits are peculiarly flattering and satisfactory; insomuch, that, were I to sit alone for a whole day in Lord Pembroke's great room at Wilton, with his beautiful *family-piece* in front of me, I should never fancy myself without company.

I acknowledge that this rule of Painting the eyes of a Portrait looking on the spectators, cramps the genius of the Painter, and confines him to a small variety of attitudes. But for the sake of preserving the likeness of a friend, which can never be very striking without displaying the eye, I would willingly exempt the Painter from exerting the powers of his imagination, and adding to the Portrait the graces of an Historical Piece.

I believe you will agree with me, Sir, that nothing teaches the force of Light and Shade, and the Art of giving a Relief, so much as drawing in black and white. I would therefore recommend to the students of the Academy to make themselves perfect in *drawing* before they attempt to *paint*. I have, in Flanders and Holland, seen imitations of sculpture that would deceive the keenest sight; and Mr. Berens, of Southgate, has a piece of that kind, by a master of Antwerp, which might be exhibited as a model of the Relief. If, then, such an extraordinary effect can be produced by plain *black* and *white*, it would surely be more easy to effect the deception when the artist has the powers of *all* the colours to his aid.

There is a custom of some of the great masters of antiquity, which is adopted by many of our modern Painters, and which is often very unnatural and absurd; that is, of painting a dark back-ground, in order to give their figures a Relief. This may be very proper, if the back ground be a dead wall, a curtain, a hanging canopy, or the wainscot of a room; but when it happens to be the sky, as frequently is the case, nothing so much offends my sight.———I do not remember to have seen such a remarkable instance of a blunder of this kind, as in a picture painted by Mr. D. when he was at Rome. I mention it because the piece is in other respects unexceptionably good. Mr. D. will doubtless recollect to have painted a young nobleman who was then on his travels *, who was in a deep consumption at the time, and whose features were strongly expressive of his disease. He is drawn leaning with his back against a tree, his gun in his hand and rested on the ground, his dog couched panting at his feet, his waistcoat entirely unbuttoned to give him air, and the whole of his countenance and figure most inimitably expressive of excessive fatigue from the sport of the day. So far the judgment of the artist was great, But the sportsman and his dog are both painted in glaring daylight, while the objects around them, and the sky above their heads, represent the darkness of night. I must confess I was much at a loss to guess what could possibly have thrown light on the figures in the picture, till I recollected an old diversion I enjoyed

* The late Lord Hope.

joyed at school, called *Bat-fowling;* which I imagined my young travelling friend in Italy had improved upon, and had gone out a-shooting by the light of a lanthorn or a lamp.

We are told, that to a person severely attacked with the jaundice, every object appears as if it were tinctured with yellow. From what cause his sight is so affected, I have never heard it determined; but I am led to imagine, that, from a similar law in optics, some particular colours predominate in the sight of many of our painters.

Who, for instance, views a painting of Mr. G.'s, but must acknowledge, that he throws a dash of the purple into every colour from his pencil:——which must proceed either from his not cleaning it sufficiently, or from a reflection of the purple colour from his eye. I remember having seen a portrait by him, of a certain nobleman, remarkable for the sobriety of his life, and who was never known to have been drunk; but his Lordship having naturally a very florid complexion, the addition of Mr. G.'s purple to the colour of his nose and his cheeks, will probably make him pass with posterity, as the damnedest drunken dog that ever lived. Mr. G. will recollect the portrait I mean, when I tell him, that the Lady he has painted for its companion, is drawn working a net; and that particular pains have been taken in polishing the mahogany table at which she sits. I cannot say that Mr. C.'s painting is entirely free from this tinge of the purple tinct.

There are other painters again, whose sight, and (of course) their pencil give every thing a cast of the *brown.* Among these our so much admired historical painter, Mr. H. at Rome, is one of the first; every one must acknowledge it, who remembers those pictures of his which have been exhibited in this town. —And here, by the bye, I cannot help remarking, how defective he is in that most essential art of a painter, towards producing a deception —the giving a *relief*. Let Mr. H.'s drawing be ever so gracefully elegant and correct, unless he study more the giving a *relief*, his paintings (as I have before observed) will ever be but *coloured plans*. But, from the last performance of his, the Death of *Lucretia*, which I have seen, I have great expectations that his taste will improve.

Mr. K. is another, who always paints in a *brown study*, if I may say so, and be forgiven the pun.

There are others who incline to the *blue*, the *grey*, or the *green*. I will instance but one. Mr. H.'s painting can be distinguished by the colouring from among a thousand pictures. But what of that (I shall be told)? Is not the painting of almost all the great masters in the Italian or Flemish schools, equally known by some peculiar tints in which they took delight? So much the worse for them, Sir. Like French dramatic writers, they laid themselves down rules of the Graceful and Beautiful in composition, but forgot to study nature and to copy it, as our immortal *Shakespear* did.

For my part, if I were a Brother of the Brush, I should think it no compliment at all to my art, were any body to tell me, " That piece is inimitably well painted; the colouring is *beautiful* indeed! one needs no other mark to know by whose pencil it is."

In opposition to these painters in *purple*, *brown*, *blue*, *grey*, and *green*, I shall only place forward Mr. *Wright* of Derby, who, of all our moderns, has shewn the most exact observance of the propriety of tints, because none other has exhibited paintings in
such

such a variety of lights: but though others had attempted that variety, perhaps he would still have remained unequalled in the justness with which he imitates the natural colours of every object which he represents. Take his famous Blacksmith's Shop, one of his candle-light pieces, and one of his landskips; place them together in one room, and I defy any man to say, that, by the colouring, he could discern them to be the productions of the same hand. Of how many of your ancient masters can you say as much? place three capital pieces of any great painter promiscuously, in a collection of pictures, and it is a hundred to one but you will discover them to be painted by the same hand. And even at the exhibitions of our Moderns, cannot every little connoisseur tell, without a catalogue, the paintings that belong to their respective painters, and the name of the master that painted any capital piece? I therefore venture to pronounce it a great defect in the art of any painter, to have his painting known to be *his*, by any peculiarity of manner or colouring, and not by the perfection of his drawing, and his superior excellence in imitating the natural tints.

Some others of our modern painters, who have exhibited historical pieces, shew a wonderful attachment to a particular set of features, and give such a family-likeness to all the faces in the same picture, that one could, without much hesitation, pronounce them to be the offspring of the same line. I am sorry to bring in Mr. H. again; but I promised to animadvert on the productions of no man who could be any ways hurt by my remarks. Every one must be sensible that he is surprisingly fond of *round* features; in almost every face of his painting, there are the same arched eye-brows, the same open, round eyes,
the

the same rounded termination of the nose, the same round chin, and the whole of every countenance exactly shaped in the same round mold. In contrast with his faces are those of Mr. P.———You may see prints from his historical pieces in almost every street; you will perceive that he has shaped the features of his faces in a kind of *square* form; the same straight line runs along the eyebrows of every face; an exact parallel one to that runs across the eyes; another at the nostrils; and a fourth at the mouth. Mr. P. has, however, great merit; his colours are very good; they are natural; and they will stand the test of time.

Mr. W. shews too great a fondness for a *Grecian* face, in his historical painting. All his young women appear to be related to the same family.

I cannot help taking notice of a fashion which some late portraits have helped to introduce, called the *Vandyke* manner of wearing the hair. It certainly saves the trouble of painting the likeness of the forehead of a child, to bring down the hair almost to the eyes; but I maintain it to be a most barbarous taste, to conceal the finest feature of the face, and make every boy and girl look like a wild bull. If to give to the face the look of surly pride be your aim, continue combing down the hair. If you want to express innocence and simplicity, part the hair at the top of the forehead, and let it gradually separate as it falls down to the ear. But if you desire to behold an open, noble countenance, that detests all guile, shew the forehead in all its glory, and let not the neighbouring nations of Europe continue to our children the character of ferocity and pride, under the ridiculous, figurative appellation of a *John Bull*.

Nor can I conclude without recommending to the amusement of the ladies, two manners of *drawing*,
which

which are far preferable to their foiling their fair hands with painting in colours in oil. The *first* is, Mr. *Hamilton* in *Pall-mall's* manner of taking likenesses with crayons, which stand the weather perfectly well. The *second* is for drawing landskips, by first shading them lightly with Indian ink, and then painting them over with thin water-colours; in the manner I have seen some drawings at Lord *Bateman's*, remarkably well executed by a young Lady whose merit deserves this applause from a disinterested anonymous writer, though she may reap more honour from the judgment of a sounder critic, or a wiser man.

The LEVELLER. N°. VI.

On ARCHITECTURE.

ARCHITECTS, like Portrait-painters, are often, by the bad taste of their employers, circumscribed in their operations. I should, therefore, first chuse to be informed, whether the plan or design of any building had been left to the free choice of the Architect, before I would venture to call his Taste in question. Some Gentlemen are fond of a house as squat as a barn, others of a dwelling as elevated as a church-steeple; some prefer windows from the

the floors to the ceilings, and, following the Taste of France and Holland, make of their dwellings the likenesses of green-houses or lanthorns. Others, again, chuse to have their windows appear like the holes of a pigeon-house, or the port-holes of an armed vessel: In short, there is no pleasing these people with any thing in true taste or proportion. Yet the eye of a person of Taste cannot be pleased, without an observance of due proportion in building. Who views from the fields the North front of Bedford-house, without wishing, for the sake of grandeur, that another story had been added to its elevation? And would not the neighbouring house of the late Lord Baltimore have appeared in better proportion, if, in raising it, the bricklayers had been spared a little of their labour?—As, therefore, a certain proportion is required to be observed between the height and length of the front of any building, so is there a requisite proportion between the elevation and extent of that front, and the number and size of the windows which it should contain. That proportion I have seen nowhere more justly observed than in the front of the Queen's Palace. I could quote too Hopetoun-house in Scotland: but few of my Readers will have seen it. In both buildings, however, there is such an agreement between their fronts and the windows which they contain, that each, at the proper point of view, diminish the magnitude of the other, without lessening in the mind of the Beholder the idea of grandeur. In like manner, we may have sometimes seen a very tall man so exactly well-proportioned, that, at a few yards distance, he appeared nothing beyond the common size; but, as we drew nearer, and examined him limb by limb, we were surprised at his prodigious stature.

From

From the Queen's Palace, it is but a short walk to that row of houses which overlook her gardens, and where the Duke of Athol's house stands. You will there see some of those lanthorn-houses I have before mentioned, and by them you may judge, if my remarks on French windows are agreeable to reason. Many of the hospitals in and about London, will give you an idea of the pigeon-house fashion, which was in general followed in the private buildings of twenty or thirty years standing. I do not know any street in London where the windows are better proportioned than they are in Cumberland-street, near Tyburn. Whoever was the Architect or Builder of some of the houses in that street, deserves my acknowledgement of so much as I have seen of his good Taste in building.

A former publication of Critical Observations on the Buildings and Improvements of London, has left me little to add on the subject of their *Outsides;* but I will beg leave to take a look at them *within.* Here the first great innovation of our modern Taste that strikes me, is the gaudy painted cieling; and yet it was but by accident that I first discovered it, as I was one day leaning back in my chair, to have a bone taken out of my throat at dinner: it happened to be at a certain *Great House,* where I had something else to mind, than, like a country-booby, to be gazing at the cieling.—A couch, indeed, is the only place from whence one can get a convenient view of those gaudy cielings. I have several times attempted to admire the cielings at the Pantheon, but have always been so unlucky as to make somebody suffer by my attempts. One time I trode upon the toes of a tall fellow of a Horse Officer, who was near making me swallow the hilt of his sword; another time I ran my chin,

chin, plump, into the eye (fortunately for me his only one) of a Captain of a Man of War, who damned me moſt bitterly for *taking my obſervation* to the prejudice of his ſight; and a third time, I ran foul of a big-bellied lady, who mildly reproved me, by aſking me if I came there to play at *blindman's-buff?* The loading a cieling with a profuſion of expenſive decorations, is like ſquandering ſo many ornaments on a certain ſtool, which is commonly placed in that part of a room the leaſt conſpicuous to the ſight; with this difference, however, that to examine a fine cieling is often attended with much pain or inconvenience to one's neck; whereas the ſtooping to admire the ornamented ſhrine of Cloacina, would contribute very conſiderably to the eaſe of the body, as well as to the temporary amuſement of the mind.

I have juſt now bethought myſelf, however, of one good reaſon for painted cielings being in faſhion in the houſes of the Great: That as it is reckoned extremely vulgar to take notice of any thing *beneath* one, it certainly muſt be the ſummit of politeneſs to fix one's attention on thoſe objects which occupy the *higheſt places* in the room.—But the greateſt objection that occurs to me againſt theſe painted cielings, is this: They are generally ornamented with ſuch beautiful colours, that they make the ſides of a room look comparatively dirty and mean; ſo much ſo, that on ſeeing a plain dull room with a painted cieling to it, I could not but compare it to a chimney-ſweeper dreſt out on the firſt of May, with his face bedaubed with flour, his wig ſtuck full of ribbons, and his hat bound round with gilt leather by way of coſtly lace. In this chimney-ſweeper's Taſte is the library at Woburn-abbey; the ſides of the room are all covered with books, in appearance as dirty as a chimney-ſweeper's sweeper's coat, and its cieling is loaded with a profusion of gilding and paint. Yet the Architect in this may have had a very judicious design: reflecting that few people, now-a-days, go into a library to look *into* the books, and considering, that to look *at* their musty covers is, at the best, but a dismal sight; he perhaps imagined it was highly becoming the dignity of his Grace the Duke of Bedford, to suffer no visitor to enter his library without some *elevation of thought*, without feeling his ideas ennobled and raised to *things above*. If Sir William Chambers gave the design for this cieling, as I have been informed he did, it is but justice to his Taste in Architecture (however I might differ with him in *Oriental Gardening*) to add, that the Music-room in the same house, which, I was also assured, was finished from his designs, is really beautiful and elegant, and is far superior in taste to the tawdry French cabinet-work in that other room, where hangs the portrait of the French King. —I cannot conclude without making one more observation on many of the painted cielings which I have seen: The painters or designers of them frequently forget the distance from whence they are to be viewed. What is very beautiful and striking at the distance of a yard, may be nothing but confusion or intricacy of design, when beheld at the distance of twenty feet. The same remark might be made on other modern ornaments about our houses, which seem to approach too near to the diminutive minuteness of the Gothic scale. They are like the finishing of a Dutch picture, which commands our admiration of the curious industry of its painter, but which leaves no impression on the mind of the Sublime.— Those artists who work at the cielings by the help of a scaffold, would do well to follow Sir Joshua Reynolds's

Reynolds's method of painting, who, after every few strokes of his pencil, retires some paces from the canvas, to see what effect his painting has at that distance. The exercise of running up and down a ladder, from the cieling to the floor, and from the floor to the cieling, would certainly retard their operations; but then it would contribute greatly to the health of their bodies, and (it is to be hoped) to the improvement of their minds. This, at least, I am certain of; Dr. Cadogan himself could not prescribe a better preventive for the gout, to which painters in general are very tributary subjects; and their Taste could not but be corrected by their placing themselves sometimes in the situation of those for whose amusement their minutely ornamented cielings are designed. I would neither make choice of a wife nor a snuff-box from the opposite side of a street, because they are, in their use, intended for a *nearer* inspection; but a pair of buckles that are not designed to be examined in the hand, I would try in my shoes before I bought them; and I would keep my nose from offence by chusing the external ornaments of a certain temple at the full extent of my garden walk.

The LEVELLER N°. VII.

On the SAME.

I CONSIDER these cursory Observations of mine as practical Essays on Taste, in contradistinction to the theory or systematical writings of others. I have, therefore, avoided entering into any examination of the nature or principles of Taste, already so fully considered by more ingenious Authors, and have been satisfied with laying before my Readers some few examples, which sufficiently prove that there is no defining, to any kind of purpose, the principles of a thing, of which every man, by his senses, his imagination, or his judgment, may have a different notion. What does it signify to say, that we all agree in our Taste of things that are sour, bitter, or sweet, when there are a thousand dishes, which to as many thousand people will have a different relish? What better purpose can it serve, to advance, that the principle of pleasure derived from sight is the same in all? that what appears light to one eye is light to another? and that light is more pleasing than darkness? It will not convince another man that my mistress is handsome, though I should admire her above all other women.—But I will split the matter with those systematical writers. I will allow there are things in which we all agree in Taste, and the definition of which is certain:—I will allow that sour, bitter, and sweet, are sour, bitter, and sweet to
every

every natural palate; and that light is more agreeable to every eye than darkness; if they, on their parts, will be so obliging as not to skrew their mouths up at any plain dish that may be agreeable to my palate; nor to stop their noses at any scent that may please *me*, however uncommon or offensive to *their* smell; nor to shut their eyes to the many strange objects which are every-where to be seen around them, and which, but from the *uncertainty* of Taste, would never have been seen at all.—They must also allow me, that as habit or custom has a principal share in forming our Taste for almost every thing in this world, I may be permitted, without imputation of self-conceit, to give my own reasons for not relishing any such particular customs, however highly relished, or enthusiastically followed by others.

Having said thus much by way of apology for any *singularity* in these my observations, I must now beg leave to make some remarks on our houses in the country. By what I have observed in the course of my travels in England, it seems to have been the fashion, among the Gentry, some centuries ago, to build their houses in the bottom of the vallies. Whether for the convenience of fish-ponds and potable water, or to be hid from the distant view of an enemy, they chose this situation, I will not pretend to determine; but, in general, the old houses so situated have a dull and melancholy appearance; and from being placed in a stagnated air must be very unwholesome. In opposition to this Taste is the situation of many of our *modern*-built houses in the country, which are generally placed on the summit of some hill, to command an extensive prospect. I would avoid *that* extreme as much as the other; for, when I can behold, from my windows, the whole beauties of of the country around me, I have nothing new to entertain me; no new prospects, in my walks, to give me pleasure;—and I view, with indifference, those fields which my eye has already so often travelled over. I would therefore place my house on some small eminence, with a brook or river a few hundred paces below it: on the opposite side of the water should be a hanging field, at such a distance from me, that every object in it should be perfectly distinguishable. This situation, however, should be in the neighbourhood of high lands, from whence, when I chose it, I could enjoy a grand and extensive prospect, which from its rarity would afford me double pleasure. If constantly beheld from my windows, it would, as I have before observed, soon lose its novelty, and would appear as dead as if the landskip was in miniature painting. A *near* prospect, on the contrary, is occasionally enlivened with cattle grazing, ploughs going, carts driving, corn-reapers, hay-makers, and a variety of other moving objects. A house, placed aloft on an open lawn, has a very diminutive appearance, when contrasted with the wide sky, and spacious bare field around it: I would therefore confine the eye, as I approached the building, within a short, broad avenue of trees, and have the top of a grove to be seen towering at a proper distance behind it. People of Taste all agree, that a building should be concealed from the sight till one has approached it to the proper situation, where the view of it will strike the beholder with admiration. The approach to Hopetoun-house (mentioned in my last Essay) is in this respect admirably well directed. At the distance of two miles you have a view of the house, from whence, indeed, it appears nothing extraordinary, and seemingly so near, that you

expect.

expect to be at it immediately: you then lose sight of it intirely, and see nothing of the building again till you are within a quarter of a mile of it, where the ground rises with an easy ascent, and is levelled in such a manner, that the horizon before you, and the top of the building, run exactly in two parallel lines; so that, as you approach the house, it seems gradually to rise out of the ground, and presents to you a front far exceeding your expectation.

A house placed at the very bottom of a hill may be *beautiful* but it can never be *magnificent*. The view of such a vast natural object beside it, must make it appear comparatively small and insignificant. I will give but one instance of such an injudicious choice of a situation; 'tis that of the house at Woburn-abbey. Immediately behind the building rises a hill covered with lofty trees; and opposite to each angle of its front, within pistol-shot of the windows, are two eminences, one of which overtops the house by many feet; by which means it resembles a cistern, or reservoir, intended to collect the water from all the heights and woods that surround it:—To appear like any thing else the house should be at least a story higher.———The recollection of this house puts me in mind of the inattention of many Architects to conceal their chimneys. When they are shewn on the top of a building, they should certainly serve as much for ornament as possible, and not be left like so many nine-pins among which the bowl has made a devastation. The mention of chimneys, again, reminds me of a hint I have to offer to all Architects and Builders, to prevent a chimney from smoking; they shall have it *gratis*, though I well deserve a *Patent* for the discovery. I deserve, at least, the thanks of all sober housekeepers; for if I deliver them from a smoking a smoking chimney, it was perhaps the *second* plague in their house; against the *first* there is no remedy but patience.—My observation is this: That it has been the custom with the Architects of almost all the modern-built houses (at Bath, Liverpool, Lancaster, and many other places where stone is used) to run up the chimneys in the gavel-ends, or outside walls of a house; from which I have noticed this consequence to follow: That as sure as a cold, bleak wind beat upon the wall where the chimney was, so sure did that chimney return the smoke of its fire into the dwelling. And I account for it in this manner: Most chimneys will smoke a little when a fire is first lighted, after any intermission of the custom; the wall, and the soot in the vent were become damp, which chilled and condensed the air in the vent so as to resist the smoke, till the air became gradually rarefied and heated, and then it dilated itself through the top of the chimney.—That this is not an *imaginary* but *natural* resistance of the condensed air, the atmosphere of the city of London will demonstrate any frosty morning.———Now, as this occasionally happens to almost every chimney, much more is it likely to happen, when wind and rain beat on a chimney built of porous stone, or of stones not well cemented together; and it does so happen in many houses within my knowledge, where the chimneys smoke at no time but when the wind beats on that side of the house where the chimneys are; and the smoking ceases as soon as the wind changes. This custom of building the chimneys in the gavel-ends of the house, is very much followed in the neighbourhood of Edinburgh. Many little country-boxes are lately run up there, *prefaced*, as Mr. Foote says, with white-painted rails, and *prologued* with a brass

N knocker;

knocker; but it is a pity that the hospitality of their owners should be so often counteracted by a smoky chimney. My Readers will be pleased to observe, I do not hint this as the *sole* cause of a chimney's smoking; but only as *one* evident cause, which might, at the first building of a house be easily prevented. The running up the vents in the partition-walls of a house will indeed alter the fashion of the roof, and occasion some additional expence in the building. But who would not be at *some* expence to get rid of a scolding wife, or a smoky chimney?

The LEVELLER. N°. VIII.

On LOVE.

THE great materials with which Mr. Locke composed his Essay on the Human Understanding, he confesses to have been produced from a candid examination of the rise and progress of the ideas in his own mind; and from thence the various operations of the *judgment* were most minutely ascertained. The various degrees and effects of our *passions* might, in like manner, be as accurately traced, were every one, with equal candour, to confess the feelings of his own breast. But some there are, whose pride will not allow them to acknowledge one sensation beyond the dictates of Prudence and sober Sense; and from such (with their own free-will) there is no making any acquisition to our knowledge of the human heart. Nor for them do I pretend to write. I address myself chiefly to those, who, young and unexperienced in the ways of Love, may persuade themselves they feel that soft and tender passion, when perhaps gratitude, compassion, or ambition, is the latent spring that moves them to bless a Lover, and pronounce consent. In these days, then, of infidelity to the marriage-bed, when the husband, the imagined Lover, is frequently supplanted by some gallant really and sincerely beloved, a few of my Observations on Love may be attended with some public good.—

Love is, by most authors, defined to be a compound of friendship or esteem, and of a desire of possessing or enjoying the person beloved. The ingenious author of the Essay on the Sublime and Beautiful gives to that passion no greater sublimity of appellation, (nay, he even makes use of the grosser word of Lust) though *my* sensations have taught me a more accurate definition; a definition more refined, equally pure and sublime. My feelings have informed me, that the passion of Love, between two persons of a different Sex, consists in a *constant* mutual friendship and esteem, and in a *temporary* or *occasional* desire of an embrace. Love has ever, in this progressive manner, affected *my* heart:—With the greatest purity of mind, and without the most distant thoughts of the pleasures of the Bed, I feel a constant desire to be in the presence of the object beloved, for the sole delight of her company and conversation. When I am in her company, I as constantly feel a desire to draw near to her; and when placed at her side, I cannot help as constantly wishing

ing to take her in my arms, and prefs her to my breaſt. Without forming ſuch a wiſh at the ſight of his Miſtreſs, I really think a young man, in perfect good health of body and mind, cannot be ſaid to be ſufficiently in love with her as to make her his Bride. If, on the contrary, that wiſh ſhould be uppermoſt in his thoughts when abſent from the object of his deſire, it is much to be apprehended he is not truly affected by Love; it is perhaps but a brutal paſſion, that, after its gratification, would turn from its object with loathing and diſguſt; whereas Love, as above defined, would ſhew itſelf, even after enjoyment, in the ſame fervent deſire of union of Soul with Soul, and Heart with Heart.—Thus we ſee it becomes equally hazardous for a man, without friendſhip or without deſire, to unite himſelf to a woman for life. In either caſe, there is a danger that his happineſs will not be of long duration in the change of his ſtate: he may ſoon feel a deſire for ſome other woman, or he may loſe the deſire which alone attached him to his wife; when he would become miſerable, in the poſſeſſion of the very object he once thought would complete his bliſs.—The firſt part of my definition of Love is eaſily underſtood: Virtue, good-ſenſe, good-nature, great and numerous accompliſhments, and a ſimilarity of diſpoſitions, may command my eſteem; but how it happens, that I ſhall behold ſome beautiful faces with the ſame indifference as I ſhould view ſo many inanimate blocks of marble, while a ſmile from certain ordinary features ſhall inſtantly inflame my breaſt, is a little incomprehenſible indeed. A Philoſophical Friend of mine has, however, attempted to account for this phænomenon, by ſaying, that the ſoul or ſpirit of Man was originally of the ſame eſſence in

our

our firſt Parents, and would be ſo found tranſmitted to *us*, did it not vary in its operations and effects, according to the different organs or conſtitution of the human body, through the medium of which the ſpirit acts; and that when now two bodies, of a corresponding organization, happen to approach each other, however different in outward form they may appear, they feel a ſecret impulſe of attraction, which, producing a deſire of union and adheſion, my Friend pronounced to be the Paſſion of Love. But I objected to his hypotheſis, by obſerving to him, that a Lady will, with the warmeſt affection, preſs to her boſom a dog, a monkey, or a cat, none of which I could ſuppoſe were endued with the organs or intellects of a man.——Others, again, will account for the operations of Love, from the force of a certain ſympathy, which they allow to be as inexplicable itſelf.——As for me, ever ſince I read Mr. Brydone's Tour through Sicily and Malta, I have laid all the bleſſings and miſeries of Love to the account of *Electrical Fire.* I only intend to give it a new name; let others *explain* it who can. Yet I cannot help thinking, that moſt of our Poets and love-ſick Swains have had a glimmering of this reaſon of mine, when they ſo often exclaim—" You have ſet my Soul on " fire:"—" The Flame you've kindled in my " Breaſt:"—" The Fire which darts from your bright " eyes;"—with many other fine phraſes, which were certainly intended to convey *ſome* meaning, tho' perhaps not underſtood in the Electrical ſenſe I comprehend.—I am confirmed in this my opinion by the general obſervation, that the older we grow, the leſs effect this *Electrical Fire* has upon our mortal frames, whilſt we daily behold younger bodies affected by it to the higheſt extreme. I have alſo remarked, that

it

it is the power of the Electrical Fire, in the person beloved, which attracts us as much as we are impelled by the flame in our own breast: we cannot but feel for those who feel for us; and those, on the contrary, who shew themselves cold and indifferent to us, attract us in no violent degree. For my own part, I could never sigh long for any Woman who was insensible of affection for me. And in this I am not very singular, though perhaps pride and vanity may be at the bottom of it; for, *L'Amour ne se paye que par Amour reciproque*, is a proverb among the vainest of all earthly people. Nay, most of your Lovers of other Nations have been of the same feeling:— *Esto mihi, ero tibi;—ut ameris, amabilis esto,* say the Latins. *Ama a chi t'ama, rispond a chi ti chiama,* is an Italian saying,; which the Dutchmen have very literally and ingeniously translated, *Antwoord die je vraegt, Min die je Liefde draegt:* to which we may add another of their Proverbs, *Vriendschap van eener zyde en duert niet lang;* and something in the same Sense is the German Proverb, *Gleich und Gleich gesellt sich Gern;* which the Spaniards again translate, *Cada oveia con su pareia;* or, in other words, *Toma tu ygual* (which is to be understood, *equal* in *electrical Love*) *y vete mendigar.*—— Many other authorities I could produce in support of my argument; but as I hold it to be impertinent, and pedantic, and inconsistent with the character of a Man of Taste, to deal out quotations in any language but that in which he is actually writing, I hope those I have already given will be thought sufficient, to prove the truth of my Remarks and the amazing profundity and universality of my Learning.—Those being granted me, I promise never to offend against my own given rule of politeness in future.

My Readers will be pleased to observe, I only pretend, from my own feelings, to account for the cause and effects of Love in the *Male* Sex; the sensations of the *female* heart I shall leave to be described by some *female* pen.——It is, however, not difficult for a Man to guess when a Woman has but little affection for him :—If after the fullest declaration on his part, and the most convincing proofs of his love, the Object of his affections continues secret and reserved; if by frequent little tokens of friendship, and particular attention, she seems to insinuate what, in words, she is careful shall neither be expressed nor understood; if she encourages him to attend her, and seems pleased with his attachment to her in public, whilst in private she refuses him the most innocent favour, or the smallest mark of her esteem;—that Woman is either insensible of Love for her admirer, or she is a Coquette or a Prude; one whose vanity prompts her to encourage a number of followers, or whose pride will not allow her to acknowledge one feeling beneath the character of a Saint.

An instance of Prudery, and another of Coquetry, occur to my mind, which, to teach young people not to be precipitate in their determinations, it may not be improper to relate.—A Friend of mine had held a correspondence with a young lady for upwards of two years, under the name of Friendship and Esteem, although *Love* was certainly understood; but on her side never properly expressed. An offer being made by another Gentleman of much superior rank and fortune, she consulted with her Friend by letter, whether she should accept of it. He made her no answer; but packing up all her letters in his possession, he returned them to her in a blank cover, by way of a gentle reproof. This packet expressed his indignation

tion more fully than any thing he could have wrote; and the Lady was candid enough immediately to confefs her affection for him, and to acknowledge that, by her conduct, fhe had merited his contempt. The other inftance was far lefs juftifiable, and deferved the fevereft rebuke. I learnt it from another Friend of mine, who made no fcruple of telling it me, as the Lady it concerned had long fince been dead. He was, he faid, once connected with a Lady, who had given him a moft folemn Promife of Marriage, but who fuddenly broke off their correfpondence, without vouchfafing to give a reafon for her inconftancy, even to the hour of her death. Such a behaviour in a *Man*, after poffeffing himfelf of a Woman's affections, would be pronounced to be infamous, bafe, or difhonourably inconftant and unjuft:—in a Woman we only give it the gentle appellation of Coquetry or Flirtation, thro' complaifance to the ficklenefs of her fex.—My Friend had, however, a better opinion of the Lady, than at firft to imagine fhe could be ferioufly forfaking him; he flattered himfelf, for fome time, that fhe only intended to try his temper; but on her afterwards repeatedly refufing to account for her change, he gave up his purfuit, he pocketed the affront, and quietly fubmitted to his fate. It was, in fact, of fmall importance to him, whether fhe had jilted him for another, or whether fhe had deferted him from the mean opinion fhe had conceived of his honour, and the fincerity of his regard. Be that as it may, the Lady, by her precipitation alone, would have loft the heart of a Man of any pride; at leaft, the opinion *I* have of the fulfomenefs of profeffions of Love from a perfon beheld with contempt, would have prevented *me* from renewing my addreffes to the Lady, and I fhould have
been

been loft for ever, unlefs fhe could have fubmitted to have given me fuch encouragement as *I* could not have mifunderftood. I doubt if ever I fhould have thought her ferious again, till the Parfon had joined our hands in holy wedlock, and the old-fafhioned ftocking was on our bed.

I have known fome Women make, of their filial duty, a cloak to their own inconftancy; and to one of them, if fhe were fincere, I would beg leave to declare, that until fhe could transfer her love from her Parents to the Man whom fhe chofe for the partner of her fortunes, fhe was not fit to enter into the married ftate. I have known too fatal effects of divided affections, to counfel any Woman to leave Father and Mother and cleave to her Hufband, (as the Scripture faith) unlefs fhe can diveft herfelf intirely of her infantine attachments. Yet I would not be underftood to advife a Child to commit an action that would render a tender and worthy Parent unhappy; a Parent endeared to her by the treatment and behaviour of the friend, and to whom gratitude is due, not for being merely the inftrument of her earthly exiftence, but for an education calculated or intended to promote her fubftantial happinefs;—I only mean to fay, that a bafe compliance with the will of a proud or ambitious parent, in marrying contrary to one's own inclinations, is an action offenfive to the laws of God and Nature, and can be called by no fofter name than *Proftitution;* for a marriage contracted to gratify Pride, Vanity, or Ambition, is furely as culpable in the eye of the Almighty, as the forced proftitution of the Wretch whom misfortunes have reduced to want.—If thefe fentiments fhould prove difagreeable to any friends to arbitrary and defpotic meafures of Family Government, I have but this apology to make them: That my Father never taught me to look on myself as his property, to be difposed of like an African Slave; and that I at prefent regard him as the beft friend and companion I have upon earth. I have alfo the pleafure to obferve, that my own Son feems to think he has found no harfh Monitor in me; nor do I think that either of us is more wicked or lefs happy than many of our neighbours, whom their Parents have taught to tremble at their nod.

But 'tis not on *Platonic* Love I am writing; 'tis on a tenderer *Senfation*, and I have not yet finifhed my tafk.—Young Women fometimes perfuade themfelves they are really in love with a Man, when perhaps Gratitude only for favours received is miftaken for the fofter paffion: I have alfo known a heart melting with pity and compaffion for the misfortunes of a friend, which felt not one fpark of its celeftial fire. Yet the Ladies cannot fo eafily deceive themfelves, as they can impofe upon us, poor credulous Men. I will not awaken jealoufy by quoting examples of deceit; for, as it is a pleafing deception, the fincerity of a Woman's attachment ought not readily to be fufpected; excepting indeed, when, in licentious amours, it is evidently for her intereft and advantage to profefs the moft ardent affection.—I cannot omit this farther advice to my young Readers: A Man who has any value for his own happinefs, ought to be cautious how he attaches himfelf to a young Woman, who, in the lefs confequential purfuits of life, appears to be volatile or inconftant, and is not miftrefs of her refolutions for any long duration; and far lefs ought he to form a connection with that woman, if fhe has feen but little of the world; for he either may be deferted before his wifhes are accomplifhed, plished, or she may afterwards repent of her choice, when, alas! it is too late. And yet one might, without much vanity, venture to unite himself to such a Lady for life, if, from his former connections with other women, he had experienced that, by intimacy and long acquaintance, he had gained on their love.

Since it is *scientifically* I write, and not in a religious sense, any thing seemingly indelicate, in this Essay, must be charitably understood. As an Anatomist is permitted to call every part of the Human Body by its proper name, why may not a Moralist be allowed the same freedom in describing the feelings of the Human Heart? Our Pride alone forbids it. Should therefore that Pride, from my definitions above given, revolt at the name of Love, I beg my fair countrywomen will, in future, give it the sublimer appellation of *Electrical Fire*. I shall then make no manner of doubt, it will in time become as fashionable to say,—" My dear friend, you have quite electrified me;"— as it is now thought indelicate by some Women to avow their Love, or indecent in a Man to ask a Lady to undress.

Having now spun out my Essay to a tolerable length, in a kind of incoherent, unconnected style, perfectly correspondent with the subject on which I wrote; I must beg leave to conclude with an Epitaph, which I formerly composed for a young Lady, and which, if not sufficiently expressive, or poetically good, has at least the recommendatory merit of being short:—

   Here, sunk in Earth, O justly sunk in dirt!
   Lies tasteless, fickle, cold, unfeeling *Flirt*;
   Each Youth admir'd her, but admir'd in vain;
   Her sole delight—to aggrandize her Train;
   She smil'd on All, to All denied her charms,
    Till Death, indignant, dragg'd her to his arms.

The LEVELLER. N°. IX.

On the SAME.

I Intend this Essay to be a comment on my last. The subject was tolerably liked, and I had also the pleasure to find that my manner of treating it had given very little offence.—But I have a longer preamble to make ere I renew the subject.

In most of our Grammar Schools, an old Monkish custom at this day prevails, of obliging the Scholars, of a certain standing, to compose verses in Latin; when perhaps not one-tenth of those Boys have the least spark of poetical genius in them, and when speaking or writing that language is in this country almost totally in disuse. The Orations delivered at the Universities, the Compositions of their learned Students, or the crabbed Prescriptions of our Medical Gentry, cannot be termed of much consequence to the bulk of mankind. This Monkish custom I once ventured to throw in the teeth of a late learned Master of Westminster School; and had even the presumption to debate the matter with him, notwithstanding he had been used to claim and obtain assent by his sole dictatorial and magisterial nod. "It is the readiest manner, said he, of teaching the Boys to read and pronounce the language with its proper accents." "Any Lad, said I, in return, that has the perfect use of his ears, will, in a very short time, learn the proper accents, by reading the Poets aloud; and then, as for your pronunciation, with your *a*'s and your *i*'s, your Latin is understood nowhere without the boundaries of England."—" Then, resumed he, it whets the Invention amazingly, and brightens the Imagination." " True, replied I; but, Doctor, do not you think that the *Judgment* is a little neglected, which would be better improved by giving your Scholars longer Themes in their own Language?" Here our debate was interrupted; and the Judgment was left by the Doctor to shift for itself. Not so did *my* old Master, however little I may have benefited by his instructions. The same antient custom, however, existed in his school. A boy, more remarkable for his invention than for his industry or application, brought him, one morning, a couplet of very good Latin verses, which the master could not but recollect. " Why, Dicky, said he, you are prodigiously improved, or else these two pretty lines are stolen from Ovid's Metamorphosis." " Indeed, Sir, quoth Dick, they are my own; it is very possible that Ovid may have had the same thought before me."—" Well said, Dicky! Then, since you are so clever, my Boy, I desire you will bring me a dozen such to-morrow morning;—but remember, Dicky, if they are not more original than these, you and I shall talk together in that corner."—Thus, if any of my Readers have found, or shall have found, that I have repeated, or shall have repeated, any thing in my last Essay, or in this, which they have long since read in Ovid's Art of Love, I humbly beg leave to make use of my old friend Dicky's Apology; That it is very possible for me to have hit on the same thoughts with *Ovid* who has gone before me. But I can, in regard to his *Art of Love*, say, (with more truth than Dicky of the Metamorphosis,) that I never looked into it

in

in my life; and that even the Latin quotation in my last (if it was Ovid's) I wrote entirely from hear-say. The *Art of Love* was not read at my School; and since my Schooling-days were over, I have had sufficient to do in the *practical* part of it, ever to desire to study its theory. Yet I shall look into it out of mere curiosity, however little I may expect instruction from the perusal of it. *Nature* must have been the same in Ovid's days as in the present; but *Art* is always varying; and that part of it which may have been instructive in his time, may be of very little use to us of this Age and Nation. To be more serious; what I just now said is mere evasion. Where *Art* is to be used in Love, I disclaim all knowledge of it; excepting what I may have learnt in my observations on the conduct of others; and even *That* is not very easily obtained. I can tell what passes in my own breast; but to ascertain, from words and expressions only, what passes in the breasts of others, would be possessing a knowledge altogether divine. Whoever expects it of me is as unreasonable as a certain Foxhunter I have heard of, in Northamptonshire, who insisted on his Apothecary's telling him, on hearing him helloa, what complaint he had in his lungs.— The 'Squire was, by nature, endued with a remarkable strong voice, which, one day that he was out a hunting, he imagined was suddenly fail'd. On his return from the chace, he sent immediately for his Apothecary. The Apothecary happening not to be at home, his apprentice came. " Here, my lad, said the 'Squire; can you tell me what's the matter with me? I feel myself, some-how, in the inside, not perfectly well." The young man, as usual, took hold of the 'Squire's wrist, and began to feel his pulse. The 'Squire withdrew his hand with sovereign contempt.

tempt. " Poh! boy, who can tell, from feeling the pulse, what ails a man's lungs?—I tell you my complaint is here—within. Now, hear me holloa, my lad;—*yoix! yoix! holloa!*—can't you hear how my voice is fail'd?"—" Upon my word, Sir, I can perceive nothing the matter with your lungs; I wish to God, mine were as sound. But my Master will be at home presently; I shall send him, and he may possibly be able to tell." The Apothecary himself came in the evening, prepossessed, as you may imagine, from the report of his apprentice, that it was the 'Squire's *Brain* that was affected, and neither his Liver nor his Lungs. On his entering the room, the 'Squire immediately addressed him in the former strain. " That was a modest well-behaved lad you sent me, Sir; but he seemed not to understand my case very well: I told him my inside was wrong, and he went to feel for my complaint at my arm. Now, come here, and tell me if my voice is not prodigiously fail'd. Only hear me holloa:—*yoix! yoix! holloa! holloa!*—don't you think there is something decay'd within?"——Now, was any kind-hearted Damsel, with the greatest vehemence of *words* and *expressions*, to protest she had a most affectionate regard for me, she would puzzle me, as much as the 'Squire did his Apothecary, to tell what she felt within; unless, by her *actions*, she gave me some symptoms of her flame. I am not, however, in any danger of having my skill, in such a case, put to the trial; for my Readers will easily perceive, from the stories I have given them, that I am verging towards narrative old age, when people are seldom consulted in affairs where the *Feelings* alone are concerned. Yet, from past experience, my opinion ought to have some weight; and, let me add, too, from my apparently

rently profound erudition. A very antient Author has written, that, to the age of twenty, Man is ruled by Love; from twenty to forty he is governed by a mixture of Love and Ambition; from forty to sixty he is guided by Ambition and Avarice; and from sixty upwards, Avarice entirely engrosses the Heart. Though these stages may vary, sooner or later, in proportion to the different constitutions of men, I believe it will be found that our ruling passions in general succeed each other, according to the order above described. And I therefore lay it down as a maxim, That if a young man of twenty can subdue a noble and generous passion for a woman, on account only of the imprudence of his attachment with regard to pecuniary affairs, he will never after have a *disinterested* affection for any Woman; for his Prudence will but encrease with his years. If a Woman, too, under the age of twenty, can, from the motives of Prudence, refuse the Man whom her heart has approved, I would advise him not to build his hopes of happiness on such a sandy foundation; they will too readily be swept away by some Rival's more prosperous and resistless gale. When Inconstancy happens from such a cause, I call it *premeditated*, in contra-distinction to that kind of Inconstancy which may proceed from the discovery of Vices and Imperfections in an object, which the Imagination had at first painted of unblemished Form. This last Inconstancy I really think one ought most charitably to forgive; for the Feelings may be *surprized* into an *Engagement*, but no force can *command* them to *Action*.

The

The LEVELLER. N°. X.

His DEFENCE of LAUGHTER, against Lord CHESTERFIELD's unwarrantable Attack.

HOWEVER serious and grave some of my *Levellers* have been, and however incapable I may be of entertaining my Readers with sallies of Wit and Humour, no one can laugh more heartily than I can, at the witty sayings of other people.

This disposition for Laughter in me may proceed from pride; it may proceed from a certain turn in the imagination to the burlesque; it may proceed from lively spirits, a gay fancy, or any other cause hereafter to be sought for;—but I am very unwilling to believe it to be, as *Lord Chesterfield* terms it, "the characteristic of Folly and Ill-manners." Since no man, then, likes to be thought a greater fool than he is in reality, and since I cannot always confine the expressing the joy of my heart to the mere grin of a monkey, I must, for my own sake, write something in defence of frank, open Mirth and Laughter.

" Having mentioned Laughter," (says Lord Chesterfield, in his fashionable Letters to his Son) " I
" must particularly warn you against it; and I could
" heartily wish, that you may be often seen to smile,
" but never heard to laugh while you live. Fre-
" quent and loud Laughter is the characteristic of
" Folly and Ill manners; it is the manner in which
" the mob express their silly joy at silly things; and
" they

"they call it being merry. In my mind, there is nothing so illiberal and so ill-bred as audible Laughter. True Wit, or Sense, never yet made any-body laugh; they are above it: they please the mind, and give chearfulness to the countenance. But it is low buffoonery, or silly accidents, that always excite Laughter; and that is what people of sense and breeding should shew themselves above. A man's going to sit down, in the supposition that he has a chair behind him, and falling down upon his breech for want of one, sets a whole company a-laughing, when all the wit in the world would not do it; a plain proof, in my mind, how low and unbecoming a thing laughter is—Not to mention the disagreeable noise that it makes, and the shocking distortions of the face that it occasions. Laughter is easily restrained by a very little reflection; but, as it is generally connected with the idea of gaiety, people do not enough attend to its absurdity. I am neither of a melancholy nor a Cynical disposition; and am as willing and as apt to be pleased as any-body; but I am sure that, since I have had the full use of my reason, nobody has ever heard me laugh."

Writing to a young Man, that was likely to be employed in the affairs of a Court, his Lordship certainly gave him very proper advice:—to acquire, if possible, a perfect command of his countenance. One needs not shew all that one thinks, tho' there is no occasion either (as his Lordship in other parts advises) to put in practice seduction or deceit. Sir William Temple disclaimed them both; and though he could laugh, too, was esteemed a *wise* Politician.

In Private Life, *Gravity* is undoubtedly becoming in a Divine, in a Judge, in a Physician, a Surgeon, an Apothecary, a Schoolmaster, an Undertaker, a Midwife, a Ratcatcher, or a Thief, during the time they are employed in the exercise or function of their respective offices, professions, or trades. It is also prudent and becoming in all Ladies, at all places of public resort; and it is equally proper to be observed by all persons in all companies that are to be treated with decency, decorum, or respect. Due regard ought, likewise, to be paid to the difference of customs and manners in the different places at which one resides:—The frolics of a youth in *London* would be treated as the actions of a madman at *Amsterdam*, (where, indeed, an Englishman and a madman are synonimous terms;) and the smiles of a frank, open-hearted girl, educated at *Paris*, or at *London*, would be regarded by the formal prudes of some country-towns, as indications of the most wanton mind.—— But I can see no reason why the same serious, stupid face should be continued in a private company of friends; *Prudence* requires it no longer, among those to whom the rate of each other's understanding must be sufficiently known.

Nor can I suppose that true *Wisdom* and *Good-sense* are incompatible with *Laughter* at any time. The Archbishop of York* can relish a piece of Wit and Humour as well as any man; and no people can laugh more heartily at a good joke, than the present Lord Chief Justice of England, and another learned Judge, the Lord President of the Court of Session in Scotland. From these three eminent examples it may be fairly presumed, that Laughter is not, as Lord Chesterfield alledges, the characteristic of Folly;—nor yet of *Ill-manners*, tho' the Mob thereby express their silly joy at silly things. His Lordship,

* Drummond.

by parity of reasoning, might as well have said, it was vulgar and ill-mannered to eat, drink, and sleep, because the Mob with great enjoyment do the same.

His Lordship is the first person I ever heard give to Laughter the name of a *disagreeable noise;* or, to its expressions on the countenance, the epithet of *shocking distortions of the face*. The very sound of of a laugh, and the sight of people laughing, have frequently the effect to make us join in the mirth of others, of which we know not the cause. It gives such a comical cast to some features, that there is no resisting the sympathetic force of them without being uncommonly dull. I remember an instance of a whole company of sensible people being diverted for a quarter of an hour by a facetious friend of mine, who, instead of returning thanks after dinner, arose with great solemnity, and said, " Come, let us have " a Laugh;" then, putting both his hands on his sides, he forced a Laugh in such a variety of notes, and with such a drollery of countenance, that he set the whole table in a roar. Some people will tell me, the joke was as silly as the pulling of a chair from behind a man, to make him get a fall; nor will I pretend to say, there was any wit to bring out a Laugh upon us, instead of the expected Thanksgiving Prayer; all I mean to affirm by it, is, that the sympathetic power of a Laugh is sometimes so strong, that whoever should have seen my friend's very comical face, and heard the merry sound of his voice, would have had but little mirth in him, to have kept himself grave.

I leave to Anatomists to account for it, why one man is more readily convulsed than another; but certain it is, that when I hear any thing very laughable, let it be in the Church, the Senate, or the Court, I can no more refrain from grinning, than I

can

can from weeping at any affecting misery or distress of a fellow-creature. Every one must recollect some, among his acquaintance, whose risible faculties are as little under command as mine, and who stand as little in awe, as I do, of the censure of a superior. For my own part, without being guilty of self-approbation, I never liked a person the better for his not shewing the passions on his countenance. I hate a *masked* face; and whenever I discover one, I always guard myself against the possessor of it, as I would against a thief or a pick-pocket. Can the sincerity of that man be depended on, who can look grave when he is inclined to laugh, or who will put on a smile when he wishes me perhaps at the Devil?—I know I shall be taxed here with writing against *Good-manners*; for to the vanity of mankind *Bluntness* is displeasing; but I recommend it not; I mean only to say, that as Dissimulation is ever to be suspected, there is a manner of being *sincere* without being *blunt*: There is a wide difference between a suppression of the truth, and saying nothing but the truth. I would not, therefore, have a man laugh in another's face, if it were to give him any offence; and so far a command of countenance is desirable. But to smile on a person towards whom at the time you bear neither friendship nor love, is saying *more* than the truth;—'tis dissimulation; 'tis deceit; 'tis wearing a counterfeit face.

I intimated at the beginning of this Essay, that I hated to be thought a greater fool than Nature had made me; and I therefore must strenuously maintain, that neither the *Wise* nor the *Silly* are more to be distinguished by Laughter, than by any of the natural functions of the human body, which are common to both of them. And if it should still be objected to me, that fools are apt to laugh at many silly conceits

ceits which affect not the man of wisdom, I am ready to answer, that full as many fools will be grave at a witticism, through stupidity or a want of sense to comprehend it. There certainly are grave, stupid, dull fools, as well as merry-ones; and there are merry wise-men, as well as wise-men who have not the least relish for Wit and Humour.

Granting me, then, that Gravity and Laughter are not the signs either of Wisdom or Folly, I will proceed to account for the different causes of Laughter, after my own manner; that is, agreeable to what I have perceived to pass within myself on laughable occasions: and if I am not a very extraordinary creature, some of my Readers, from the experience of their own feelings, must surely assent to the truth of my observations.

In the first place, then, I will honestly allow, that Self-sufficiency and Pride often provoke us to laugh at the follies or absurdities of others, when we should look confoundedly grave, if the like follies and absurdities of our own were maliciously and satirically told us.

Secondly, a natural liveliness and sprightliness of spirits make some people more prone to Laughter than others, in the same degree as a Frenchman (without being the greater fool for it) will be more chearful than a Native of Britain, or as a Boy is generally more merry than a Man. Both the Frenchman and the Boy will become the more sedate, as they grow older; but it is not always found that their Wisdom encreases in proportion to the gravity of their deportment. Their lack of Laughter is, therefore, occasioned by the loss of youth, and the approach of old age.

Laughter is also the effect of a fertile imagination, which, on some story being told, or some event happening,

pening, will start many things in addition to the circumstances, which a person of a dull genius could never imagine.——This too we find in youth much stronger than in men advanced in years; tho' some, in spite of chilling blood, retain it to the oldest age.

To this sprightliness of spirits, and fertility of imagination, we may add a turn to the buffoonery or burlesque. A look of *Ned Shuter*'s on the Stage has frequently said as much to me as a speech of many words; to another, it would not have said so much; on a third, it would have been entirely lost.—On such an occasion, however, I am not certain whether instinct or sympathy does not provoke us, without thought or reflection, to join in the laugh at the sight of a droll look, as naturally as we gape when others gape, commiserate when we see others grieve, and tremble at any sudden expression of fear. I have laughed as heartily at the sight of Hogarth's print of the *Laughing Pit*, as ever I did at any witty speech in my life.

Some men are apt to laugh when others will be serious, from an intimate correspondence between the countenance and the heart; which is equally the cause of our expressing, without reserve, our mirth, our grief, our anger, our fear, our scorn, our horror, our pleasure, or our pain.—Others, again, give loose to their mirth, from a want of that kind of prudence, or circumspection, which teaches the Selfish to keep a constant guard over their words, looks, and actions, lest, by their genuine expression or interpretation, they should prejudice their worldly interest.——That kind of prudence is no where more fully exemplified than in the Circle at St. James's, or at the Levee of Lord North. A man may be able to laugh very heartily, whom neither the King nor his Minister, at either of these places, ever perceived

to

to alter a muscle in his face. It is certainly one of his Majesty's prerogatives to laugh when and where his Royal pleasure is; but, otherwise, I agree with Lord Chesterfield, that Laughter is the characteristic of Folly *at Court*.

Last of all, (though I ought to have placed it in front, because it is one of the first things by which a human creature is pre-eminently distinguished from a brute) there is an involuntary convulsion in Laughter, to which some people are more subject than others, which children even shew before they come to the use of reason; and the power of which, from infancy to manhood, gradually declines till it is almost lost in the infirmities of old age. This involuntary convulsion may be tried by titillation:—tickle only a few people's sides, and its various effects you will instantly perceive.

To a proneness to this convulsion, in me, to a turn for the burlesque, and to an imagination not incapable of improving on events, I chiefly attribute the cause of my laughing at the recital or appearance of many things, which give not half so much entertainment to another person. Tell me a comical story, and it is ten to one but I start many incidents which never struck *your* fancy. Give me a droll one to read, and my imagination is ever ready to paint it *droller*. I must, no doubt, on these occasions appear a fool to many; but I think it unfair to pronounce me intirely guilty of folly, till it be known what passes within me.

I remember the first time I read *Tristram Shandy*, it was in the company of two very sensible men, who were each entertaining himself with his own reading. —I happened to come to the unfortunate rencounter of Dr. Slop and Obadiah, at the short turn of the
garden-

garden-wall; and the whole scene presented itself so lively to my imagination, that I laughed, as Lord Chesterfield would say, like a most egregious fool. I thought I saw before me the little, fat Doctor, mounted on his diminutive poney, that was waddling through the narrow, dirty lane, at every step sinking to the knees in mire; I thought I saw the hasty Obadiah, mounted on a great, unruly brute of a coach-horse, galloping at his full speed; I thought I saw him, with this tremendous velocity, bounce upon the unsuspecting Doctor, at the sudden turn of the garden-wall; I painted to myself the terror and consternation of the Doctor's face; the vain attempts he would make, in the dirt, to turn his poney out of the way of Obadiah's horse; his crossing himself, like a good Roman-Catholic, on the apprehension of inevitable death, his dropping his whip, through hurry and confusion, in crossing himself; his catching most naturally, and as if by instinct, to recover his falling whip; his losing his stirrups in consequence thereof; his falling, like a windmill, with legs and arms extended; and then sticking, when he reached the earth, like a pack of wool in the mud;—then the trepidation of Obadiah at the sight of the Doctor's dirty and dangerous state; the trouble he was at to stop his great, hard-mouthed, stiff-necked brute, which he could by no other means effect, than by pulling him round and round the prostrate Doctor, and bespattering him all with mud; the rueful face of Obadiah, and the aukward apologies he would make;—All these, I say, with many other additional circumstances, painted themselves so strongly on my imagination, that I laughed most immoderately loud. My friends, with surprize, asked the reason of my mirth; and I made them no other answer than by reading

reading them the passage forthwith. It tickled the fancy of one of them as much as it had mine, and he joined very heartily in the laugh: but it did not touch my other friend so much. He could not see, he said, any thing so very witty in the misfortune of a poor, harmless, inoffensive, man-midwife, who was travelling the road on a visit of civility and complaisance; it was cruel and insulting to laugh at his distress; and as for the unlucky rencounter of the poney and coach-horse, the thing was natural and common enough; it might happen in the neighbourhood of London any day of one's life. In short, he was quite out of humour with us, and peevishly pronounced us to be a couple of idiots for being diverted with such silly conceits.—I need not tell my readers, that my grave friend, though a man of a good solid understanding, had neither a sprightly imagination, any taste for humour, nor the least turn for the burlesque.

From what has been written, I think it is sufficiently plain, that *Laughter* is no more the characteristic of *Folly*, than *Gravity* is of *Wisdom*; and my Lord Chesterfield might, with greater propriety of reason, have said, "Laugh if you are wise:" for it is the greatest folly on earth to grieve at any loss or misfortune, not immediately caused by our own misconduct, but, for purposes unknown to us, permitted by the Will of *God*.

The

The LEVELLER. N°. XI.

An ESSAY on the NATURE and MUTABILITY of STILTS.

Projicit ampullas & sesquipedalia verba.
Decipimur specie recti.———
Aut dum vitat humum, nubes & inania captat.
                                    HORAT.

THE curious *Tristram Shandy*, among the rest of his singular opinions, hath given us a Dissertation on *Hobby-Horses*; but it is left to *The Leveller* to write an Essay on the Nature and *Mutability* of *Stilts*.

As a *Hobby-Horse* is defined to be a thing, in the possession or pursuit of which a man places his chief delight; so are *Stilts* such things, especially, in the use of which he takes a particular pleasure, because they raise him, in his opinion, above the rest of mankind, and eminently flatter his pride.

What principally brings this subject to my mind at present, is, the recent perusal of a *Journey to the Western Islands of Scotland*; in which I had not proceeded many pages, before it fully exhibited to me what I call an *Author upon Stilts*, stalking with most mighty and gigantic strides. The Writer of that Journey is generally supposed to be Dr. S———l J———n; but I should rather believe him to be some one employed by Dr. J———n's Bookseller, with a view to bring his Dictionary into greater repute. Be it as it may,—that Author, not contented with his own uncommon ftature, (that ftrength of reafoning, folidity of judgment, juftnefs of obfervation, and accuracy of remarks, which pre-eminently raife him above the fcribbling tribe) muft elevate himfelf on the Stilts of pompous diction, and endevour to ftalk more confpicuoufly towering in the croud. Yet one cannot help fmiling to hear common events recorded in the phrafe of monumental infcription or plain facts related, and familiar fights defcribed, in the language of Hiftory, and the cadence of Blank Verfe. I not only fmiled, but I moft certainly laughed ; and it was a confiderable time before I could determine within myfelf, whether the Journey was really a *ferious* performance, or whether it was written by the Author of *Lexiphanes*, as a fecond compofition of burlefque. Hear, only, how curioufly the Writer of that Journey tranfpofes fome familiar phrafes into pompous words:—for, *the road takes a turn*, he gives it a new turn indeed!—" The way makes a *flexure*." (p. 69.) For, *taking a walk through the town*, he moft elegantly writes—" We rofe to *perambulate* the City." (p. 6.) And *for giving his horfes their feed of corn*—" We fed the poor animals *liberally*." (p. 370.) But from the following extracts, my readers will judge for themfelves, if the author is on a level with them; or if, as I afferted, he is mounted confpicuoufly on ftilts.

" At an hour fomewhat late, we came to St. Andrew's, a City once Archiepifcopal, where that Univerfity ftill fubfifts in which Philofophy was formerly taught by *Buchanan*, whofe name has as fair a claim to immortality as can be conferred by modern Latinity;

nity, and perhaps a fairer than the inſtability of vernacular languages admits.—And, in the whole of our ſtay, we were gratified by every mode of kindneſs, and entertained with all the elegance of lettered hoſpitality (p. 5. and 6.) Of the architecture, the poor remains can hardly exhibit, even to the artiſt, a ſufficient ſpecimen." (p. 7.)

A monumental inſcription, indeed!

"One of its ſtreets is now loſt; and in thoſe that remain, there is the ſilence and ſolitude of inactive indigence and gloomy depopulation.—The Chapel of the alienated College is ſtill ſtanding; a fabric not inelegant of external ſtructure! (p. 9.) The Library, which is of late erection, is not very ſpacious, but elegant and luminous. The Doctor, by whom it was ſhewn, hoped to irritate or ſubdue my Engliſh vanity by telling me, that we had no ſuch Repoſitory of Books in England." (p. 10 and 11).

"The road beyond Aberdeen grew more ſtony, and continued equally naked of all vegetable decoration." (p. 35.)

If there were neither trees, buſhes, nor graſs upon the *fields*, the Author was very unreaſonable to expect that any ſhould grow upon the *high-road*.

"Lough Neſs, though not twelve miles broad, is a remarkable diffuſion of water. (p. 62.)

"The Country, at the bridge, ſtrikes the eye with all the gloom and grandeur of Siberian ſolitude. (p. 69.) The country is totally denuded of its wood. (p. 73.) They pollute the tea-table with large ſlices of Cheſhire Cheeſe, which mingles its leſs grateful odours with the fragrance of the tea. (p. 124.) We had

had, from this time, our intelligence facilitated, and our conversation enlarged by the company of Mr. Macqueen. (p. 129.) I honoured his orthodoxy, and did not much censure his asperity. (p. 280.) I, though less eager, did not oppose him." (p. 323.)

No Theatrical Prince could talk in a more important strain than this.

" There is yet another cause of errour not easily surmounted, though more dangerous to the veracity of itinerary narratives, than imperfect mensuration. An observer, deeply impressed with any remarkable spectacle, &c.—how many particular features and discriminations will be compressed and conglobulated into one gross and general idea." (p. 342. and 343.)

Sure the Author cannot expect, that the Ladies will suffer their tea-tables chat to be *polluted* with this incorporation and transubstantiation of thoughts.

" To this dilatory notion must be imputed the false relation of Travellers, &c. (p. 343.) The walls were always too strong to be shaken by such desultory hostilities. (p. 362.) At last we came to an inn, not only commodious but magnificent. The difficulties of peregrination were now at an end. After two days stay at Inverary, we proceeded southward over Glencroe, a black and dreary region, now easily passable by a military road, which rises from either end of the *Glen*, by an acclivity not dangerously steep, but sufficiently laborious. In the middle, at the top of the hill, is a seat with this inscription—*Rest, and be thankful.*"

And

And my readers, I think, will not be *unthankful* for giving *them* a rest. I have produced an extract sufficient for them to judge, if this kind of writing is really, what the pedants call, *enriching* our language. —As for my own part, where words are multiplied without adding to the idea; or whene'er a polysyllable is used for what a monosyllable could equally express, I deem it an unnecessary circumlocution, that ought ever to be discountenanced. We see no such art or false taste in the compositions of Mr. Pope: some of his most beautiful lines consist of the plainest and shortest words.

Hark! a glad voice the lonely desart chears;
Prepare the way! a God, a God appears:
Lo, earth receives him from the bending skies!
Sink down, ye mountains, and ye vallies, rise!
With heads declin'd, ye cedars! homage pay;
Be smooth, ye rocks! ye rapid floods! give way;
The Saviour comes! by ancient Bards foretold;
Hear him, ye deaf! and, all ye blind! behold.
The MESSIAH.

'Tis not enough no harshness gives offence;
The sound must seem an echo to the sense:
Soft is the strain when Zephyr gently blows,
And the smooth stream in smoother numbers flows;
But when loud surges lash the sounding shore,
The hoarse, rough verse should like the torrent roar.
When *Ajax* strives some rock's vast weight to throw,
The line too labours, and the words move slow;
Not so, when swift Camilla scours the plain,
Flies o'er th' unbending corn, and skims along the main.
ESSAY on CRITICISM.
Next

Next hear, in softer strain, a few of *Eloisa*'s lines to *Abelard*.

Yet write, oh write me all! that I may join
Griefs to thy griefs, and echo sighs to thine.
Tears still are mine, and those I need not spare;
Love but demands what else were shed in pray'r;
No happier task these faded eyes pursue;
To read and weep is all they now can do.
Then share thy pain, allow that sad relief:
Ah! more than share it, give me all thy grief.
—Thou know'st how guiltless first I met thy flame,
When Love approach'd me under Friendship's name.
—Guiltless I gaz'd; Heav'n listen'd while you sung;
And Truths divine came mended from that tongue.
From lips like those what precept fail'd to move;
Too soon they taught me, 'twas no sin to love:
Back thro' the paths of pleasing sense I ran,
Nor wish'd an Angel whom I lov'd a Man———
—Come, with thy looks, thy words, relieve my woe!
Those still, at least, are left thee to bestow———
—No; fly me, fly me, far as Pole from Pole;
Rise, Alps! between us, and whole Oceans roll!
Ah! come not, write not, think not once of me,
Nor share one pang of all I felt for thee.
Thy oaths I quit, thy memory resign;
Forget, renounce me, hate whate'er was mine.
Fair eyes, and tempting looks! (which yet I view)
Long lov'd, ador'd ideas, all adieu!———

I am afraid I have already tired the patience of some of my readers, unused to the melting mood; and yet I cannot forbear transcribing the pathetic description that follows next.

See, in her cell, sad Eloïsa spread,
Propt on some tomb, a neighbour of the dead.
In each low wind, methinks, a spirit calls;
And more than echoes talk along the walls.
Here, as I watch'd the dying lamps around,
From yonder shrine I heard a hollow sound:
Come, Sister, come! (it said, or seem'd to say)
Thy place is here; sad Sister, come away!
Once, like thyself, I trembled, wept, and pray'd;
Love's victim then, tho' now a sainted maid:
But all is calm in this eternal sleep;
Here Grief forgets to groan, and Love to weep;
Ev'n Superstition loses ev'ry fear;
For God, not Man, absolves our frailties here.

 I could dwell for ever on some of Pope's Poetry, where the smoothness, force, and dignity of our language is occasionally shewn, without having recourse to words a foot and a half long. Yet, some may be of opinion they could make richer language of those lines above quoted, by writing, " Hark, a loud acclaim the solitary desart exhilarates," and so forth; but I should answer them in the words of *Boileau;* which, as every common reader, now-a-days, understands a little French, I hope I may venture to quote, without stalking upon stilts myself.

J'aimerois mieux qn'il déclinât son nom,
Et dit, Je suis Oreste, ou bien Agamemnon;
Que d'aller, par un tas de confuses merveilles,
Sans rien dire à l'Esprit, étourdir les oreilles.
Le sujet n'est jamais assés tôt expliqué.
      L'ART POETIQUE.

I shall now dismiss our Author upon Stilts with a card I lately wrote to an admirer of his Journey, in answer to a common invitation to play at cards and spend the evening. It will serve as a further specimen of the true manner of writing on a familiar subject in pompous diction; and will prove that nothing is more easy than to adopt the *ſtiltic* ſtile, if one will but take a little time to employ his memory or recollection.

" At an hour ſomewhat late, your moſt benevolent
" invitation I received. As I deteſt indeciſion, ab-
" hor irreſolution, and abominate a declaration in-
" explicit, reſerved, or incomplete, rather than re-
" ply to you, that I will attend you *if I poſſibly can*,
" I muſt inform you, I will not come at all. My
" head, now tortured with rheumatic pain, is as un-
" fit for the intricacies of whiſt, the required atten-
" tion to the game, or the expected ſolicitude about
" your betts, as it is incapable of enduring the tur-
" bulent vociferation of convivial mirth."

After your *Writers upon Stilts*, of which I have touched but upon one claſs, the next, who take a pride in elevating themſelves above the common level of mankind, are your *Speakers upon Stilts*; and theſe are a very numerous race. Since it is impoſſible to ſpeak of them in this paper as diſtinctly as I could wiſh, I ſhall only mention a few of them as a ſample of the reſt.—A man who is continually ſtunning my ears with citations from the books he has read, I readily allow to have ſtudied hard; but then his ſtudy is oſtentatiouſly ſupported by Stilts. A man, who, in diſcourſe, takes every opportunity of throwing in a ſcrap of Latin or Greek, (of which your *ſtiltic Authors* are equally guilty) may be both an orator and a scholar; but he talks from a rostrum, which his vanity has mounted on stilts. A man who is eternally tormenting me with his bastard Italian, or broken French, I allow to have travelled; but I willingly stop him from making a *second Grand Tour* upon stilts. My method of *levelling* these Gentry is by rumbling out a bit of German or Dutch; by which, as these are languages in this country but seldom understood, they instantly perceive I have travelled, for their comprehension, a little too *far North*.—In short, affectation of *every* kind is walking upon stilts. The using terms of art, for instance, which serve not to distinguish or explain, or technical words which contribute nothing towards making yourself understood, are only so many elevating stilts.

From the frequent mention of the Bagpipes, in the Journey above quoted, Music, of all things, comes first into my head at present. The words made use of here, to signify the length of time in the notes of music, as semibreves, minums, crotchets, quavers, and semiquavers, are, in other countries, as properly described by a whole note, half a note, a fourth, an eighth, and a sixteenth. And, applicable to that, a story occurs to me, with which I shall conclude; warmly recommending it to the Author of the late Journey to insert it in the next edition of his book.

A Highland Piper, having a scholar to teach, disdained, with the stilts of semibreves, minums, crotchets, and quavers, to break his head.—Here, Donald, quoth he, tak yere pipes, mon, and gie us a blast. (But as I cannot make him, in character, speak *Erse*, he may as well talk English, and his lesson will be the better understood.)——Here, Donald, said he, take your pipes, my lad, and give us a blast.—So, very well blown, indeed! But what is sound, Donald, without sense?—You may blow on to all eternity, without making a tune of it, If I do not tell you how the queer things on that paper must help:—you see that fellow with the white, round, open face (pointing to a *semibreve* between the two lines of a bar); he moves slowly from that line to this, while you beat one with your foot, and take a long blast:—if, now, you put a leg to him, you make two of him, and he'll move twice as fast.—If you blacken his face, thus, he'll run four times faster than the first fellow with the white face. But if, after blackening his face, you bend his knee, or tie his legs, he will hop you still eight times faster than the white-faced fellow I shewed you first.—Now, whene'er you blow your pipes, Donald, remember this—the tighter those fellows' legs are tied, the faster they will run, and the quicker they are sure to dance.

The LEVELLER. N°. XII.

Another ESSAY on the SAME.

Medio tutissimus ibis   OVID. Metam. Lib. II.

THOUGH the *Journey to the Western Islands of Scotland* led me into the immediate consideration of the elevating powers of Affectation; Pride, Vanity,

Vanity, and Ambition, are the *grand Stilts* which invite men to mount above the level of their fellow-creatures. Instances of these are too numerous to be particularly mentioned. I will not therefore pretend to enumerate them; nor will I range the few, which readiest strike me, into any kind of order. Let them stalk about in the same irregular manner in which my imagination starts them.

Half the Nation, at this moment,* are mounted on the Stilts of Pride and Ambition, and are, in idea, wading the Great Atlantic, to kick down the antient and accustomed Liberties of America. But they will possibly exchange them, before the expiration of the ensuing summer, for those of Vanity and Affectation. Upon these we may soon expect to see them mounted; for, ever since the last Treaty of Peace, when the neglect of a grand fire-work occasioned so much national dissatisfaction, it has been the constant practice of the *Cabinet* to contrive something to amuse the people, and to give them and their representatives a harmless subject of conversation at their respective retreats during the summer season : " I have nothing to recommend to you, but that you will carry into your respective counties the same affectionate attachment to *Luxury* and *Dissipation*, and the same unconcern for the public welfare, which have distinguished all your proceedings :"—And so they are dismissed with a farce or an entertainment, immediately defrayed or powerfully patronized by a Great Person :—a *Coronation*, real and represented ;—a *Jubilee* at Stratford, conducted by Mr. Garrick, Master of the Revels, and acted again at his Theatre ;—an *Installation* at Windsor, and another at Westminster; besides the second Exhibition of the Knights on the Theatre;
—*Cox's*

* April, 1775.

—*Cox's Museum*, which terminating soon, will be a *Raree-shew* no longer; a *Royal Expedition* to Portsmouth; a Ministerial *Encænia* at Oxford; and, lastly, a *Fete Champetre;* which, however, was so far premature as to stop for a day the more weighty proceedings of the House of Commons.—Besides these, there are every Spring Masquerades and *Bals-pares* without number; which help to keep the Nation *elevated* and in good-humour the whole Summer; for *stiltic* amusements are the more perfect, as we enjoy them under a preternatural or improper figure.—As I do not recollect that any of our modern writers have made mention of these Political Stilts of Vanity, I must here claim the honour of detecting them, whoever has the merit of their invention.

But of all *Stilt-walkers*, none cut a more ridiculous figure than your *Lovers* upon Stilts; those, I mean, who heartily wish to come together, but whose pride and dignity will not allow the Gentleman to make the least concession; nor the Lady, (without the most abject demeanour and the most earnest supplication of her Lover,) the smallest surrender. *Honorius's* Love for *Gloriana* was founded on reason, and not on a doating fondness, which disgraces a man of prudence. He considered her person as an object he should be soon tired of in the possession, were she not endowed with good-nature, and an understanding which rendered her a most desirable companion. But *Honorius* would never stoop to fawn and flatter, and used the freedom to tell her of her failings. This proceeding disgusted *Gloriana*, who naturally imagined that the man who could talk in that undisguised strain to her when she was free, would be an absolute tyrant to her if he had her in his power. Nor would she ever acknowledge that she felt the least inclination

for

for him, or for any of his sex. Though she would on every occasion shew her affection for *Honorius*, 'twas mere *Platonic* Love; her dignity was hurt, if he presumed to construe it into any other. And that her behaviour towards him might not be understood to proceed from any tenderer sensation, she always took care that her words should be delivered like the words of an Oracle, which none but a *Priest* should ever interpret into a declaration fixed and certain. In short, their courtship was like the courtship of cats; an eternal scratching and caterwauling: the more pressing *Honorius* was, the more squalling noise *she* made about her *friendship*, and the more averring screams that she could never *love*. As *Honorius* would not submit to supplicate, he was on the point of giving the pursuit entirely up. He began to consider, however qualified *Gloriana* was for a friend, that she who would think it humiliating to allow a husband any freedoms, would, in his arms, be found to be but a cold and indifferent wife. But happily, one evening that he had the charge of her at Ranelagh, instead of conducting her into her own coach, he handed her into *his*. With a special Licence in his pocket, he then hurried her away to his friend Parson *Tiefast;* and this was the last *force* which *he* ever used; the last *resistance she* ever made.

How very different the character of *Gloriana* from that of *Constance*, in the Comedy of *Le Fils Naturel* of *Monsieur Diderot!* The Lady, there, reasons with her Lover on the procreation of their species (not with the calmness indeed, but) with all the chaste confidence of a Philosopher. And she pushes her arguments so closely to the Gentleman, (who rather wants to shun an engagement) that he is at last obliged in plain terms to tell her, that he shudders at the

very

very thoughts of having children: "*Dorval, says he, oseroit-il se charger d' une femme? Il seroit pere! il auroit des enfants!—Des enfants! Quand je pense que nous somme jettes, tout en naissant, dans un cahos de prejuges, d' extravagances, de vices, & de misere, l' idee m' en fait fremir.*" To which *Constance* very readily answers: "*Dorval, vos enfants ne sont point destines a tomber dans le cahos que vous redoutez.— Vos filles seront honnetes & decentes. Vos fils seront nobles & fiers.*"—And her imagination firing as she proceeds, "*Tous vous enfants seront charmans!*"—At this, as might naturally be expected, "Dorval *prend la main de* Constance, *la presse entre les deux siennes, lui sourit d' un air touche, et lui dit . "Si, par malheur,* Constance *se trompoit; si j' avois des enfants, comme j' en vois tant d' autres, malheurex & mechants, (je me connois) j' en mourrois de douleur.*"—To cut short the conversation, after reasoning the matter with him through a dozen pages, *Constance* modestly concludes with assuring him—"*Je ne crains pas qu' une ame cruelle soit jamais formee dans* mon sein *et de* votre sang."—That is *French* sentimental Comedy for you; at which perfection, praise the Vestals! our's is not yet arrived. But our Play-wrights would do well, from this little sample, to remember, that there is as thin a partition between Sentiment and Sensuality, in a friendship of the two sexes, as there is said to be between superior wisdom and downright folly.—The world, at least, seem to be of that opinion, in the case of the inconsiderate *Fulvia*.

Mounted on the Stilts of Vanity, *Fulvia* is never happy unless she has some young Officer, or some man of distinction in the Polite Circle, to attend her as her friend and sentimental companion. It is to her the highest delight in imagining the World will suppose,

pose, the young man is actually dying for her; while, ignorant of the uncharitable conſtruction put upon their intimacy. She irretrievably loſes her reputation. *Fulvia* is married, and were I her huſband, I ſhould certainly tell her—"The care of your *Virtue*, Madam, as I mean not to be tied to your apron-ſtrings, I leave to your own diſcretion; but, as your huſband, I muſt ever conſider myſelf to be the Guardian of your *Reputation*. When a man pays a conſtant attention, and, by a continued attendance, ſhews himſelf particularly attached, to a married woman, you may depend upon it, it can be for no diſintereſted purpoſe; and though he ſhould not have gained his ends, the the world will not fail to ſuppoſe it. I inſiſt upon it, therefore, you will drop that friendſhip. Chooſe *friends* among your own ſex, and *acquaintances* among mine; for no *man* but your huſband ought to ſhare your confidence." *

Celia is attacked with the ſame rage or unbounded deſire for admiration. No ſooner does ſhe deſcry a man whoſe addreſſes ſhe thinks will do her honour, than ſhe employs every art to attach him to her perſon. Though bleſſed with a beautiful face and an elegant figure, ſhe uſes the mean deceit of painting her cheeks, and blackening her eyebrows, to render herſelf more certain of her conqueſts. As ſhe is endowed with a good underſtanding herſelf, ſhe will never marry a fool; and men of ſenſe, in time, will deſpiſe her. When they diſcover the *rouge* and fictitious eyebrows, they will be apt to doubt whether every ſeeming beauty about her is not an impoſition. When they perceive her capriciouſly flying from one

---

* Some caſes excepted, where the Lady cannot do without her Man-Midwife.

man to another, they will dread being united to her, lest, after marriage she should prove unfaithful.

A handsome woman ought to be particularly careful how she exalts herself above the common level; for, the eyes of every-body attending her motions, if she does not manage her Stilts dexterously, she runs innumerable hazards of tumbles and shameful exposures. And, indeed, what with the lowness of their Stays (which exceed, now, all bounds of decorum), and their occasional lapses in foxhunting, there are some Ladies whose shape I can exactly tell, from three inches (I dare venture to say it) above and below the apron-string.

But when once a woman gets upon Stilts, and proclaims that she does not care what the World says of her, I pronounce her to be utterly incorrigible; she is then in a fair way of breaking her neck, and going headlong to the Devil.—Yet her actions partly belye her very declaration; for she courts, in fact, the praise and admiration of mankind, in her every attempt at being singular. Thus, in endeavouring to become conspicuous for a moment among the beholders in general, she may render herself ridiculous and contemptible among her friends and companions for ever.—So much for Vanity and Affectation.

As for the subject of Pride, I have formerly made the distinction between not stooping unworthily to those above us, and the haughtily attempting to raise ourselves out of the reach of those below us. To me (who am happy if, at the small expence of a hat, I can oblige the meanest of my fellow-creatures' it always gives particular satisfaction to see a Stilt-walker of the last class ridiculously dismounted.

My Readers cannot but observe, that I have dwelt less on the Stilts of Pride and Ambition, than on
those

those of Vanity and Affectation. The reason of it is plain:—These *last* are more the failings of the Moderns; and as the Ancients were more given to the *former*, sufficient is already said about them in ancient writ.—But we no where read that the Ancients had such a place as a *Ranelagh*, where they occasionally met and stalked about, for the mere empty satisfaction of interchanging looks; of seeing a number of strange people, and being seen by them. A *Pantheon*, indeed, they had; but their piety raised That in honour of their Gods. It was not erected by Vanity, nor was it supported by the gratification of Self-conceit. Their Writers therefore chiefly attacked them on the score of their Ambition and Pride. As long since as the building of the Tower of Babel, we find an account of the dispersion of the ancient walkers on the Stilts of Pride and Ambition through every kingdom of the known Globe. They must have been no less numerous in the time of the Roman Empire; for *Ovid* has a severe cut at them in his Fable of Phaeton and the Chariot of the Sun, from which I have taken my Motto for this Essay. But, between these two mentioned æras, *Homer*, in his immortal Poems, has particularly pointed them out. Nay, a friend of mine is actually in possession of an ancient Manuscript in *Erse*, which, in commenting upon *Homer*, says, that the true cause of Achilles's confining himself to his tent, the great Bard (for the honour of his Hero) hath thought proper to suppress; for this, continues our Commentator, was the real fact:—Prior to the story of the Armour, an incident had happened which I am going to relate, and which, indeed, was the principal cause of the Armour's being made. *Vulcan*, whose lameness, at times, obliged him to use crutches, was requested to lend them to *Achilles*, and to work them up for him into a stupendous

pendous pair of Stilts. *Vulcan* was a good-natured, easy, *cuckoldable* * kind of a fellow, as may be gathered from the story of his catching *Venus* with *Mars*; for instead of knocking both their brains out with his great hammer (as some *modern* Cuckolds would do in their wrath), he only threw a thin veil of an iron net over them, and diverted himself with exposing them to the derision of his Brother-Gods. He accordingly complied with the request. *Achilles*, with the counsel and advice of all the Grecian Chiefs, mounted his Stilts in the dead of night, and stalked towards the walls of Troy, with silent but gigantic strides. The concerted plan of operations was, that he should, by the help of these Stilts, scale the enemy's walls; put the Trojans at one of the gates to instant death (for he alone was reckoned a match for the whole guard), and then admit the Grecian army at that surprized gate. But *Hector*, who, as Captain of the Guard that night, was vigilantly going his rounds, (except butchering their fellow-citizens, no duty was deemed beneath the Heroes and Generals of those times) happened to espy *Achilles* just as he had made his last stride, and got against the parapet with his breast.——Upon this, without knowing who he was, *Hector* brandished his mighty sword, and levelled a furious blow at his head. Down dropt the son of *Thetis*; and thanks to his trusty helmet! or that blow would have finished his life. It had, however, a sufficient effect; for, in the very scientific words of the original account, *Achilles*, in his tumble, fractured his nose against the wall, excoriated his shins with the Stilts, and dislocated his shoulder in the *fosse*.——No wonder, then, he should have kept to his tent so long, or should even have been

---

* *Cuckoldable* is heartily at Dr. Johnson's service, for the next edition of his Dictionary of English Words.

been confined to his bed! The truth of it was, that after this disaster, by which he had so piteously bruised and disfigured himself, *Achilles* was for some time ashamed to shew his face. The cause of his confinement, therefore, (adds our learned Commentator) ought by no means to be laid to *Briseis*'s account; since, Heaven knows, the poor women have mischief enough to answer for, without our charging them with *fictitious* events.

As many learned Critics and Antiquarians may be curious to see this *ancient Manuscript*, I will inform them where it is to be found. It is in a Collection of *Original Papers, yet unpublished*, and which are now deposited, for the inspection of the Curious, at Mr. B.'s house, in the Strand.—A *late* Translator of Homer, who collected these papers in the Highlands of Scotland, gives of them this true and genuine account:—That a Highland Chief, being taken prisoner in the memorable battle between Agricola and his Romans and Galgacus and the Scots, was soon after conveyed to Rome, where he won so much on the good graces of the Emperor, that he obtained leave to examine the imperial *State-papers;* among which he found one containing many *secret Anecdotes* of the Siege of Troy, written in *Æneas*'s own hand, and which that unfortunate Hero carried off with him in his flight; the papers in his pocket, and old Father Anchises on his back. The most remarkable of these papers the Highland Chief translated into *Erse*, and after his ransom brought them home with him to his Caledonian cot. From *these* he wrote the Comment upon Homer, of which we have made this honourable mention; and from *these* he would also make it appear, that the noblest and most valiant of the Trojan Chiefs were not possessed of one drop of Patriotic blood;

blood; for, at the very time the Greeks surprised the town, those illustrious Heroes were plotting to deliver it up.—Hence the *English* Translator, exploding at once all Patriotism among *us*, drew this consequence in private to me, which I think myself at liberty to impart:—" Since, said he, the sincerity and disinterestedness of those antient Heroes were not to be depended on, who can rely on a *Temple*, a *Chatham*, or a *Wilkes?*"

The LEVELLER. N°. XIII.

A Short DISSERTATION on MASKS.

" To cover the Mask afresh, was more than the Mask
" was worth; and to wear a Mask which was bald,
" or which could be half seen through, was as bad
" as having no Mask at all.—This is the Reason,
" may it please your Reverences, that in all our
" numerous Family, for these four Generations,
" we count no more than one Archbishop, a Welch
" Judge, some three or four Aldermen, and a single Mountebank."
TRISTRAM SHANDY, Vol. VIII. Chap. iii.

SINCE perfection is not to be expected in this world, I am glad to choose my companions according

cording as their virtues preponderate, and their failings are found light, in my esteem. Agreeable to this maxim, I should also regulate myself in the choice of the Fair-one I would marry, or in the preference of the book I would peruse; provided always the *first* had good-nature, and the *last* had common-sense, without which my happiness or entertainment could never be compleated.—*Sterne* being one of those Authors whose excellencies greatly over-balance their their defects, I frequently amuse myself with him. Yet I cannot but confess, he is sometimes above my comprehension; for, in his Life and Opinions of Tristram Shandy, he has singly undertaken what *Pope*, *Swift*, and *Arbuthnot*, in the Memoirs of Martinus Scriblerus, jointly began—a Satire on the Abuses of Human Learning. One must therefore have a smattering of every thing, thoroughly to understand him. —He is, moreover, in his endeavours on all occasions to be witty, not a little guilty of playing upon words; but, when he does lay earnest hold of a subject, it must be acknowledged he treats it in a manner inimitable by any body else. I wish, for that reason, he had left less to the imagination of his reader concerning the subject which I have now taken in hand; my friends would then have been better entertained with *his* observations, than they can possibly be pleased with *mine*.

Not excepting the Savage of the Woods, which of us, almost from his cradle to his grave, wears not the *Mask* at times? We all wish to appear better than we are; and our very endeavours so to appear have often, in example, the effects of *real* Virtue. I would not, therefore, unmask the whole human species. It is, besides, an invidious task to attempt pulling the mask off those who wish to be concealed; and though
the

the Author of the Fable of the Bees had only expatiated on this text of Scripture—" If we say we have *no* sin, we deceive ourselves, and the truth is not in us;"—though he had allowed us *some* virtue, he would still have acquired a character of ill-nature, which I should be sorry to get by my Writings.

I am no enemy to a *Mask*, as long as it is put on with a good intention. A Clergyman is, by his profession, entitled to wear one; for, with the appearance of an extraordinary sanctity of manners, he is to enforce his precepts by a good example. When he is to say grace at table, he is not to mutter a few hasty words, as if he were ashamed of the office; nor is he to rise up, in the middle of his story, to return thanks, and, instead of the Amen, to conclude his thanksgiving with, " This is by way of parenthesis." Nor is he, in reading prayers at church, to smell at his nosegay, to push back his wig, and wipe his sweaty brow with his handkerchief; to loll lazily with both elbows on the desk; to recline with his cheek on one hand; nor to be continually scratching his head. He is to address his God with solemn voice and serious demeanour, that he may not, by his careless manner, strengthen the incredulity of unbelievers.

A Judge is another that ought undoubtedly to be masked during the time he is executing the duties of his office; for he is to impress the minds of his beholders with the highest notions of the austerity of the Law against its offenders, and of its due administration with the aid and interpretation of his own superior wisdom. When he pronounces sentence of death on a criminal, he ought to deliver himself with the most awful dignity, with the most composed and serious countenance. A Judge on the Bench ought not suddenly to interrupt his jocular discourse with
the

the ladies who fit near him, to put on his cap fmiling, and pronounce fentence of death as a thing of the leaft importance.—An Alderman, for the reafons affigned above, is alfo entitled to wear the Mafk; and fo is every Country Juftice.

As for a Phyfician, I am not quite fo certain if a grave wife face is always of as much fervice to his patients, as it is of ufe to himfelf, in procuring the public opinion of his experience and learning. If he be to wear a Mafk, then, let it rather be of the *comic* kind; for the cheerful, good-natured looks of fome Doctors are an antidote to low fpirits; whereas the fad folemn features of others may (in hypochondriacal cafes) be as bad as the Undertaker's.

It is generally allowed, that the Members of the Houfe of Commons would receive confiderable addition to the dignity of their appearance, were they to attend the Houfe in *ferious* Mafks and Dominos; I mean, that if they were never to fit there but in robes and graver faces, more refpect would be fhewn to the Reprefentatives of a great people, and lefs trifling would be fome of their Speakers, than when fo many of them attend in boots and leather breeches.

But no one has certainly greater occafion to wear a Mafk, than the Sovereign of a mighty Empire. Yet our good and gracious King wears the Mafk but feldom; and I verily believe it proceeds from his utter diflike to one, or the being obliged to put a reftraint upon his features, that he paffes his life in that reclufe, domeftic manner. Were I, however, of his Majefty's *favourite* Council, I fhould advife him to put on the Mafk much oftener; and, being fo mafked, I fhould alfo advife him to invite the principal men of the kingdom, now and then, to partake of a family dinner. Were his Majefty in that familiar way to have, in rotation, at his table, the chief of the Clergy, the Army, the Navy, and the Law, he would in time be acquainted with every man's character, from his own experience and observation, instead of having it upon trust from the partial report of the *so-named King's friends* who immediately surround him.

Self-defence justifies the use of a Mask at any time. When I perceive a man speaking to me with a seeming sincerity and candour, at the same time that he is only tempting me to lay myself open to him, that he may ridicule me in my absence, or take some private advantage of what I disclose to him; I immediately mask myself too, and let him see no more of me than I desire should be seen by the whole world.

As my two last Essays were levelled at those who from pride, affectation, vantiy, or ambition, are restlessly endeavouring to render themselves conspicuous in the world; I would, in this, willingly expose those selfish or mean-spirited wretches who live in an eternal dread of what men might say of them, or in a continued hypocritical disguise, with the sole purpose of serving their own private interest.—'Tis certainly a most laudable desire to wish to stand well in the esteem of our fellow-creatures; and, in trifling concerns or amusements, I would cheerfully give up my own taste or opinions, rather than I would forfeit the good-will of my neighbours; but, in the great and important transactions of life, a man ought to be guided by the noble motive alone of pleasing his Creator; and the fear of offending *Him* should be the only restraint upon his actions. One had better be born to a mild servitude or slavery, than live under a constant apprehension of his neighbour's censure. —I have an ample fortune, which enables me to live in affluent and independent circumstances; shall I

marry

marry Pamela, born of honest and worthy parents, and blessed with every virtue and accomplishment to render our marriage happy? No; I must not think of it: she is but a Farmer or a Tradesman's daughter, and I should be the ridicule of all my gay acquaintances.—I cannot join in every prayer of the Church service, and I disapprove of its forms and repetitions;—but I must attend the Church; for if I dissent, and go to the Meeting, I shall be laughed at by my episcopal neighbours. Or, perhaps, though educated a Presbyterian, I should wish to join in *some* form of prayer, rather than endure the absurdity of my Minister, who will sometimes, at pleasure, (as it is left to him) invoke God for me in impertinent nonsense. Yet I must be masked, and attend the Meeting, or I shall pass for a graceless apostate, among a congregation of very religious people.—Nay, if I am born among Roman Catholics, I must be doubly masked; (as Mr. B————e tells me in his Tour to Sicily and Malta) and I must kneel, however against my opinion, to the Host and to all the saintly images; and I must pay adoration to the Virgin Mary. That considerate gentleman even blames a blunt Englishman for standing up unmasked, one day, when the Host passed him; at the same time, he is so ill-mannered himself, as to publish to all the world a book ridiculing the Roman Catholic religion at almost every stage of his journey.—I cannot forbear making another remark on the masked conduct recommended by the same Writer. If every good Christian in the Protestant countries had formerly been of his opinion, we should never have seen any religious reformation. To which I may add, that if the great and learned, (instead of being instrumental in opening their eyes) assist designing Priests in blinding the vulgar and illiterate

literate people, they will hereafter have to anſwer for every evil conſequence attending ſuch confirmed ſuperſtition.

This would naturally lead us into the conſideration of forms and ceremonies of every denomination; but I muſt confine my obſervations within the limits of a periodical paper. Forms and ceremonies are oftentimes but Maſks, which the crafty make uſe of to impoſe on the ignorance and credulity of mankind; and ſo far as they tend to maintain the peace and good order of ſociety, they ought undoubtedly to be ſupported: but when they are employed, by the great and opulent, to keep the poor in the groſſeſt ignorance, and in the moſt abjeƈt ſtate of dependence, the Maſk ſhould be pulled off, the cheats deteƈted, the ceremonies levelled, and the forms aboliſhed.

Every man's obſervation muſt make him ſenſible how cautiouſly religious ceremonies ought to be put in practice. In the Roman Catholic Church, they have eminently the aſcendant over the moral duties, and the true ſpirit of Chriſtian adoration. *Baptiſm* the Papiſts look upon as eſſentially neceſſary to Salvation; and the *Holy Communion*, which commemorates the ſufferings of our Saviour, they have actually deified by their belief in Tranſubſtantiation. What profound veneration is even paid to the laſt by many of the Proteſtants! ſome of whom regard it as a ſign by which they enter into a covenant never to commit a ſin. Vain, preſumptuous men, to pretend to promiſe they will never ſin! But their reſolution ſeldom continues for any long duration; for after much preaching and praying in weekly preparations, no ſooner have many of them ſwallowed the Bread and Wine, than they return again to their old courſes. Thus, in our own Church, ſome ceremonies remain,

which

which the superstitious regard with the same reverence as the most essential parts of their Religion. As another instance:——How many good people imagine their friend would be damned to all eternity, were they to suffer his corpse to be buried without the previous reading of the funeral service? No time, surely, could be more proper to convey admonition to the Living, than at the burial of the Dead, when the minds of the mourners are sadly affected at the loss of a dear and valuable friend or acquaintance. The custom, therefore, however mistaken by Ignorance and Superstition, had for its institution a most laudable purpose. So had the custom of congregations of people assembling once a-week in Church, to perform public worship to their Creator; yet many pious Christians seem now to think, that in the mere frequenting the Church consists the chief merit of their devotion. What numbers of devout old women do we see trotting, every day in the week, to the tinkling of the mattin-bell! as if the Almighty would not listen to their prayers, unless they were spoken before witnesses, or offered up for them by a man in a white surplice. I have no quarrel with those acts of supererogation, if their incentives be pure and upright. But when I perceive no fruits produced by them, no acts of charity or benevolence, I then suspect them to be but Masks to cover the designs of self-interest.

And, in fact, if we look round us in the world, we shall see that they are the prudent and selfish, who are, in general, reputed to be over righteous.—In attending regularly the Church, and scrupulously observing its ceremonies, they mistake the *means* of becoming virtuous for *real* virtue. Some of them, indeed, may excel in the negative virtues:—they will not

not drink, they will not whore, they will not swear,—all perfectly commendable. But what good have they done to their fellow-creatures? Their virtue, therefore, centers in self: but the virtue of the noble and generous, like the light of the sun, diffuses itself on every one around them.

I would not be understood to discourage the attending Church on the Sunday. As that is the only day of the week in which the laborious part of mankind have opportunity to improve their understanding, the rich (were it only for example's sake) ought to keep it holy. Nor would I be thought to cast any reflections against frequent private prayer to the Almighty. On the contrary, the effusions of a grateful heart heighten the enjoyment of every blessing in life: and a due resignation to the Divine Will, with a firm confidence in the goodness of the All-wise Disposer of events, are the best comforts under every misfortune that may befal us. Besides, no ingenuous mind can be constantly humbling itself before God, without as constantly recollecting, and forming a resolution to amend itself.

I once knew a Gentleman so well persuaded of the truth of that remark, as even, in a dangerous sickness, to be deterred by it from praying for the recovery of his health. Going one day to see him when he was severely attacked, I asked him how he found himself? "Oh! very ill, indeed! I never had such an inclination to pray in my life." "And why don't you pray, then?" said I.—"To say the truth, my friend," replied he, "I could not bring myself to promise never to sin again; without which I thought my prayers would have little effect."

I knew another Gentleman as little given to implore the daily protection of God.—He belonged to

the

the Army; and happened to be fishing with another Officer in one of the rivers which empty themselves into the St. Laurence, not a great distance from Quebec. They were in a little canoe, which they had suffered to float so long with the stream, that, without perceiving it, they were got into a strong current, and were precipitately driving to a cataract: there they must have been dashed against the rocks, sunk, and inevitably perished. They tugged and laboured at the oars, as soon as they saw their danger; but they were still approaching the fall, and could not get out of the current. One of them then, despairing, threw down his oar, and fell on his knees in devout invocation to God. The other stuck to his oar, perfectly ashamed, in his perilous situation, to implore the Omnipotent assistance. "I thought," said he to me, when he told me the story, "that as it had been a long time since I had prayed to God before, he would look down on me with utter contempt: I thought I heard his tremendous voice reproaching me in these words: 'Are not you a pitiful, cowardly ' rascal, to be praying to me now you are going to ' death?—You, who forgot me in the days of your ' prosperity, what expectation can you have that I ' should prolong your existence?'—So I took both the oars, added he, and while my companion prayed, I rowed with all my might; and I tugged so tight, that at last, with the blessing of God, I got the canoe safe into a creek."—These men had souls above dissembling virtue; and deplorable as their situations were, I leave it to Casuists to determine, whether their inward conviction of unworthiness would not lead as readily to salvation, as the feigned sanctity of some Methodists, or the useless maimed life of a Monk.

The

The LEVELLER. N°. XIV.

Another DISSERTATION on MASKS.

———————————— There's no art
To find the mind's construction in the face.
MACBETH, Act I. Scene 6.

SHAKESPEARE is perfectly in the right, with regard to the faculties of the understanding. A man, with a most stupid, dull look, may nevertheless be a very clever fellow; while another, with a most sprightly countenance, will be found to be exceedingly shallow. But, in the mind's construction, as to the tyranny of the *Passions*, there is certainly an Art to find it, and I think it is attainable by any man of common observation. I have seldom found it fail, that the person whose features resembled those of a man perfectly known to me, was more or less governed by the like passions as ruled that well-known character. Let a continued habit of hypocrisy ever so much mask the countenance, I shall discern its natural lineaments in some unguarded minute of anger, grief, or laughter. What face, for instance can be more thoroughly masked than that of a Dutch Parson? Yet, if he is at all capable of feeling, the discomposure of his features must sometimes discover to me his true character. Nothing has been more entertaining to me than the sight of one of those Hypocrites, when he has suddenly recollected

lected himself in his laughter, and with a sigh resumed his saintly look, as if he would have said, "God forgive me! what a sinful mortal I am to laugh in this manner!"—Next to a Dutch Clergyman's, the most settled countenance in the world is that of a Prudish Woman; and yet the very manner of her turning her eyes from an object (for *them* the mask cannot conceal) will often shew us the bent of her inclination. As, then, there are moments in which a good Physiognomist can, from the expression of the features, pronounce which of the passions bears the greatest sway in the bosom, and the mask of dissimulation is of little more use than to impose upon the ignorant or unobserving; it were to be wished we would give less attention to appearances in the world, and pay greater regard to the practice of real and intrinsic virtue. But, on the contrary, it does often seem as if a sin consisted not so much in the *commission*, as in the *discovery* of it.—I am led to make this remark by having lately seen a woman do penance in church for an occasional weakness. It is a common observation with historians, that no men are so fond of power as the clergy, and that no men are worse politicians. Can it otherwise be conceived that such a power should be continued in the Spiritual Court, as that of publishing a woman's shame to a whole congregation of people? It cannot, sure, by the Clergy be considered as a punishment, for they are in Scripture expressly prohibited from inflicting any: *He that is without sin amongst you, let him first cast a stone at her*, are the words of our Saviour; and, with an exhortation *to sin no more*, he dismissed the Adulteress.—But I shall be told that public penance is intended as an example *in terrorem* to other women. It might with as much plausibility be said, that the cries

cries of a woman in labour would terrify all maidens from venturing on matrimonial pleasures.—Few people, who yield to the tender impulses of a natural affection, can coolly reflect on the bad consequences that may follow; and the more cautious who are possessed of that cool deliberation, are but indebted for it to the phlegm of their constitution, or to a certain prudence and circumspection, which only render them the more guarded in their conduct—the more hypocritical in their character. The good proceeding from this custom is at the best but problematical; the evils resulting from it must be acknowledged by every considerate person. It has seldom been found, in the parishes where the custom has been mostly continued, that the women were more chaste than the rest of their country neighbours; but, on the contrary, it is a melancholy truth, that the murder of bastard children has, on that account, happened to be more frequent; and thus women, to conceal one sin, have inhumanly been guilty of a greater. The dread of punishment cannot *amend the heart* (which alone should be the province of the Clergy), nor prevent the commission of any one sin that can be safely committed in secret. Instead of amending an unfortunate girl, the publishing her shame but accelerates her ruin. A young woman, with no other fault in her composition than the having a too tender and susceptible heart, has yielded (I shall suppose) to the importunities of a man possessed of her esteem; her weakness is perhaps known but to one family, or to a few friends: some relentless Priest or Churchwarden shall drag her from her obscurity, present her to the Spiritual Court, and expose her character to a whole town.—From the hour she has done public penance she becomes desperate; she either flies the country,

country to shun the contempt of her neighbours, or, heedless of what farther can be said of her, she prostitutes her person, becomes totally abandoned, and thoroughly practised in every Wickedness. But where we ought to expect the most tender indulgence, the greatest rancour is frequently found: her own sex have been the most inveterate against her; the *modest women* have turned their backs upon her; and the unfortunate girl, having found herself shut out from the society of the virtuous, was it to have been expected, that in the company of the vicious, into which from solitude she had fled, that in a repetition of her follies, she should ever have been reclaimed? *Bigots*, indeed, may imagine that such a conduct, towards a young sinner, will produce her reformation, and that they do a thing well pleasing to the Almighty in making themselves the instruments of his vengeance; but every one, the least acquainted with the world, knows it to be a melancholy truth, that more women become prostituted and abandoned, in consequence of the contempt of their own sex, than from the treachery or inconstancy of our's.——But for *one* woman who, out of a false zeal for the interests of religion and virtue, shews her resentment against the conduct of the frail-hearted, there are *twenty* who, from far different motives, affect to be equally sincere in their detestation. Of these, the most violent in their expressions of contempt and abhorrence of the *filthy creatures*, are many of the poor, neglected *old maids*, who would willingly make us believe that a disgust of the joys of wedlock had been the occasion of their celibacy, and not any defect or deformity of their own persons. A second set of *abhorrers* are your ladies of *suspected virtue*, who industriously attempt to render less conspicuous the stain on their own

own characters, by blackening or painting hideously the conduct of their neighbours. And a third class of avowed enemies to sensual pleasures, are your prudes or devotees; women who have set up for a character of eminency in religion, who are ambitious of being esteemed in the world as the very patterns of piety, and who, by shewing any indulgence to a woman that had a flaw in her reputation, would dread any diminution of their fame, any exposure of their own masked virtue.——But as these, by their conduct, shew themselves only apprehensive lest the mask of sanctity should be disfigured which they had so carefully put on, so will they, who are virtuous for Virtue's sake—they, whose actions are governed by motives alone of pleasing their Creator, and not by the censure or applause of men—they will ever, with Christian charity, compassionate their neighbour's failings, and be ready to forgive and amend. They will reflect, that there are stages or degrees of vice; that no one becomes instantly abandoned; that the loss of chastity implies not the want of every virtue; and, instead of driving a weak woman to despair, they will humanely use every method to reclaim.

The want of fellow-feeling is not, however, peculiar to the Women;—by those who wear the mask, imprudence of conduct is as little forgiven among the Men. How many promising young fellows set out in the world, befriended and protected by their relations for no other reason than because they wish to make them rich or eminent! As their aggrandisement would reflect honour on their family, their friends strive emulously to push them on. Some, perhaps, depending more on expectancies than on the fortune which they actually possessed, have lived beyond their income, and in a few years have been

totally

totally undone. Their friends, thus difappointed in their views, regard their want of œconomy as the greateft of fins, believe them for ever void of induftry, and incapable to act in bufinefs again; then drop them and forfake them as the moft vicious and moft profligate of men.——Not fo fared it with the gallant, gay Lothario, related to Lord Maynard, who is lately dead and gone. Lothario, in fome difficulties, applied to his relation for his affiftance and advice. His fituation he difclofed to his Lordfhip by a letter, to which he received the following anfwer by the return of the poft:

" Dear ———,
" AS my eyes are very weak *, and can bear but
" little writing, and as the correfpondence between
" us, at this time, is of a private and fecret nature,
" I think it moft advifeable for you to haften down
" hither, even at the time fixed for your journey to
" ———, whereby we may be able to talk over your
" affairs privately between ourfelves.
                " I am very faithfully your's,
Eafton Lodge,   MAYNARD."
April 7th, 1775.

The fame cover tranfmitted a bank note to defray Lothario's travelling expences, and pay his little debts in town.—He repaired immediately to Eafton Lodge, where Lord Maynard received him as the Father did his Prodigal Son. Waving all reproaches on the imprudence of his paft conduct, which had been fo oppofite to his Lordfhip's plan, Lord Maynard invited Lothario to live with him, and fettled on him for life a very handfome income.——Lord Maynard

---

* His Lordfhip was then about ninety years old.

Maynard in this letter shews such a delicacy of sentiment, so much generosity of mind, and such charitable indulgence for the frailties of mankind, that few examples of the like will be found. One would imagine that the business of it concerned his Lordship alone; that some affair was depending in which he had a sole interest, and not that he had a benefit to confer.—The sight or recital of a noble action will often force tears of joy from my eyes, in exultation at the thought of so much goodness in a fellow-man! Thus, at the first reading of this letter, my heart overflowed with benevolence towards the generous Lord by whom it was penned. My mind was suddenly impressed with the highest veneration for his character.—I was resolved to record this instance of his beneficence (his *many* † noble acts being then to me unknown); and, for the honour of true religion, I gladly now proclaim, that in *Charles Lord Viscount Maynard* much piety, much virtue, without a mask, was found.

The

† I have been since informed that his Lordship expended in charitable donations 3000 l. per annum.

The LEVELLER. N°. XV.

His ANSWER to SCRUTATOR's Remarks on his laſt LEVELLER.

SIR,

I AM but an anonymous writer, and have little concern about the fate of my *Levellers;* ſome anſwer is, however, required to your ſtrictures; becauſe the character of my friend is at ſtake, and the reputation of the Weſtminſter Magazine.

It might eaſily have happened, that Mr. Wright, in the multiplicity of affairs, ſhould have iſſued from his preſs an improper publication; and two or three other Printers might have been equally inadvertent, who have done me the honour to *reprint* the *Leveller* you have ſo critically cenſured. But I am unwilling that inadvertency ſhould be any excuſe for their having committed, in your eyes, an act of evil tendency. I ſubmit to defend my writings; and, in the explanation I ſhall give you, I hope to make it appear, that a Printer, even in the hurry of his buſineſs, is no incompetent judge of morality.

If your zeal had not blinded you, Sir, you muſt certainly have perceived, that we were both writing in the ſame cauſe of virtue. However groſsly, and in general terms, you have miſrepreſented me as an immoral writer, if you will deſcend to particulars, I believe you will find it difficult to prove any thing either

either impious or immoral in my compositions. You may, indeed, call me *irreligious;* for the religion I profess is *Christianity*, according to the gospel, and not according to your belief of the infallibility of the Church discipline. I confess to have sneer'd a little at the *ostentation* of devotion, at the parade of some people trotting every morning in the week to church; because I have remark'd the generality of the people in Holland, Scotland, and Geneva, who are supposed to say prayers in their closets, to be equally virtuous with the rest of mankind. I have also been so free as to give my opinion on some of the ceremonies of the Church, without the observance of which I have known so many good Christians live and die in the hope of salvation.

But, in delivering these sentiments, you will be pleased to remember, that I glanced only at those designing Hypocrites who wish to impose on the world by the *shew* of Religion; or at those well-meaning people who deceive themselves, by vainly imagining, that, in repeating like parrots a string of prayers at church, they are before God superlatively virtuous. I was far from saying any thing against keeping holy the Sabbath-day, or privately lifting up our thoughts to heaven in devout meditations.

On the contrary, Sir, were I disposed to entertain my readers with a sermon, I should recommend prayer to them in a much more serious manner than you imagine. I should exhort them never to address the Deity, without composing their minds, and banishing as much as possible all earthly considerations; without considering the importance of the occasion, or without the utmost awe and reverence of expression. A man, who entertains that just idea of prayer, and who has any worldly concerns to occupy his time and reflexion,

cannot

cannot kneel to God at the ftriking of a clock, or at the tinkling of a bell from a church fteeple —Even at the hour of relaxation from bufinefs, at perodical family prayer, fome time is neceffary for pious preparation.—One night, as I fupped with a friend, whofe cuftoms had undergone fome alteration,—juft as the clock ftruck ten, and in the middle of a merry difcourfe that had raifed the whole company's laughter,—the fervants fuddenly appeared in the room, formed in a line, and kneeled before me in regular order. I ftared; but looked to the right like a foldier a drilling, and took from my friend the mechanical motion. My friend then opening a prayer-book, compofed his countenance to a ferious expreffion of features, and went through the prayers with the greateft decorum. When the fervants retired, he refumed his jocular humour: "Well! my friend, did not I "take you nicely in, for a bit of prayer?" True, faid I, it was the fartheft from my thoughts at that moment. Your cuftom, however commendable, over a bottle a little furprized me. But as I am one of thofe giddy mortals who cannot always command their attention; as I cannot inftantly jump from your witty difcourfe, your table and your fire-fide, to invoke the Great God that made me, I beg that, the next time I attend you, my friend, you will read me a previous chapter or two, to prepare my mind for adoration.

Though thus particular, to the Public, in the explanation of fome of my late expreffions, I fhall not be furprized, Sir, if you and I fhould continue to differ. For one man, who, in fearch of truth, exerts the powers of his own underftanding, there are a thoufand who give implicit faith to the doctrines and opinions of others. For one *Prieftley*, for one

X *Lindfey,*

Lindsey, there are twenty superstitious Parsons. *You* may have been taught to revere some of the ordinances of men as sacred and indespensible, which *I* discern to be instituted either to impose on, or, for wise purposes, to govern the illiterate and vulgar. *You* may, therefore, regard *me* as a reprobate; and so would a Monk, if I refused to worship his Wafer. But pronounce not a man to be wicked, because he disagrees with you in the Church discipline; nor yet from the integrity of your own heart, judge of the good intentions of other people. The Clergy are not immaculate; relentless Priests exist not alone in my imagination; I could name you relentless Priests; if I were given to be personal, I could name you a relentless Prelate. Say not, then, in support of that power which may be abused by a bigotted Priest, " I " hope his authority would not be employed on im- " proper objects;" for, on the same presumption that the King would do no wrong, we might invest him with unlimitted authority.—However these expressions may offend *you*, Sir, I mean not the least disrespect for the Clergy. I know many valuable men in the Church, who teach Christianity to their flocks thro' the example of their every action; men, who endeavour to amend sinners, by eating and conversing with them, and not by punishments and persecution; men " who put not on a sorrowful countenance, for to be seen of men,"—but, " in this world so light and trifling," can shew themselves cheerful and happy.—

I shall now, Sir, more immediately reply to your strictures on my last *Leveller*.—You must be very ignorant of the professional arts of a Printer's business, not to perceive, that *An Apology for Prostitutes* was merely a *catching Title*. I suppose Mr. Wright imagined, such a Title would naturally awaken the
curiosity

curiosity of some people who might accidentally look at his Magazine, and would induce them to purchase it, that they might read what could be said on the subject. But nothing was certainly farther from my intention, than to apologize either for Prostitutes or Prostitution. On the contrary, Sir, I detest the sin, though I most compassionately pity the sinner. Instead of an Apology for Prostitution, I gave you a natural description of a woman, who, after the loss of her character, by a common gradation in vice, becomes totally abandoned. I said, there were degrees in vice, and I made an express distinction between an *occasional Weakness* and *Prostitution*. An *occasional Weakness* I define to be, the yielding, as opportunity offers, to a powerful impulse of nature, in favour of a beloved object, without a consciousness of sin, or any reflection on its consequences.—Surely, Sir, such a sinner is not equally guilty, in the sight of God, with the loose woman who prostitutes her person. Nay, should she continue faithfully attached to one object, without having received the Parson's blessing, I believe her to be less sinful than the woman, who, marrying, gives up her body to a husband for the sake of lucre. However sanctified by custom, the ecclesiastical ceremony of marriage is but the confirmation of a civil contract. In the union of the minds of the two sexes, after a solemn vow of constancy made before God, is comprised the *real* holiness of its institution. That vow, that contract, 'till of late years, could in England be made before a private person; in Scotland, it can still be made before a Justice of the Peace; and, in Holland, no marriage is valid that is not solemnized by the Civil Magistrate. It was not, Sir, 'till the time of Pope Innocent the Third, that the intervention of a Priest to solemnize a contract of marriage, was deemed either *juris naturalis aut divini* But I am attacking again the authority of the Church, and shall draw down more of its thunder upon me.—Yet, 'tis some comfort to have the right reverend Bishops on my side; who, in all Bills of Divorce, certainly consider the *Ceremony* of marriage as no divine, indispensible part of its institution. They would never consent to put asunder those whom God hath joined together, did they not consider the *Vow* as the *Spirit* of the union, and on the breach of which alone the Gospel permits a Separation.

Though I have said thus much to remove that horror you express at an *occasional weakness*, I repeat my detestation of promiscuous amours, and I would by no means be understood to recommend particular illicit attachments. I acknowledge the wickedness of *prostitution*, and fully admit the *inexpediency* of *keeping*; but I think the *sinfulness* of the *last* may be reasonably doubted, where a mutual vow of constancy is made, and faithfully kept, before the God that heard it. With *him*, it must be the *vow* that constitutes the union, and not the presence of any particular people who administer the oath, or by whom it is witnessed. If, therefore, the parties so living together, without the Parson's blessing, can provide a sufficient maintenance for their children, the Clergy may deem it a sin, but Civilians will scarcely call it an offence against *their* law, wisely instituted to ascertain and make known the father who is bound to provide for his offspring. Leave it then to the Civil Magistrate to be judge in such wanton offences. When a frail woman can shew no honest way of getting her livelihood there is a Bridewell, or a House of Correction. If she follows any lawful profession, and

demeans

demeans herself decently in public, the law humanely winks at her *sins*, (for *such* must inevitably be) and reckons those only as her *crimes*, which hurt the community by idleness and a dissolute example.

In addition to my last *Leveller*, it is unnecessary to say any thing more about the inexpediency of making a woman do penance in church for an *occasional weakness*; excepting that, notwithstanding the *boldness* of your affirmation to the contrary, I have known the case happen, and I have known it to be attended with all its evil consequences. But I cannot help animadverting a little on the propriety, you maintain, of bringing a woman of an *abandoned character* to do penance, as an example, *in terrorem*, to the modest women. What! Sir, do you make so slight of a solemn promise of amendment uttered before God, as to oblige a woman to make it in the presence of a whole congregation of people, who are fully persuaded that she will continue to earn her bread by prostitution? Is not *that* adding one sin more to her wickedness, by tempting her to sport with God Almighty? And must it not lessen the solemnity of an oath in the minds of the people? Surely, Sir, you could not be serious in the proposal, unless, like *Hudibras*, you thought to take off the sin of perjury from her:

He that *imposeth* an Oath, makes it;
Not He that, for convenience, takes it.

I am very much afraid, Sir, that the custom of obliging only prostitutes to do penance, would answer little other purpose than to render some others of the Sex more guarded and hypocritical in their conduct. It would be a mere bugbear to frighten children; for the grown girls would soon be cunning

ning enough to fee, that, if they faved but appearances with the world, they would never be exhibited on the ftool of repentance. Once more, then, let me recommend it to you, to leave the judgment of the *criminality* of the frailty in queftion to the Civil Magiftrate; for, as to the *finfulnefs* of it, our Saviour, when he *fufpended* the fentence of the law againft the Adulterefs, virtually *prohibited* punifhment.

Nor am I very fingular in this charitable indulgence to human weaknefs:—the Magdalen Hofpital, projected by that excellent good man Mr. *Jonas Hanway*, and fupported by fuch liberal benefactions, plainly demonftrates, that a very different fpirit prevails with many Chriftians, in confidering the infirmities of our nature, than that of punifhment or perfecution. Men educated with Monks, or confined to their clofets, aufterely judge the world as *it ought to be;* men, bred in the world, indulgently rate it as, by experience, they find *it really is*.

It happens a little unluckily, Sir, that the only two quotations you give from me, you have totally mifapprehended. "It does often feem, as if a fin "confifted not fo much in the *Commiffion* as in the "*Difcovery* of it," evidently implies, that an unfortunate woman, who had given birth to an illegitimate child, (which conftitutes the *Difcovery* of her weaknefs) was often brought to public fhame; when many others, who were reputed to be more vicious, would, for want of proof, efcape the punifhment. We know that nobody, by the civil law, can be convicted of a *Crime*, unlefs it can be proved upon evidence; but we alfo know, that moft of us have committed *Sin* in private; againft the repetition of which the fureft preventive is, for the Clergy to continue preaching amendment.

"*Nam*

" *Nam quid faciet is Homo, in tenebris, qui nihil
" timet nifi teflem et judicem.*"—Cicero.

In the other quotation I find an error of the pen, or an error of the prefs, which the whole of the fentence plainly evinces. For *virtuous* read *cautious*, and my meaning, Sir, is fufficiently obvious: that " few people, who yield to the tender impulfes of " natural affection, can coolly reflect on the confe- " quences that may follow; and the more *cautious*, " who are poffeffed of that cool deliberation," (and who, neverthelefs, yield to thofe tender impulfes; not the rigidly *virtuous*, who refift them) " are but " indebted for it to a certain prudence and circum- " fpection, which only render them the more guard- " in their conduct, the more hypocritical in their " character."——If I had that levelling idea of the Sex which you impute to me, I fhould fhew very little thankfulnefs indeed for my paft happinefs, and no fmall difrefpect to many valuable friends at this moment.——I have been married to a moft amiable and virtuous woman, and I am acquainted with feveral of her Sex, who, though they poffefs not my love, equally command my efteem.——I agree with you, Sir, that virtue doth not confift in an apathy of mind, but in a firm, efficacious refiftance againft temptation; but while I acknowledge that, I abjure the levelling principle which you feem to retain, That, becaufe a woman has yielded to the man fhe had an affection for, fhe would give her embraces to any indifferent perfon that fhould afk her.—Carrying with us my definition of an *occafional weaknefs* and the geneial received idea of proftitution, I muft ftill maintain, that more women become proftituted and abandoned, in confequence of the contempt of their own Sex, than from the treachery or inconftancy of our's.

ours. If I had said, " than from the *Seduction* of
" our Sex," your objection would have had greater
weight. Where a man, to gain a woman, employs
assiduity, entreaties, persuasion and art, I call that,
Seduction; and he will have much to answer for, if
that woman should be drawn deeper into vice. But
where two people unpremeditately meet, and by the
force of attraction mutually embrace;—to lay the
whole blame of the woman's future wickedness on
the man, is like loading the tree with reproaches of
which our mother Eve did eat the fruit.—

I shall now take my leave of you, Sir, for I must
decline answering any more of your remarks. He is
a bad writer who cannot intelligibly express himself;
and I would much rather be reckoned such, than, by
repeated explanations, be drawn into a dry dispute.—
I cannot, however, conclude without presenting you
with some lines, which I formerly wrote in a young
Lady's Bible, and which, you may think, could be
as properly addressed to any *Bigot*, who finds himself disposed to preach.—

[teach?

Read'st thou this book, as *Monks* and *Abbots*
As *Calvin* taught us, or as *Lutherans* preach?
Doest thou torment thy brain, or beat thy head,
To find two meanings to what here is said?
Expounding Texts, to common-sense most clear,
Explain'st for types, where none in fact appear?
Or, passive in th' opinions of thy mind,
In Tenets treading as are led the blind,
Believ'st in such, (howe'er absurd, abhorr'd,)
Because a Parent taught, or priestly Lord?
Doest thou neglect our Saviour's words and rules
For Creeds, for rites, for forms of wrangling
 Schools?

His

His name forgetting for a *Sect*'s, doest hope
And trust in *Calvin, Luther,* or the *Pope?*
If so thou form'st thy mind, peruse no more
This sacred Book, for shut's true Wisdom's store;
By no proud sect her learned treasure's found;
Who seeks for truth, his faith in none must ground;
Each hath it's errors, to this Book unknown;
Mark then its precepts, common-sense hath shewn,
Those lead to Heav'n; all else beyond our reach,
(Which deep Divines dogmatically preach)
Man may *believe*,—but *God* alone can *teach.*

The LEVELLER. Nº. XVI.

Some THOUGHTS on MUSIC and DANCING.

THOUGH no person can be fonder of Music than I am, I confess, I never sat out an Opera or an Oratorio without being heartily tired of it. A man must certainly have few ideas of his own, or at least have a perfect command of his attention, to be able to listen, during the greater part of three long Hours, to the tiresome *twing-twang* of the *Recitativo*.—It is more than probable, that the inventors of this musical accent (if I may so call it) borrowed the first thought of it from the chanting in the service of the cathedral churches. They may have imagined,

that

that if it were natural and becoming to chant a Prayer or Petition to God Almighty, it would surely be allowable, if not entertaining, to make their Heroes on the Stage speak in *Recitativo*.—But they mistook the case entirely;—the similitude will not hold:—for when a heavy, dull Priest, with a drowsy, drawling drone of a voice, has, in the tedious repetition of ceremonious prayers, read his congregation half asleep—a chant of the Litany, of a Psalm, or even of the Lord's Prayer, is a happy relief. In the Opera, on the contrary, Music is that for which the audience are assembled; and they impatiently expect a song: their organs of hearing ought not, therefore, to be fatigued with the continued sound of the Recitativo, before the song is begun. The hearing, like our other senses, is palled by long enjoyment, and recovers its vigour by relaxation. Would not then the Songs of an Opera have a stronger effect, were the rest of the piece to be acted and spoken, and the Recitativo to be dropt? It is, undoubtedly, nothing but custom that continues the Recitativo in Taste. The English and French, in their Comic Operas, have properly omitted it; and, I think, with very good success. If the number of Songs in *Love in a Village* had been burdened with a Recitativo, I dare say no one would have had patience to have heard them to the End. I shall perhaps be told, that there are, very judiciously regulated, two pauses in an Opera, between the Acts.—Very true;—but my ears, for all that, have no mercy shewn them—not the least relaxation. There is the music for the Dancing as noisy as the Opera itself; and *there* the vain Catgut Scrapers exult; having no longer any competitors whose voices they would willingly drown with the instruments of their numerous band.

Each

Each voice now hush'd;—save in the Orchestre loud, 'tis silence all, and pleasing expectation. *Heinel*, lo! on stilt-like tip-toe, makes her grand approach. Behold her stand with arms outstretch'd, as when we see a broom-stick, across the shoulders of a scare-crow tied, resisting every wind! And now, her petticoats forming a Pantheon dome, celerous she whirls, on thin shank spindling round; a solitary shank it stands, yet gains the applause, the admiration, eke it's sister's due, and which between the twain more justly I would deal.———So have I seen arch, little Miss open her rusty scissars wide, and, one point fixing on some polish'd board, turn them, ah! swiftly round, to make her sport.——But that is Grace, and it is fashionable Grace.—Mr. Slingsby, with all your ease and agility, unless you can improve your Taste, you will shortly lose your bread: you will, at least, be soon discharged the Opera-house, if you will not learn to dance a little more à *la Heinel*. You can, indeed, throw your legs and arms about pretty sufficiently already; but you have not yet learnt to stiffen your back-bone, and rest on one leg like a goose—the great perfections of French dancing. Next to these, you have to observe few other Graces in dancing, except to jump up and down, in a perpendicular Direction, like the Jacks of a harpsichord.—I shall never be a fond Spectator of dancing, till I am past dancing myself; and then I shall admire a grave solemn dance on the Theatre, as I would a Parson dancing a Hornpipe at a Burial, while the Funeral-service was read by his Clerk. At present, I must own, I would rather join in a favourite Country-dance myself, than be a looker-on at the best caper that two legs (male or female) ever cut.

We will therefore leave Madame Heinel to spindle away unrivailed, on her stilts; and before we quit the subject of dancing, will just drop a hint to the Cotillon-dancers at our fashionable assemblies.—— They forget themselves greatly when they imagine, that people subscribe to Balls to see four couple figure it away before them like so many Stage-dancers.—It is highly impolite for such a small number to take up the Music, and the whole floor of a Room, from the rest of the Company; and let them dance ever so well (which to them, perhaps, may appear the highest accomplishment) they will still, in my opinion, be ill-bred people. Custom, indeed, and the tacit consent of seated assemblies, have made it legal, in the rules of politeness, for a Gentleman and Lady to take a walk in the figure of what is commonly called a Minuet, within a circle of idle Spectators; but we hold, that a Cotillon cannot be danced at a public assembly, without transgressing the Law of Civility, (which we acknowledge is sometimes oppugnant to that of *modern* politeness or good-breeding) unless a Room be appropriated for the use and conveniency of such Cotillon-dancers, in like manner as is provided at the Great Pantheon.

Of all our Musical Entertainments, Bach and Abel's Concert, to my Taste, is the most agreeable. There is a *variety* in *their* Concert, and there are besides two pauses for conversation and chit chat. As for that matter, truly, I never found that Conversation was wanting either there or at the Opera, if I had an inclination to divert myself, to the annoyance of those good people who wished to be musically entertained.—I hope, however, that Messrs. Bach and Abel will provide themselves with a capital Performer on the *Violin*, and, in future, give us less of their

Piano

Piano Forte, and *Viol de Gambe*. I have not attended them this year, but they used formerly to give us a great deal too much of these two instruments, for such a spacious room as Almack's.—The first time I had the pleasure of hearing Mr. *Abel*, was, some years ago, at an Inn abroad. He had heard me, from his room, scraping some of Tartini's Solos on the Violin; and judging, from my attempts, that I was fond of Music, he obligingly sent his compliments with an offer of bringing his Instrument, if it would be agreeable, to play with me. I had accordingly the honour of accompanying him while he played me a few Solo's, and I must acknowledge, nothing could sound more delightfully sweet than did then his *Viol de Gambe*.—I dare say I should receive the same pleasure from it now, in any private room; but it is utterly lost at *Almack's*.——Mr. *Bach's Piano Forte* is thrown away too, for it is not heard by one half of the people in the Room.——I recommended to their consideration, the providing themselves with some excellent Violin-player; but who shall they have? Let them choose which Violin-player they please, I hope they will pitch upon none of those new-fashioned Fidlers from France, who, whatever Music they play, seem to think, that the whole excellence of a Master consists in playing with life and spirit, and in sawing at the strings till they crack.—Let them remember, that each piece of Music has its peculiar Taste; that the first excellence to be attained is to stop in tune; and consequently that all their tricks, at the top of the board, will not compensate for the many scratches and discordant squeaks, with which they are intermixed; and let them also have in mind, that the second excellence to be attended to, is the Tone, or Sound produced by the drawing of the Bow.—Without

out these two accomplishments, I think no man ought to presume to play a Solo on the Violin, or any other instrument sounded with the bow.——As for the *Violencello*, it is a very pleasing Instrument, when confined to grave, solemn, or plaintive Music; but, in the hands of the first Master, it fails under any thing quick; it is no longer a *Violencello*, and its beauty is lost. The same remark I might have made on Mr. *Abel*'s *Viol de Gambe;* and the same remark, with additional observations, I shall now make on the *Bassoon*. Let the performers on that instrument take my advice, and never attempt at any music of too quick a movement; for, when they do, they seldom fail to expose themselves.—I remember it so happened to the Sieur *Comi*, when he played us a Solo on the *Bassoon*, at a Concert last winter at Bath. The slow Movement went perfectly well; but when he came to the quick Time, he gave us such a variety of windy notes, in so many surprizing and unexpected tones, that the whole Company were in a titter, and the Ladies were obliged to have recourse to their fans.—There are, indeed, some Instruments that are not at all calculated for cheerful Music, and that shew their impotence in attempting the expression of it. A Bassoon and a Violencello give a solemn and grave tone, as I observed above, whatever Music you play upon them; and the German Flute and the Guittar are ever soft, plaintive, or melancholy. —I can never hear a Jig or a Hornpipe played on the Guittar, without thinking of an old woman singing a jolly merry song, with a voice half broken, and expressive of disease and pain.—What pretty music, too, a man would make of *Nancy Dawson*, were he, in a fit of the gout, to tune his Ah! Oh! Oh's! to the notes of that song!

I do

I do not recollect ever to have heard the various Inſtruments of an Orcheſtre employed with a more ſurprizing good effect, than in a ſolemn March in the Oratorio of *Ruth*, compoſed by Giardini, which is performed once a-year in the Chapel of the Lock-Hoſpital. There is ſuppoſed to be a Funeral Proceſſion preceded by a Chorus of Singers; and the Inſtruments which play the Dead March, as a prelude to the Chorus, are ſo judiciouſly varied, that any one, with a fancy leſs lively than mine, would imagine he heard voices, at ſeparate diſtances, taking up the tune in ſucceſſion, and continuing the funeral-ſong *.

---

* Written in the year 1773.

The LEVELLER. Nº. XVII.

ADDRESSED to the NOBLEMEN and GENTLE-MEN, who have accepted COMMISSIONS in the MILITIA, established for our NATIONAL DEFENCE.*

My Lords and Gentlemen!

WHEN, in history, we read how innumerably the *Te Deum* has been sung, in gratitude for the conquests of frantic kings; when it is related by his biographer, that Charles XII. of Sweden, with a pious regularity, attended the public worship of his Creator, during those victories that deluged the one half of Europe with innocent blood;—we may believe the devotion of princes to be sincere; but we must deplore their mistaken method of pleasing the Deity, and, sighing, drop a tear on many a cruel and unchristian deed.—If the slaying our fellow-creatures be at any time *justifiable*, it is on the principle alone of self-defence; if the profession of arms be at all *honourable*, it is only so when we bear them for the protection

---

* This Address was written in the Year 1776; and it will be allowed there was occasion for it, if we recollect how indifferently the Militia was then officer'd. Nor will the Republication of it, at present, be deemed unnecessary, when we are told that the Militia, in some Counties, is still neglected by the Country Gentlemen. To *their* Indolence we must principally ascribe it, if such a noble Institution should ever be perverted.

protection of our king, our country, and our own rights. The officers of our national militia are, therefore, the most honourable of all military men. They are neither under the arbitrary commands of a despotic King, nor are they liable to be sent abroad to fight the battles of a haughty or avaritious Commonwealth. They fight not, they slay not, but on some just and necessary call.

That necessary occasion for your services, my Lords and Gentlemen, may arrive much sooner than some of you imagine. Our natural enemies regret the loss of Canada; they regret the diminution of their trade to the East-Indies. It would also be a most desirable object for them, to have a free commerce with our American Colonies. The French Islands stand greatly in need of the lumber, flour, and live stock, with which the Colonies could supply them; and excepting the Birmingham and Staffordshire ware, there is scarcely one article of the European manufacture, with which the French could not serve the Colonists at an easier rate than the English can; and those products of our Colonies which the French consume, they would certainly receive cheaper, if transported directly from the American lands.

Thus, from their mutual wants, an intercourse between France and our American Colonies will naturally begin. Merchants will be meddling wherever there is a profit to be gained. French adventurers will be smuggling their manufactures into our Colonies; our cruizers will intercept some of their ships, and as lawful prizes they will be condemned. France will resent these captures, and a rupture will ensue. Tho' she may be unwilling to encourage a spirit of resistance in the Colonies against their Parent State; tho' she may deny the Americans an *open* and *avowed* support;

support; to serve her own ends, she may endeavour to prevent the success of our arms in America, and draw our attention to a war at home, while so many of our forces are employed abroad.—Under whatever pretence she may quarrel with us, it is certain that France could not harrass us more, than by the invasion of an army of thirty or forty thousand men. They would put a stop to every branch of manufactures, wherever they carried their arms; the people would be reduced to that unsettled, unprotected state, into which they were often brought by the invasions of the Scots, before the union of the two Crowns; the credit of our funds would be lost for many years, both abroad and at home; and they would ruin our navy and our trade, by destroying the docks and harbours of our sea-port towns.—Let not the Lords of the Admiralty give me here a contemptuous smile. My apprehensions are too well grounded. I have spoken with several experienced French Officers, and with many able commanders in our navy, who have all agreed, that a landing in England could not be prevented, if our enemies chose to execute the plan.—The same storm that would blow our fleet of observation off *their* coast, would, when abated, waft their ships to *our* shore before our fleet could return. How the French are to get off again, is another question; but if they fight their way well, we shall be glad to let them depart the country, on a capitulation little dishonourable to them.

The practicability and probability of an invasion being granted, it behoves the Militia of *England* to stand to their arms. It is, however, with real concern I learn, that, in some counties I could name, the gentlemen who have the largest property to defend, have the most disgust to the militia service. Tho' I trust,

trust, when the hour of danger comes, men of spirit will abundantly shew themselves; yet gentlemen ought to consider, that to learn the duty of an officer requires some practice, without which they will at least be as aukward in the evolutions of the army, as they would be perplex'd with the figure of a country-dance, had they never received instructions in the art of dancing. This unwillingness in our modern gentlemen, to the military service of their country, demonstrates more than any thing, to me, the necessity for having an established Militia in England. Ease and luxury, already so prevalent amongst us, would render us at last so effeminate, that, like many other nations before us, we should become a prey to the first foreign invaders. The case is not similar in Scotland. The Scots are several centuries behind us in their trade, manufactures, and agriculture.—They have the recent use of arms to forget, and they have much to improve in their industry. But so different a spirit prevails among the English, that I knew a regiment of militia disbanded last year, out of which the recruiting officers of the regulars got but three men; and all the rest, to the number of 637, returned peaceably to their former vocations at home. This circumstance I mention, because it is a great argument with the opposers of the militia, that its service gives the men a habit of idleness and dissipation.—I can also add, to the honour of the same regiment, that, during the three years I knew them, but one man was confined for drunkenness, or irregularity of behaviour.*

As, to secure victory, a mutual confidence ought to subsist between the officer and soldier;—(an opinion

* The Northamptonshire Regiment.

opinion of the abilities of the one, and a sufficient dependence on the courage of the other;) let not, my Lords and Gentlemen, this vulgar notion have any weight with *you* :—" That the soldiers of a standing army must have the superiority, in courage, over the soldiers of a militia, because the militia men are drawn by ballot, from among the herd of mankind; whereas the soldiers of regular troops are volunteers, men who offer to serve their king and country, feeling themselves bold, and imagining they can beat an enemy." Whoever adopts that argument, must know as little of human nature as he shews himself ignorant of the arts of the recruiting service. An unwillingness to broils and bloodshed is as little a sign of cowardice, as a bullying, hectoring spirit is a demonstration of true courage; and of the men who are enlisted by the regulars, there is not one in twenty that is not elevated beyond the pitch of sober reason at the time of enlisting.

Let us not despise our militia as unfit for our protection. Tho' they should be defective in military discipline; with a few experienced generals at their head, (of whom we are not destitute at home) I should think them able to cope with the best regular troops of the French King. Personal courage, an implacable hatred of the enemy, and a mutual confidence between the officers and soldiers of a new-raised army, have often defeated the mechanical motions of well-disciplined men. Have we not heard how the militia of Sweden, under General Steinbock, in the year 1710, defeated and cut to pieces the best disciplined regiments of Denmark? Did not the united militia of the Low Countries repeatedly defeat the Spanish armies, then composed of the best infantry in Europe? Have we not heard what a few ragged Highlanders

effected

effected in the year 1745? Have we not heard what Elliot's light-horse performed, the very first engagement they were in? And has not our own army been kept at bay, and cooped up at Boston, by the militia of the American Colonies.* I repeat it, then, let us not despise our militia; but let us rather consider by what means it can be brought to do us most effectual service.

In the first place, my Lords and Gentlemen, I would advise you, by no means to attempt to render your men equal to the regular troops, in all the tricks of their manual exercise. Since the regulars, in time of peace, have more leisure on their hands than they know what to do with, it may be proper, in *them*, to contrive as much employment as they can for their soldiers; in order to add grace to their appearance, and to preserve them from a habit of idleness. But as *you* have only one month in the year, in which to exercise your men, you ought to curtail every thing in the exercise, that is not really useful in the day of battle. I mean not to wage war with the Adjutant-General, and far less to increase the number of volumes that have been written on military discipline. I only intend to throw out a few hints for the consideration of the militia-officers.—With regard, then, to the manual exercise, I would humbly propose to have nothing done in *three* motions, that can be done in *two;* and nothing in *two* that can be performed in *one*.

Officers will agree with me, how material it is to make the men load and fire regularly, and with expedition, without incommoding each other in the ranks

---

* Another unfortunate instance has been since given us in General Burgoyne's defeat.

ranks as they stand. But that regularity and dispatch cannot be attained without much practice; and it is for that reason I am so strenuous for curtailing the exercise of all unnecessary motions, and words of command. The more a man is confined to any particular motion of the hands, the more expert he will daily become in performing it. He will be found to perform that motion with considerable more dexterity than another man, whose hand is spoilt for expedition in any one thing, by practising many motions of a different kind. A clock, or any other complex machine, could not be finished in half the time it is, if it were to be the workmanship but of one man; and the very making of a needle or a pin is the employment of several hands.—Unless, however, the loading and firing exercise be performed with powder, the men will be so aukward with their cartridges in the field, that they will have half their task to learn.

I cannot approve of the posture in which a soldier is first ordered to stand. He is directed to join his knees, to keep close his heels, and at the same time to hold himself perfectly easy, and without constraint. How can this be expected of a bow-legg'd man? The strongest men and I may say the generality of men) are bow-legg'd, and cannot close their knees without forcing their whole frame. I have seen some recruits so constrained by it, that their bodies tottered as they stood, and one might have pushed them down with the least touch of the hand. Nor is it more easy for an in-kneed man to close his heels, than for a bow-legg'd man to keep his knees joined. And, as for the few straight-legged soldiers, the compressing the thick of the legs disfigures the shape of them in *any* man. I therefore maintain, that the standing with the legs closed, is only the posture of a woman

too

too modest to be seen with open thighs. A man should stand firm on his feet, with a space of at least four inches between them. Every man's leg would shew best in that posture; and tho' he might lose, in appearance, a little of his height, he would certainly find himself more at his ease; and his body would be more graceful, by deviating a little from the stiff, straight line.—But, provided a soldier does not turn his back in action, it signifies little in what posture he *stands*.—More attention, however, ought to be paid in teaching the soldiers to *move;* and, after the firing exercise, the evolutions are what I would particularly recommend. In *these* the militia ought to emulate the regulars, as being more within the compass of their time.—Instead of misspending so many days, my Lords and Gentlemen, in teaching your men a number of monkey-tricks, that would be of little use to them in actual service, let them practise all possible evolutions, in companies and divisions, in the open field.—When I see a battalion drawn up on a smooth plain, where all mole-hills have been levelled with the spade; when I see the men dressed in their ranks, according to straight lines marked parallel on the ground where they stand; when I see them exercised by words of command, following in accustomed order, like the questions of a Catechism;—it brings no grander idea to my mind, than the discomfiture of Mr. *Foote*'s *Commissary*, or of the *Burgeois Gentilhomme* of *Moliere*, who was prepared to receive his adversary's sword in quart, when, to his utter astonishment, he was hit with a *tierce* thrust.

What a farce it is, to see a regiment firing in *divisions* and *subdivisions*, alternately to the right and left, when we know that, in action, the officers think themselves happy, if, after the first discharge, they
can

can make their men fire regularly in *platoons!* What a parade, in marching and forming, according to the order of the Major's notes, when the officers and soldiers ought to be taught to be prepared, as much as it is possible, for every thing unexpected and unforeseen!—Will that man ever have a firm seat on horseback, who has never mounted an unruly horse?—No;—the rider who has always been accustomed to pace it round the *manege*, on a tame animal of a dressed horse, would be confounded with the tricks of a vicious brute, that obeyed neither his hand nor his heel.—As much perplexed, too, would a gentleman be, to parry his antagonist's thrusts in open fencing, who had never practised but the regular lessons against his master's breast, or in pushing quart and tierce at a brick wall.——It will, indeed, be necessary, in the first teaching the evolutions, to keep to the same following rules; but, after they are once learnt, I would never let either the soldiers or subaltern officers know, after one evolution, what was to be the succeeding one. I would sometimes form the battalion into two divisions, that should each act under a separate command; they should be opposed to each other like two fencers, each ignorant of the other's intentions; they should march and countermarch, prepared to parry, ready at fronting wherever an attack was made, wherever the enemy unexpectedly assailed. It is the common attempt of Generals to attack their enemy before his troops are formed; and had not the French been alert in shewing a front before Quebec, General Murray would have beat them off the field.——The battalion might sometimes be dispersed too, as if it were broken by an attack of the horse or dragoons; and the men should then rally themselves

themselves as well as they could, under whichever officers were nearest to command them.

Should you be called out on actual service, my Lords and Gentlemen, the *aids* of courage must by no means be neglected. It is a known truth, that few men are to be found, who, in cool blood, can face danger with the same bravery with which they would encounter it if they were heated. This many gentlemen must have experienced, even in a foxchace; and some savage nations are so much convinced of it, that they inflame themselves by *dancing*, before they venture to attack their enemies. The assailants have in general the advantage of their adversaries; for, by marching briskly up to the attack, they acquire in the exercise such an uncommon flow of spirits, that it banishes the recollection of their own danger.—Most of our conquests last war were gained by such precipitate attacks, as inspired our own soldiers and intimidated the enemy. Nay, so eager were our troops at the taking of the Moro Castle, that many of the very men who, in the assault, ran nimbly along the narrow, dangerous rock that led to the breach, durst not afterwards cross it, in cool blood, but by creeping on their hands and knees.—Good feeding is another requisite to make an Englishman fight, and, if procurable, should never be omitted. Some historians have been so much of my opinion, with regard to the effects of a good meal in giving a temporary courage, that they have not scrupled to affirm, the Carthaginian General gained his victory at Trebia, by ordering his soldiers a warm mess, and by attacking the Romans in a cold morning before they had *their* breakfast.——Philosophers may smile at these remarks; but *officers*, who have to deal with many of the unthinking part of mankind, must know that

A a courage

courage often borders upon mechanism; and they will confess, that howmuchsoever reason may teach us to face death in the closet, we shall encounter it in the field as resolutely by banishing thought and reflection, or by raising the proper passions.———The love and esteem of the soldier ought of all things to be courted by his officer. They have ever, with Englishmen, been the greatest incentives in the day of battle; and they are obtained with a very little trouble. As authority, among freemen, is better supported by love than by fear, give your orders, my Lords and Gentlemen, with firmness; but avoid all haughtiness of words and behaviour. Shew that you command, by virtue of the powers vested in you by your commission, and not through any conceit of your own dignity, or through any contempt of the soldier's inferior station. Be not above assigning a reason, to a young soldier, for every instruction which you may give him; for the more he knows the utility of any motion of the manual exercise, or of any part of the evolutions, the more attentive will he be to his duty, and the more respectful to that officer who gives himself the trouble of an explanation. In short, give not way to the *insolence of office*; but, in all your commands to the soldier, remember he is your fellow-citizen.—What carried Alexander and Cæsar, through all their conquests, more effectually than their soldiers love? What was Charles XII. of Sweden's best shield, in all his battles, but the love his soldiers bore him? What stronger incentives had the Highlanders to fight, in the last rebellion, than the love and veneration each man felt for his chieftain? What rallied our troops so soon at the late attack on Bunker's Hill?—Superior to the thought of self-preservation, superior to all sentiments of honour,

compassion

compassion arose in the breast of every man, when he saw the general he loved in danger of being left on the field.

The LEVELLER. N°. XVIII.

His SALUTIFEROUS CREED, or His WASSAIL* for the Year 1776.

SITTING at my fire-side one evening in the dreary month of December, an account was brought to me of the death of a young man in the neighbourhood, who accidentally shot himself under the violent effects

---

* *Wassails* are New-Year's Wishes, said or sung by some of the poorer people, in the country, to get money out of the pockets of their betters. To this vulgar but antient custom the *courtly New Year's Ode* probably owes its institution. I mean not, by this supposition, either to affront the *Poet-Laureat*, or to derogate from the dignity of his character.—The word *Wassail*, says Bailey's Dictionary, is taken from the old Saxon *Was hael*, and signifies Good health to you! But the meaning of it is as well explained to *me* by the two *modern* Saxon words *Was heil*, Some welfare, or prosperity. Or, perhaps, it is of Low-Dutch origin; for *Was heel* in that language signifies, Become whole, or grow healthy; *Wafs* coming from *Waffen*, to grow or become— as it is used in *Wafs goed, Wafs ryk, Wafs magtig,* Grow good, grow rich, grow powerful or mighty.——As by omitting only the aspiration of the *h* I have retained the pronunciation of *Wassail*, the Antiquaries cannot think me too far-fetch'd in my derivation.

effects of intoxication. An event, so melancholy and unexpected, could not but afford employment to my mind for that evening. I could not help reflecting how many lives were lost, and how many constitutions were impaired, by the intemperate indulgence of one sense—that vulgar sense of Tasting. It gave me pain to think that, to satisfy a brutal appetite, so many heedless beings should sacrifice a thousand pleasures and enjoyments, which, from their other senses, they are capable of receiving. For my part, though I hope never to be afraid of hazarding my life in a good cause, I am not ashamed to own, that I wish to enjoy a perfect state of health, and to retain the full use of my faculties, as long as I am destined to live in this earthly habitation.—In this train of thinking, my Readers will suppose me seated again in my easy-chair, where the sight of a warm fire-side contrasts the appearance of a most horrible storm. For these twelve days past I have not seen the face of the sun; nor have I been able to take any bodily exercise, excepting on a road—where, through drifts of thick-fallen snow, some peasant-pioneers have dug a slippery path, (tremenduous to behold!) ten feet, at times, in depth. I must, of course, be uncommonly stupid. Unless with hoar and icicles at my head, (and they, too, would soon thaw at the fire-side) it is impossible, under these circumstances, for *me* to shine, who, at no time, am allow'd to be shining.

I shall not then attempt it; I shall only present my readers with a few dull remarks, in the form of my *Salutiferous Creed;* and I sincerely wish that their health may be preserved until the fatal disease, when my writing can do them no service.

I believe that Physicians are very much at a loss to account for the manner in which the stomach performs

forms its Digeſtion. Tho' many explanations of it have been attempted, ſome of the moſt learned and experienced of the Faculty candidly confeſs, they are yet much in the dark with regard to that ſubject.— I believe that it is fallacious to judge of the conſequences of a mixture of aliments in the ſtomach, from their viſible effects upon each other when commix'd in the air. There is ſome hidden property in the ſtomach, which changes as it were the very nature of things, by making one ingredient often aſſiſt in digeſting another, that otherwiſe would have preſerved it in the open air. Thus, fiſh and fleſh will, with moſt people, digeſt better after a glaſs of Brandy and Wine, than after a draught of cold water; altho' we find that, out of the ſtomach, they are in the former longeſt preſerved, and in the latter ſooneſt corrupted. I believe that the firſt act, in the proceſs of digeſtion, is to reduce to acidity the nutriment we have taken. In oppoſition therefore to Dr. Cadogan's opinion, I believe that Bread and other aliments which become ſooneſt ſour in corrupting, are, for that very reaſon, if not always the moſt healthful, at leaſt the moſt eaſy of digeſtion. They muſt, in their effects, materially differ from vinegar, lemons and other things, which, in their natural ſtate, the palate diſtinguiſhes to be acid. Theſe no man can ſafely take, in any great quantity, unleſs they are properly corrected; but 'tis not yet proved that unadulterated bread can do injury to any one.—When, to this uncertainty of the conſequences of mixture, we add the difference of Conſtitutions in men, and the difference of digeſtive power in the ſtomach, I believe that to adviſe every man to the ſame kind of Diet, would be acting like any Quack that ſhould preſcribe the ſame Medicine to every one who conſulted him. As every man of
ſenſe

sense and observation is, by experience, capable of judging what are the Aliments that best agree with him; he ought not to eat of any thing, accounted never so innocent in its nature, if he finds it to disagree with his stomach; for that which does not properly digest, can never be wholesome for the person who takes it.—I believe that a regular diet is necessary for one who has a weak stomach, and can tell what best will suit it; but I would not advise a person in a perfect state of health, to stick to any kind of regimen. A variety of food is certainly what nature intended for the human species; yet, from the uncertainty of the agreement of mixtures, I believe *that* variety to be most wholesome when taken at separate meals.—I believe that Fish, Flesh, Beer and Wine, nourish the blood and recruit the spirits; but that Bread and Vegetables more certainly harden the sinews, and supply us with muscular vigour. The Scots, the Irish, and the Dutch, who live perhaps on porridge, potatoes or salads, are, in general, stouter-built men, and will lift with an Englishman any weight; but they will want spirits to continue the work of a coal-heaver, unless they have strong beer and Porter to drink, and can dine on their beef or mutton. This disadvantage, however, attends the Englishman's food: If you deprive him of it, he will under labour become languid and faint; whereas the other-named Countrymen (if you give them but time) will, on their poorer food, be able to go thro' with their work.

I believe that the natural food for a child, 'till a little time before it is wean'd, is its mother's or its nurse's milk, provided that either have a sufficient supply for it.—I am bless'd with three blooming Boys, who never tasted any thing but the milk from the breast, 'till they got a crust of bread to mumble a few days before they were wean'd.

I believe

I believe that feeding children entirely on animal food, as I have seen practised by the advice of the Physician, in some families in London, was the certain cause that I seldom saw the Physician out of the house.—I believe that the proper food for children, immediately after they are wean'd, should consist of milk, with flour, or bread, 'till they are, by degrees, accustomed to the addition of vegetable, and a smaller proportion of animal food; which last, thro' the whole life of man, I think not should ever prevail.— I believe, that keeping young people too long on farinaceous and vegetable food, as is frequently the practise in Scotland, is too often the cause of their being carried off by Consumptions; for, when grown up, they come to a change of animal food, the blood-vessels become suddenly overcharged, and the lungs are greatly obstructed in their operation.—I believe that the dipping of children every day in cold water, is the cause, by stopping the pores, of most of their cutaneous disorders; but as it braces their nerves, and adds to their muscular strength, the custom is certainly of use in hardening them, when they are intended to live in the camp or the country. If, on the contrary, they are designed for some business or life of confinement, they ought neither to be too long accustomed to the country air, nor will the hardening their bodies be found of any material service. The inuring children to that kind of life for which they are intended, when adults, is principally useful in guarding against the sudden transition from one manner of life to another; for otherwise, after the first seasoning is over, we find, that, making allowance for the difference of constitutions, all bodies are soon rendered equally hardy or equally tender, according to any continuance of a rough or delicate treatment.—

ment.——Bring a hardened Country gentlemen to London, and after a short residence there, in a life of inactivity and confinement, he will become as susceptible of cold, and will suffer as much from the inclemencies of the weather, as any Citizen who has been born and educated within the sound of the bells of Bow-steeple.——On the other hand, carry that Citizen to the camp, and if he survives the first seasoning, he will endure any hardship of the field as safely, tho' perhaps not so easily to himself, as the hardened Countryman.——One ought not, therefore, to let any manner of life become so habitual to the body, that the disuse of it should be dangerous or hurtful, for, tho' excess of all kinds be prejudicial to the health, I believe that any uniformity or regularity in air, diet, or exercise, is productive of many inconveniencies, and exposes men to many consequential distempers.—I speak of mankind in the bulk; for as to men of independent fortunes, who may have it always in their choice to continue in the same even track, there is no doubt but the country air is preferable to that of the city; that the nutriment which is reckoned most innocent, and is found to agree best with the stomach, is the most eligible food; and that moderate and regular exercise is more healthful to the body than hard labour, or a sedentary life.

I believe that the fashionable practice of sea-bathing ought to be used with more precaution than it is. —A thin, muscular man, as I am, may use freedoms with cold water, which a fat, corpulent man should not. I have frequently gone into the water in a profuse perspiration, after two or three hours exercise— but then I staid no longer in the water than I would remain in a cold bath.——It sometimes gave me the sensation of so many pins stuck into every pore of my

skin;

skin; when, dressing myself immediately, and resuming my exercise, I soon recovered my former heat. —I took these liberties with myself, because I did not apprehend, that what an old Roman, or a savage American, could safely bear, would do a temperate Englishman any hurt.——Having always bathed for my pleasure, and not for my health, I must own I deviate a little from the common track: I never go into the cold bath in Winter, as the Physicians prescribe, because I have not the least inclination for it — and I find myself, by the cold air, sufficiently braced. But, in hot weather, when, like any amphibious animal, I feel a longing desire to be in the water—I bathe to the height of my wish. I have sometimes gone thrice a-day into the sea at Brighthelmstone, which so effectually cooled me, that I have had the most profound and refreshing sleep at night, while every one else was complaining that he could not shut his eyes for the heat. Tho' I am only telling what a lean, temperate man has safely practised on himself, I believe that most men might save themselves from fevers, if they were to bathe in cold water when they feel a desire for it, and feel themselves, without exercise, intolerably hot.—A Director of the East-India Company told me, that when he commanded a Company's ship, he ordered every man aboard to bathe once a-day, at least, after they came into a warm climate; to which custom he ascribed it, that he lost very few men in any voyage, while other ships suffered a considerable loss.

I said that the practice of sea-bathing ought to be used with more precaution than it is, principally on this account—Because I believe the custom, if diurnal, is dangerous when it is suddenly left off.—I am confirmed in this belief, not only from my own experience,

experience, but from the inconvenience or misfortune which others have felt.——The firſt year I was at Brighthelmſtone, I bathed, for two months, conſtantly every day, after which I was called to London in ſome haſte. On the firſt and ſecond day after I came to Town, I had a violent headach, felt a ſickneſs at my ſtomach, and an intolerable heat. My eldeſt Boy, who had been with me at Brighthelmſtone, and had bathed as conſtantly as myſelf, felt the very ſame complaints, but in a much ſtronger degree; and was affected in the ſame manner as I have known ſome Natives of Greenland to be, who were brought to this warmer climate by our Fiſhing Ships: He vomited, bled at the noſe, and complained very much of his head. It preſently occurred to me, that the ſea bathing having become ſo habitual to us, the leaving it off too ſuddenly was the cauſe of theſe complaints. I carried him therefore to the River: but I plunged in firſt, to try the experiment upon myſelf. After dreſſing, and finding myſelf perfectly right, I turn'd my Boy in next, and it cured him of all his complaints. Not that he was drowned; but that, after this remedy, he neither vomited, bled at the noſe, nor complained of his head. Commonſenſe told me to continue that courſe, every two or three days, till we were from the bathing totally difuſed.—I told this to a friend of mine, whoſe wife had been ſome weeks at Margate; and I deſired him to caution her not to leave off the bathing all at once. But, having neglected this advice, ſhe fevered in three days after coming to Town, and in ten days more ſhe was carried to her grave.

As the cold bathing, in hot weather, is beneficial, ſo, in cold weather, I believe the hot bath can, to many conſtitutions, do no injury, and will, to

moſt,

moft, be of infinite ufe. With regard to myfelf, I found that it removed all obftruction in the perfpiration, and revived my natural heat. I ufed to take it for my pleafure, as, in a different feafon, I took the cold bath. I have, for feveral weeks together, in the fevereft winters we have had, gone into the Kingfton-bath every other night, and I found not the leaft inconvenience in walking, the morning after it, two or three hours in the coldeft froft.

I believe that, for fuch a dry fubject, I have at prefent wrote enough; I fhall therefore poftpone the reft of my Salutiferous Creed till next month; when (I believe that) if I can get out of my eafy-chair, I fhall write lefs like an old woman, and be more original in my thoughts.

The LEVELLER. N°. XIX.

Continuation of His SALUTIFEROUS CREED

IT is a mortifying confideration to an Author, to think, that he has fo little opportunity, in thefe days, of writing any thing that has not already, in other words, been written by fome fuperior Writer. The Arts and Sciences, indeed, will ever be productive of new conceits; and new intelligence will be procured from Policy, Biography, Hiftory, or the narration of events. But from other subjects no greater novelty can be expected, than what is produced from the seven notes of Music, variously founded to different tunes; while the notes, taken separately, remain in their nature for ever the same.— Yet, after all the fine compositions of a Corelli, a Handel, a Bach, or an Abel, the capricious *Cadenza* will often please of a shallow, fantastical Fidler.——— Whatever, therefore, shall come from my pen, in future, I desire may not be understood as proceeding from any great notion I have of my own understanding; but from the opinion I entertain, that words, or expressions of the same thoughts, may, like the seven notes of music, be rung in changes *ad infinitum*.

This reflection I had in mind when I began my Salutiferous Creed. I was aware that I should say many things that had already, in other words, been said before me; and I was unwilling to deliver, in a positive, dogmatical manner, as my own sentiments entirely, what might be found to be the prior and original opinions of others.

A similar caution would be requisite in many of my brother-writers, if they would not pass for being too self conceited in their publications, or expose to the world their want of learning. A man, indeed, may imagine a thing, and deserve all the honour of it's invention, altho', unknown to him, it has already been thought of and expressed by some other person; but the merciless critics will never allow him that originality; and his fancied endowments, he will find disputed by them, of an extraordinary solidity of judgment, or of an imagination uncommonly fertile. ———Begging pardon for my numerous egotisms, which, in an anonymous writer, are readily pardoned,

I shall

I shall proceed in my Salutiferous Creed, founded chiefly on experiments freely made on my own constitution.

If a conclusion may be drawn from our observations on the *irrational* Inhabitants of this Globe—I believe that, in the cloathing of their Children, the Britons, in general, act against the intention of Nature.——The Dam of every animal, that brings its young into the world in a helpless or inactive state, is at peculiar pains to cherish it, and to protect it from the inclemency of the air, till such time as it is grown strong, and can with exercise sufficiently warm itself. The foal, the lamb, and the calf need little nursing; because, soon after their birth, they are enabled to skip about, and thereby to assist the circulation of their blood. But the puppy, the kitten, and the pig are carefully nursed, till, at least, they can walk on their legs. The same we may observe in the feathered race; the pigeon, the crow, and the finch, are assiduously covered till they are fledged; but the partridge and chicken, that, from the shell, can nimbly run about, are but occasionally under the shelter of their mother's wing; and the gosling, the duckling, and the coote, intended, if I may use the phrase, for a hardy, seafaring life, are betimes inured to it, by swimming in the river, or enjoying the pleasure of the cold bath. Why, then, should a human child, that for twelve long months cannot support himself, be clothed or dressed less warmly, than he optionally will clothe himself when he is grown up? I appeal to every man of common observation, whether he does not remember to have felt the excess, both of heat and cold, more severely when he was a child, than when he became a youth or a grown man. I believe, therefore, it is by nature designed, defigned, that we fhould be comfortably cloathed when we are young; and that we fhould afterwards be gradually ufed to that kind of drefs which we are, in our manhood, intended to wear. A man that lives temperately, is foon habituated to any drefs, as well as to any manner of life. A brother of mine, who, at fchool, was always fitting at his book, and would fcarcely ftir from the firefide, was the laft man, either officer or private, of a whole regiment of dragoons, that, in Germany, were attacked with the flux; while a coufin of his, who was not allowed to wear either fhoe or ftocking till he was four years old, was, by that difeafe, unfortunately cut off. I have known gentlemen taken and ftript naked by the Algerines, who, by feeding on nothing but bread and water, have lived feveral weeks in their buff, without any prejudice to their health. And Commodore Byron, in his travels, relates, that he and his companions, when fhipwreck'd on the American coaft, were foon accuftomed to all the hardinefs of a favage life. It may be here objected to me, " Why cannot " *we* fafely go naked, or thinly cloathed, like thofe " of our fellow-creatures who live in a favage ftate?" For this plain reafon, I think, we cannot fafely live as thinly clad as they :—We eat more luxuriant food; which certainly breeds humours in the body, in proportion as the perfpiration is ftopt; add to this, that living within doors, we are lefs expofed to the air than thofe Savages, and muft, therefore, the more prudently guard againft the weather when we walk out; and hence I infer it to be a certain rule of health, That the richer one feeds, and the lefs one is accuftomed to air and exercife, fo much the warmer he ought to clothe himfelf.—This rule the Dutch have, by experience, found to be prudent and neceffary cessary in *their* domestic way of life; and it is remarkable of the English who reside in Holland, and will not go sufficiently clad, that more coughing will be heard, in winter, in one of their churches, where the congregation consists not, perhaps, of above an hundred people, than in a crouded Dutch church of two or three thousand. The churches being of a size proportionable to the number of their congregations, I suppose them equally warmed; and that the coughs were *fixed* on the people, and not occasionally produced by a greater coldness in the atmosphere.

I believe it to be highly dangerous, after any violent exercise, to put on clothes that are damp, or have not been sufficiently aired. Few constitutions are strong enough, in such a case, to repel the cold, and prevent the perspiration being suddenly stopt; altho' the continuing one's exercise in wet clothes, or the putting on damp clothes before the pores are opened, and the blood is hot, may be done with no inconvenience to a person in good health; provided always, in the last case, that a man is not to sit still, but intends immediately to put himself in motion.

It is the *cold* damp that endangers the constitution. *Warm* damp, instead of obstructing the perspiration, will promote it, in the manner of a fomentation. I frequently leave my wet shoes and stockings to dry on my feet, at my own fire-side, when I intend repeating my walk in the morning; but I should avoid sitting down with wet feet, to be chilled, at a stranger's formal table. Neither fevers, agues, or rheumatisms need be dreaded from wet clothes, while one can continue the natural heat of the body; but that heat ought to be effected by *moderate* exercise; for immoderate exercise would put the blood into a ferment, and, should the perspiration be impeded, would render

der the case more pregnant with evil. It is, therefore, a wrong notion in a man, when surprized on the road by a storm, to put himself into too great a hurry; unless he be already over-heated, let him not hasten his pace, but continue the same jog-trot 'till he gets to the end of his stage; and then let him do something effectual to promote perspiration.

It is the common remark of Divines, that the enjoyment of our unlawful or irrational pleasures is generally followed even by their temporal punishments; and it is also one consolatory reflection afforded the poor, in their indigence, that the riches and honours of the great have frequently their attendant evils. Hence, I believe, that our immoderate participation of public amusements, and our necessary attendance at places of public business, have the evil consequence of contributing towards the debility or sterility of many of our modern married people. A free healthful air is the greatest incentive of love; but, as Dr. Armstrong says, " It is not air that, " from a thousand lungs, reeks back to thine;" in a crouded place of public entertainment, we respire nothing but a moist, foetid, putrid steam, arising from a number of human bodies squeezed into as small a compass as they possibly can be stowed; a steam void of that electrical, elementary fire which we breathe in our exercises in the open field. I believe, therefore, that all our exercises ought to be taken in the open air; for fresh air invigorates our bodies, and acts as a restorative, when we have fatigued ourselves with exercise, and carried off, by perspiration, those humours that would gather by repletion or a sedentary life.

I believe, that perspiration is the surest preventive of all our disorders; and that sudorifics, purgatives,

emetics,

emetics, bleeding, clyſtering, bliſtering, and ſalivation are, when properly preſcribed or adminiſtered, the moſt ſafe and certain remedies for every diſeaſe incident to the human body; thoſe inward and latent complaints always excepted, which ſo frequently confound the Doctors, and baffle the power of all their medicines. I would not, however, be underſtood to depreciate the virtues of alteratives; I only would ſay, that, from the difference of the digeſtion and conſtitution of patients, thoſe virtues muſt be uncertain, and muſt leave the phyſician, for ſome time, to act in the dark.

I believe, that one principal cauſe of the gout, is the eating heartily immediately after ſome violent exerciſe. Gentlemen, uſed to the turf or the ridingſchool, know, that horſes, after any ſevere exerciſe, are commonly led about for ſome time, or tied with their tails to the manger; and the reaſon, given by the grooms for this treatment, is, that if the horſes were allowed to feed when their blood was in a ferment, their bodies might contract ſuch humours as would render them totally unfit for ſervice. The ſame reaſoning may be applied to the human body; for, within the circle of my own acquaintance, I have known ſeveral ſober ſporting gentlemen afflicted with the gout, which I could impute to no other cauſe than the eating heartily immediately after hunting. I believe that the complaints, which many ſporting gentlemen feel in their ſtomachs, proceed from hard riding. It either gives a preter natural heat to the ſtomach, that produces a lethargic diſpoſition: or occaſions too great an acidity in the proceſs of digeſtion. The exerciſe of walking I therefore believe to be beſt for a weak ſtomach; and ſlow riding to be moſt adviſeable for a person that is feeble, and is afflicted with any disorder of his lungs, or any difficulty in breathing.

The rowing of a boat, or the digging the soil of a garden, I would recommend to gentlemen that wish to strengthen their voices for public speaking. The ringing of a dumb bell may be equally strengthening to the chest; but, not being practised in the open air, it cannot certainly be so beneficial to the constitution. I believe that the extraordinary circulation of the blood, by exercise, is the best preservation of the memory. I have for many years remembered every minute circumstance of a chace, when things of greater moment, and that interested me more deeply, have totally escaped me. But, perhaps, the reason of this may be, that in proportion as the blood is heated, the memory is the more capable of receiving any lasting impression of surrounding objects.— I believe, that a man who, in early life, has been accustomed to matrimony, must continue in that state; or, to preserve his health, must daily fatigue himself with exercise or hard labour.

I believe, that confining and nursing myself for a cold, is the certain way to get a fresh one as soon as I quit my confinement. It may be proper, indeed, to be more cautious with a sore throat; but I have frequently rode away a cough, a hoarseness, or a running at the head. And by treating many horses in the same manner, with gentle exercise, I have always speedily recovered them from colds; when several horses confined in the same livery-stable have died of the same distempers.

Contrary to the opinion of Dr. Cadogan, I have good reason to believe, that getting drunk once in the week or the fortnight, is much more prejudicial to the health, than the drinking of wine every day in a moderate quantity. An excefs of wine, that diforders the body for feveral days together, muft certainly be hurtful to the conftitution; and I have feen the nerves affected of many of my acquaintances by fuch a practice; whereas I myfelf, who never was drunk in my life, and who, for many years, have never drank lefs than a pint of port at my dinner, am bleffed with ftrong nerves, and know not yet what is the gout, the ftone, or the gravel. I would not, however, recommend it to every one, to drink the fame quantity. I have certainly a cold ftomach that requires it. Before I kept houfe, and was obliged to put round the bottle, I ufed to drink very little wine; becaufe I really did not like it, and the cuftom was long exploded of preffing a man to drink againft his inclination. I then had, generally, a violent thirft after dinner, and a feeming difficulty of digeftion. On the contrary, now, when fometimes I drink my bottle or three pints of wine at table, I feel no difagreeable internal heat, and (my readers will readily believe me) as little do I complain of any thirft after dinner. If I were to drink any thing elfe immediately after my wine, it fhould be fome *ftronger* liquor; efpecially after *fmall* wines, which even the French, tho' accuftomed to them, find it neceffary to qualify with *liqueurs*. I am fpeaking here of a *large* dofe of wine, that requires to be properly digefted. In that cafe, I have always found that tea and coffee, taken immediately after my wine, bring an acidity on my ftomach, which, previous to the fwallowing that wafh, felt no manner of inconvenience. As for other people, when a man finds himfelf confiderably heated with wine, and has, in confequence of it, an intolerable thirft upon him, 'tis a certain fymptom of a feverifh difpofition in his conftitution; and the wine being

being too strong a drink for him, he ought to dilute it into a beverage of smaller liquor.

My readers will perceive that I am for enjoying all the gifts of God, all the blessings of this life, only in *moderation*. I even hold the excess of lawful wedded love, to be sinful; tho' in matters of love I formerly laid so little stress upon the parson's blessing. And I reckon intoxication (as equally abusing the body) to be no less sinful; tho', for the *stomach's sake*, I would, occasionally, allow a bottle of wine, or a glass of brandy.

The LEVELLER. N°. XX.

The Conclusion of His SALUTIFEROUS CREED.

THE Head and Literary Character of Monsieur de Buffon, given in our last Magazine, recal to my mind a whimsical notion of his, with regard to the variety in shape or figure of that common animal call'd a Dog. As Prior would have express'd himself:

> This *Buffon* had an odd conceit,
> As ever enter'd Frenchman's pate.

He supposes, that the Dogs which we vulgarly distinguish by the names of Mastiffs, Bull-Dogs, Greyhounds, Hounds, Spaniels, Water-dogs, Dutch Pugs, and so forth, are all sprung from the Shepherd's Dog, or Village Cur, an animal (according to the drawing which he gives of it) resembling the Pomeranian Dog, or that kind, good-natured, civil creature, in Scotland, call'd a *Colly*. Whoever has travelled that country, on horseback, must have been particularly obliged to the *Colly* for the favour of his company on the road, and for the alacrity with which he expedited the journey. To a traveller there, the whip and spur are totally useless. A company of *Collies* meet him at the entrance to the first village, and escort him, barking all the way at his horse's heels, until they are relieved by a party from the next lordship. He may thus, in Dr. Johnson's phrase, peragrate the whole denuded country, without being under the cruel necessity of practising either incitation or flagellation on his trusty steed.

To return to the singular hypothesis of Monsieur de Buffon.—As far as I can recollect, it is built on this single observation——That the hair of a Dog's skin grows shorter or longer, according to the hot or cold climate which the animal is used to. I allow, too, that the difference of climate may enlarge or diminish the size of the breed; but I believe it would be as difficult for Monsieur de Buffon to prove, that a curl'd-hair Water-dog, or a shagged Village Cur, would ever, by transportation, become a Greyhound, as that a Sheep, by growing hairy in the West-Indies, is an animal of the same species with a Goat. Much easier would it have been to have allowed the different kinds of Dogs, as vulgarly denominated, and to have accounted for the variety of mongrels, from

the

the natural incontinency of brutes. A Sportsman would have told him, at what pains he is, to preserve the blood of his Hounds, or his Pointers, from being contaminated with that of a Cur; from which last no Hound or Pointer was ever bred. And he would also have assured him, that, in no series of generations, a Hound would ever acquire the shape of a Grey-hound, unless he allowed them to cross their breed.—When I perceive an eminent Philosopher, like Monsieur de Buffon, losing himself in the depth of his researches, and the sagacity of his remarks, and forming conjectures so much against experience and common sense, I dread the consequences of diving into profundity myself; I am fortified in my resolution of abiding by observations arising from experience alone, and of drawing no conclusions contrary to the evidence of plain matter of fact.

Considering the changeable weather of this climate, I believe it is difficult to lay down any certain rules, either with regard to clothing, or the moderate use of wine, which I have so much recommended. In the use of both, one must be guided according to his feelings. Cold, damp weather generally requires an additional coat, and an extraordinary glass of wine; while one can enjoy a mild, dry day in a thinner dress, and with a drink of smaller liquor.—I have ever been an advocate for Claret since the benign effects it once had upon me. I had travelled to a village in Scotland to drink the Goat-milk whey, after a melancholy event that had considerably affected my health. The Physician, who attended the invalids of that place, instantly perceiving my complaint to be nothing but a dejection of spirits, gave me this friendly advice, instead of prescribing any medicine: " The Goat-milk whey," said he, " will do do you no injury; take it, morning and evening, as is the custom of the place;—but, besides that, I would prescribe to you a more pleasant remedy:—drink a pint of Claret at your dinner, and, as we sup early, you may repeat the dose at night."—I did it accordingly; and in ten days time I had spirits to have climbed the mountain like a Goat, and bounded from rock to rock.—Another instance of the virtue of Claret was given me by a very eminent Physician in London, In recommending his wine to me at his own table, he bad me not be afraid of it; "for," added he, " it saved the life of my son, there, after he was given over by my Brother-physicians. He was reduced to extremity by a violent fever, but I recovered him with this Claret. After taking the chill off it, I gave it him at intervals in spoonfuls; though, before he was revived by it, he drank me at least two bottles a-day." Thus we see, that many a poor creature may be suffered to go out of the world for want of something, as the vulgar would say, only to keep body and soul together; and I believe, that weakening medicines are often given, when a cordial or restorative is all that Nature requires of us.———I believe that Claret, Burgundy, and other small wines, are the most enlivening for the spirits; but, to fortify the stomach, I would recommend Port, Madeira, and Strong beer. These last are certainly the liquors most proper to be drank in raw, damp weather; yet we should be cautious lest, by the immoderate use of them, we do not cloud our understandings, in attempting to correct the atmosphere, and render it, to our perception, serene.—Ale and Strong-beer certainly nourish the Bile. I have seldom known a Beer-drinker, but who, after his first tankard, was peevish, dull, or heavy.—Let people lay as much to the account of our climate as they please. I am perfuaded that moſt of our hypochondriacal caſes, in England, are owing to our groſs animal food, and the intemperate uſe of Ale, or clammy Strong beer —I am, however, no enemy to Beer; for, from the occaſional uſe of it, I have often found much benefit. During the laſt ſevere froſt, I got a complaint in my ſtomach, by faſting too long. As I uſed to be out in the cold two or three hours every morning, and did not dine till four o'clock in the afternoon, I was at laſt vulgar enough to ſtop at any houſe, in my walk, and to take a draught of warm'd Ale. The firſt day I tried this remedy, the complaint was removed, and my appetite returned. But, as ſoon as the froſt ceaſed, I diſcontinued the cuſtom of the warm'd Ale, leſt I ſhould acquire a bad habit of drinking in the forenoon.—In curing a cold in my ſtomach, I have frequently experienced the good effects of Strong-beer. Once, in particular, I was ſo imprudent as to travel in an open chaiſe, in a very cold day, from Calais to Dunkerque, immediately after a twelve hours confinement to my bed on ſhip-board, and before I had lined my ſtomach with any thing, after the compleat ſcouring it had undergone.—The conſequences were, that I loſt my appetite entirely, and had ſtrong ſymptoms of an ague at night. An honeſt friend of mine at Dunkerque, though leſs practiſed in phyſic than in fortification, had the good ſenſe to make me ſwallow a bottle of his Engliſh Strong-beer before I went to bed; and, as nothing is ſo grateful to my palate after a ſea-ſickneſs, it was a potion I perfectly liked. I enjoyed after it a moſt profound and refreſhing ſleep; and aroſe in the morning hearty as a Buck, and as ravenous as any Wolf on the plain.

Having

Having mentioned a cold in the stomach, I cannot help observing, that it must, for many people, be unwholesome to go out fasting into the raw morning air. I am persuaded that frequent complaints in the stomach arise from it; and the same opinion our forefathers must have entertained; for to this day a custom prevails among the inhabitants of some parts of the island, never to go out before they have their breakfast, or without taking what they call a *Morning-drink*—either a glass of spirits, or a draught of something warm'd. As for myself, if I go out, even in a Summer's morning, without lining my stomach with something (which I would rather do with a crust of bread, than with any liquor that is strong), I feel, that without violent exercise, I cannot keep myself warm.——I believe, then, that no person in health should fast in the morning; but, to avoid headachs, tooth-achs, sore eyes, the stone, the gravel, and the gout—let him fast at night, if he will.

I entertain a strange notion about ghosts and apparitions, which, as it arises from my remarks on the disorders of the human frame, may properly be included in my Salutiferous Creed. I believe that all the stories we have heard of them, have either sprung from fiction and imposition; or, during the short fit of a delirium, have originated in the brain. It has happened to me twice in my life, (when I was very young) that, being quite awake, and without any other symptom of a fever upon me, I fancied I saw the Day of Judgment, with all its dreadful circumstances, before me. Though I had few sins to answer for then, the appearance of a general resurrection and conflagration terrified me to such a degree, that I set up a most hideous scream.—The whole family, that heard me, were soon convened. I knew every

one around me perfectly well; but still I saw the frightful vision, and, till it disappeared, nothing could perfuade me that it existed only in my own brain.—As this vision, exactly similar at both times, and which happened within an interval of two or three years, did not last above five minutes at a time, I naturally infer, that the like short delirium may have seized other people, apparently healthy in body, and who, without witnesses of their folly, could not have been convicted of any disorder of their mind. If any body had been present (as in my case), these visionaries would have been soon persuaded, that all was an illusion which they had seen;—but it would otherwise be difficult to convince a man, that though broad awake he could have the visions of a dream.— Of this nature must have been the remarkable appearance of our Saviour to Colonel Gardener, as related in his Life, by Dr. Doddridge; and to which (to the best of my recollection) that learned man gives entire credit. It is true, the Colonel is said to have heard a *voice*, as proceeding from the apparition; but *that*, I believe, is no more than what is common with people in a *mania*, who will talk as if they heard strange voices, as well as they fancy they see strange things;—and when 'tis God's pleasure, by an extraordinary visitation, to convert a sinner, whether it be by the *real* or *imaginary* appearance of a messenger, 'tis equally possible to him. The *last* method, however, being less out of the common course of nature, is what we might reasonably suppose would be employed. But that suits not with the self-importance and ideal dignity of Man, or with the consequential place in the creation which he has assumed.
———Certain it is (however unaccountable to those conceited Philosophers who will believe nothing
which

which they cannot account for and explain), that we are frequently forewarned of misfortunes in our dreams.—I myself have, by a dream, been prepared for a shock, which, had it come totally unexpected, would have harrowed up my soul.———I dream'd, that thieves had broke into my house in the country, and had murdered my wife before my eyes. No dream but that had ever made any impression on me; nor has any since (though I dream every night) given me the least concern. I told my vision in the morning to a Gentleman that was with me in town; and though he endeavoured to laugh me out of it, I could not be easy until I mounted my horse, in order to go and satisfy myself that every thing in the country was well. My dream had not been occasioned by any strong impression which the thoughts of the preceding day had made upon my mind; for I had left my wife in perfect health, and then doubted not the least of her safety at home. I found her, accordingly, in the same state at my return.—I then ridiculed my own superstition; but, before the day expired, the tragical event happened which brought her to her end.—For one instance of a *real* foreboding like this, the credulity of old women will spread a hundred stories of *imaginary* warnings. Yet, tho' the superstitious fears of some, and the vanity and self-importance of others, may have given rise to many a legendary tale, it is no reason with me not to believe, that monitory visions, or preparatory forebodings, have actually existed at some time.———For what purposes God has permitted these visions, to foretel misfortunes which his Omnipotence could as easily prevent, or in what manner they are occasioned, may be difficult to determine; but many people, when broad awake, have had forebodings of what

was,

was to happen, without being able to account for it how they are produced. I remember, in particular, stopping one day under a gateway on Snowhill, when I could not help taking a particular survey of the wall in my front; and the thought instantly struck me, that it was in imminent danger of tumbling down. On the very same day, the house above this gateway fell in. Several persons were buried in the ruins of it; and tho' I have been under many a crazy old wall in my life, I never had any apprehension of being crushed, but the time above-named. Whether my foreboding, or my knowledge in building, was then the greater, the Wits will best explain.

I believe it is not derogating from the honour of God (nor yet adopting materialism), to say, that the soul is incapable of acting without the organs of the body; for the one, as well as the other, we receive from the hand of the Almighty.——If it should be asked me,—Where then does the soul reside, between the time of death and the resurrection? I shall answer, I cannot tell; but I suppose it returns from whence it came before I was conscious of existence. It is as possible for me to be unconscious of existence after my death, as that I knew nothing of my Being before I was born, or before I acquired some degree of understanding.—We see that children gradually acquire their reason, and improve in judgment, as they advance to manhood; and that men's intellects usually fail, as they become burthened with years, and their bodies perceptibly decay. We also perceive, that, from some inexplicable formation of the brain, one man's intellects are more perfect than another's; and that most of us have it in our power to improve our understanding, by exercising it, and by keeping ourselves temperate and sober. And we

may

may further obferve, that any Diforder, occafioned by accident in the Brain, will bring our Reafon at once beneath the Inftinct of a Brute. From all thefe confiderations I muft infer, that my Soul receives it's confcioufnefs of Exiftence, and the Gift of it's rational Faculties, through the Medium of the Body; and that I fhall know no future State, until the Day of it's Refurrection.——Let no one, therefore, defpife this his earthly tenement; it is the workmanfhip of a beneficent Creator; for man's happinefs it is granted to him; it is his *duty* to keep it in repair; it is his *intereft*, if he wifhes to live comfortably, and to continue long in the poffeffion.

The LEVELLER. N°. XXI.

His SPEECH to the BENCHES in both HOUSES of PARLIAMENT.*

Ye Right Honourable and Honourable Seats!

IT gives me much concern that I am obliged to condole with you on the fubject of a Speech lately delivered to your fuperiors. I would prepare *you* to receive it

---

* The fame reafons fubfifting againft the continuing the War in America, as formerly did againft the beginning it, the Republication of this Speech may not be deemed ill-timed.

it with that subordination and passive obedience becoming *your* station; but a spirit of resistance and disobedience to its mandates still unhappily prevails in the breasts of some of your superiors, which (as *they* rise in the violence of exertion) may, from diverse parts, †*break forth* in irruptions of a very fœtid, malignant, and cadaverous nature. It shall, however be my constant aim and endeavour to prevent the †*breaking out* of these †*fresh disturbances*, or of any of their peccant, itchy, or scorbutic humours; and I cannot but flatter myself I shall succeed, as I have received the strongest assurances from other well-wishers to your tranquility, that they are equally disposed to preserve you from breaking. A great Minister has got a compleat list of *King's Friends;* trusty good constables, most willingly † *disposed to preserve the peace!*—and an augmentation of the Civil List will be granted, to enable me to reward them for their faithful endeavours. A few, indeed, may rise in opposition, and may be the occasion to you of some noisy trouble:—*Wilkes* and *Glynn* may impeach; a proceeding which will doubtless be productive of fresh irruptions: but I shall depend on your firm and stedfast resolution, to withstand every attempt to weaken or impair your excellent construction; and while you stand on sure and solid principles, you will never fail to present a safe and easy support to the posteriors of any Briton. I trust in your solidity and firmness never to suffer yourselves to be disjointed, or pulled to pieces, by any mortal whatsoever. Heaven may hereafter reward your union with a quiet and honourable retreat;—carried off whole and entire, you may be safely deposited in some lumber-room of St. James's.

For,

† Expressions in the King's Speech.

For, since the *We* and the *Our* have, in certain Speeches, been changed for *I* and *Mine*, a spirit of appropriation prevails in the Cabinet of that palace. According to the interpretation of phrases, *you* are no longer the seats of the Nobles and of the Representatives of the People; you are now become the property of a greater, of a mighty and superlative Creature. If it be *my* Parliament, *my* Dominions, *my* People, it is also *my* Benches, or *my* Foot-stool. The language of the French Monarch is assumed; every thing seems to belong to the King; and the idea of a *common* interest is lost in words expressive of a *private* and particular appropriation. If I had the honour of a seat among you, I should be willing to impeach the first adviser of those alterations. The minds of men are powerfully influenced by forms and customary titles. The Gentlemen of the Army, so long stiled *his Majesty's* Officers and Soldiers, consider themselves more immediately as the *King's Troops* than as the Servants of the State;—the forces hired to defend the lives and properties of their fellow-citizens. So, in time, will the People demean themselves as the abject vassals of the Crown, instead of regarding the King, (sworn to fulfil the Laws) as the Head of the Executive Power, and the hereditary Representative of the Nation. The same spirit of Appropriation prevails in our conduct towards the Americans. *The general tranquility of Europe gives the greatest satisfaction:*—But does that satisfaction proceed from a benevolence of reflection on the peace and happiness of mankind; or from the consideration that we shall, on that account, have the fuller opportunity to inforce our arbitrary and innovating Laws with the blood of many Britons?—Our *ancient* Rights we might have supported with justice, and

might

might have inforced the long accuftomed and received Laws without danger of incurring the Divine difpleafure. But will the Almighty blefs the arms of oppreffion? or will he grant a temporal fuccefs without exacting a future retribution? "Vengeance is "mine, I will repay, faith the Lord:"—And that very repayment may be the confequence of our fuccefs againft the Americans. If the Parliament fhould obtain the power of taxing them, places and penfions will be diftributed at pleafure; the influence of the Crown will be irrefiftible; and, in proportion as the means of bribery encreafe, our Liberties will diminifh, till they are loft in the fink of Corruption for ever.

The effects of an ungovernable Pride cannot be more dangerous to an individual, than a haughty, infulting fpirit of government, in a State, may be prejudicial to its interefts.

Not to multiply examples from Hiftory, did not the Emperor Albert the Firft lofe the dominion of the Swifs Cantons, by the tyranny of his laws, and the cruel adminiftration of his governors? By his arbitrary and innovating edicts, did not Philip II. of Spain forfeit the allegiance of the Low Countries? And it muft be acknowledged, that Great-Britain, with regard to her American Colonies, is precipitately falling into the fame mifconduct[*]. It is natural in great and mighty States, as well as in the rich and noble individual, to forget the fober rules of prudence and moderation, in the vain contemplation of their own grandeur. In the conceited notion of their own importance, the councils of Albert and of Philip did imagine, that, with armies which could oppofe the force of any mighty Empire, they could have crufhed

[*] October, 1774.

crushed at once those little rebel States, and have made their subjects slaves for ever. Little did they foresee the spirit, the courage, and persevering ardour, with which men would fight, who thought themselves injured; nor did they consider the advantage such troops evidently possess over soldiers, whose passions are not engaged in the cause for which they combat.—The *Swiss*, tho' trained to war, as a trade by which they profit, have ever been esteemed as a good-natured, inoffensive people.—The *Dutch* are harmless and peaceable to a degree that makes them, to the ignorant, appear incapable of feeling; and many years have not elapsed since the *American Colonists* were reckoned so unwarlike, so patient, and long-suffering, that Officers have declared, they could, with three regiments, march from North to South, and subdue their whole country.——Yet we have seen that the tamest may be roused, the meekest may be enraged by oppression.—It matters not what the provocation is, if a people but imagine themselves injured; as little boots it to say, they are rebellious, or that they are ungrateful. Few men are grateful for the favours conferred on their progenitors. No people with the longest sword will ever acknowledge themselves to be rebels. James II. may have reproached the majority of our forefathers with being traitors, and rebelling against his government; but by their success they proved themselves to be the true supporters of Public Freedom. And so it may happen in the event between Great-Britain and her Colonists.——I mean not to enter into the *right* of our procedure; it is not the *lawfulness*, but the *expediency*, of measures for which I am contending. The *right* has already been sufficiently canvassed. A long paper-war has been carried on with our Co-

E e

lonists,

lonifts, in which, if we have not been worfted, we have been grievoufly infulted. Hoftilities have not yet ceafed; and, mortifying to our pride, we muft ftill bear with this infolent defiance, to which all their behaviour amounts: " Have you the *power* to " keep us in fubjection? If not, we fhall deny the " *right*, and vigoroufly oppofe it." Yet, in the arrogance of their conduct, they are, in fome meafure, juftified by precedents: from the beginning of the world to the prefent time, every fubordinate nation would affert its freedom, when it felt itfelf in a ftate of independence. It therefore becomes us to drop the inveftigation of the right of fovereignty, and to confider maturely what future conduct, towards our Colonifts, would be moft conducive to the interefts of Great-Britain. If we have the *power*, we have undoubtedly the *tyrannical right* to rule them, and tax them at our pleafure. But if, in the trial of that power, we fhould fail; inftead of receiving the taxes we mean to impofe, we fhall perhaps lofe the revenue to which, by cuftom, we are intitled; I mean the duties paid at our Cuftom-houfe on the products of the American Colonies. If, inftead of allowing our Colonifts the fame freedom which every Briton claims as his birth-right in his Mother-country, we fhould, with hoftile arm, with-hold it from them, and they fhould ftubbornly perfift in their attempts to wreft it from us; I dread the conteft will not terminate in our favour. Whenever we fhall draw fwords with the Colonifts, France may either quarrel with us, or join our fly neighbours, the Dutch, in granting them an underhand affiftance. It is certainly the intereft of both thofe nations, to render the Colonies independent States, for the fake of fupplying them with manufactures, in many of which their fmuggling

trade

trade evinces they can underfell our merchants. I am grounded in my conjectures of what *may happen*, by what has already come to pafs. Nor am I fingular in my opinion. Tho' the majority of the late Parliament did not forefee the fpirit of oppofition, which their haughty refolutions would raife in the Colonies; they were foretold it, at the time, by many well-meaning and moderate people. A friend of mine, among the reft, who is neither a prophet nor a conjuror, has printed it in thefe remarkable words, with which, for the prefent, I fhall conclude my Addrefs to you.

" The Houfe then refolved itfelf into a Committee to confider of the American papers; and it being moved, that the Committee fhould agree to the feveral refolutions of the Lords, fent down for our concurrence, it was carried in the affirmative. The votes were about two to one. Thefe feveral refolutions declared all the proceedings, at the late meetings of the inhabitants of our Colonies, affembled without authority of the governors, to be illegal; the circular letters from the different Provinces, to be unwarrantable and unjuftifiable; the late riots and difturbances in the Colonies, to be fubverfive of all order and government; with many further declarations equally indifputable by any-body born on this fide of the Atlantic, and too long for me to trouble you with at prefent. To thefe refolutions was added an addrefs to his Majefty, to inftruct his governors and commanding officers in America, to apprehend all perfons fufpected of treafon or mifprifion of treafon, and to fend them over to Great Britain, to be tried before the Lord Chief Juftice. If I had fpoken in the Houfe, I fhould have touched on none of the arguments againft this laft *patriotic* meafure, which were advanced

advanced by much more learned and respectable Members; but I should have begged leave to observe, that it would not be improper, before we gave our concurrence to the Address, to consider maturely of this previous question; Whether, to all human appearance, we were most likely to preserve the Colonists united to us, for a longer space of time, by allowing them all the privileges of Britons, and by treating them mildly as fellow-subjects, than by governing them despotically as a conquered people? That, by nature, that extensive country of North America has never been ordained to be *ultimately* ruled by this little island. In a few years we must expect to see the Americans become independant, and shake us off. That no one can doubt, that, with an army lately opposed to half the power of Europe, we are not *at present* able to keep the Colonies in subjection; but whether we shall be sufficiently strong to do it, when we shall have the united forces of France and Spain armed again for our destruction, is a consideration that should make us pause. That, in my humble opinion, instead of sending out a Star Chamber order, we ought to address his Majesty, to instruct the governors of the several Colonies, to signify to the Assemblies (when they were again assembled, for, at present, there is not one of them but what has been hastily dissolved) that it was his Majesty's desire, they should send Commissioners to treat with his Parliament, to represent their grievances, and to consult in what manner they should be hereafter governed by Great Britain. That tho' the late measures of the Ministry may be justifiable by precedent, and the antient method of ruling the Colonies; yet no one can imagine they will long prevail, after riches, encreased population, and amicable confederacies

shall

shall have united the Americans to oppose them; and shall have emboldened those descendants of Presbyterians, Puritans, Dutch Republicans, and Independants, to stand forth and assert those principles of liberty which lie latent in their breasts. That all the petitions and remonstrances sent over from them are scarcely, as yet, overt marks of what we may expect: And that the above measure, if it had no other effect, would at least quiet the minds of our fellow-subjects, and gain time for the prosecution of violent measures, if no agreement for an union with our Colonies could take place*."

LETTERS

* Letters on certain Proceedings in Parliament, by Myself, printed by Almon.

LETTERS on CREDIT*.

LETTER I.

To the Printer of the Public Advertiser,

SIR,

THE Causes of the extensive Credit, complained of by E. M. I apprehend to be,—a Scarcity of Money among the trading part of the Nation; our large Exportations to our Colonies in America and the West-Indies; and the income of the richest part of our purchasers, or consumers at home, consisting in Rents, or Annuities, received at periodical Payments. I explain myself thus: In Holland and Flanders, where money is plenty, the interest of it, as it was but lately, is often as low as three and an half per cent. and the longest Credit, given for Goods bought in Holland, is but six weeks, at which time they must be paid for as punctually as a bill of exchange.

---

* Though these Letters were written about the time of the Failure of the Bank of Aire, and of many capital Houses in London, the subject of them, in a trading Nation like This, can never be out of Season. I have therefore ventured to republish them in the original Form, in which, Mr. Woodfall told me, they were relished by his Readers; and in which their dry Subject will be more agreeably read, than if it was considered in a regular Dissertation.

change. The Case is very different with us; no merchant can borrow money under five per cent. and no American or West-Indian merchant can fulfil all the Orders of his Correspondents, without asking Credit of his Tradesmen till there is time to expect his Returns. Hence proceeds the long credit given for Goods, from nine months to two years. But E. M. would be for confining every merchant to trade within the extent of his own capital. To do that, he must first enable our Colonists to pay off their debts to the mother-country; and he must next give time for their sugars, their coffee, their tobacco, their rice, and all their products, to come to sale, before their factors here should send them a bale of goods. Our manufacturers at home would not thank him for his counsel.

The intended reformation would take several years in compleating; and half our manufactures would, in the mean while, be at a stand. When it is considered, that in the instance of the credit given our colonists, it is only giving time for the poor in America to pay, with the labour of their hands, the poor of our mother-country for their hard-earned work, what honest Briton would vote for its being curtailed? The first inhabitants of America and the islands must have had little else but credit, to have enabled them to settle; and, altho' that original debt be paid off, a like credit must necessarily be continued, for the increase and improvement of their plantations. Yet I own it may be abused, more from ignorance than design; a merchant here may trust planters that are not punctual in their returns, and be so far indebted to his tradesmen, as not to be able to answer their regular demands with his own stock. The manufacturer is then distressed, though he seldom meets with a total loss.

Our

Our Gentlemen of landed property come next under confideration, as the principal Promoters of long credit. A young man may inherit an eftate of five thoufand a year, and yet have not twenty pounds of ready money at command. What is he to do to live till the day comes when he is to receive his rent? He muft certainly avail himfelf of the credit which E. M. would abolifh; and fo muft every gentleman of landed property, that either inherits an incumbered eftate, or has not ready money at command. E. M.'s fcheme then for confining the retale bufinefs to ready money is entirely chimerical, and will gain *his* Judgment no *credit* in the opinion of any fenfible man. What he fays on the fubject of difcounting *fictitious* bills, I hope will not increafe the difficulty of difcounting other bills at this time of public diftrefs; for we have feen that, where there is a fcarcity of money, and an extenfive trade to foreign parts, there muft unavoidably be an extraordinary ftretch of public credit; and one chief link, in that chain of credit, is, the difcounting of bills by our national bank.

LETTERS

LETTER II.

On CREDIT.

To the PRINTER of the PUBLIC ADVERTISER.

SIR,

YOUR Correspondent E. M. in his third letter to you, asserts, "that CREDIT, public or private, is a most destructive cancer in any state;" and this he vainly defies any one to contradict. He has thrown down his gauntlet, he says, and no champion has been so bold as to take it up. But I have already entered the Lists with him; I have taken up his rusty gauntlet, and I have also had one run at him with my lance. I shall now renew the combat; but before I put spurs to my steed, I here accuse him, before the tribunal of the public, as a traitor to the state;—and thus I make good my charge.

By *credit* I understand the *trust* that one man gives another in money, or in goods, and the confidence thereby put in the honesty or solidity of the borrower by him that lends. This credit, so essential to the welfare of every trading state, your correspondent E. M. has been attempting to destroy; and not satisfied, in these times of diffidence or distrust, with attacking the credit of *individuals*, he wickedly labours to undermine the credit of the *state*.

Having in my last shewn, that it is absolutely impossible without credit to carry on the retale business. I will now endeavour to demonstrate wherein credit, in the wholesale business, is beneficial to the subject, and wherein, as in public loans, of advantage to the state.

Suppose a Merchant should have engaged the amount of his own stock in a venture beyond sea, and should perceive an opportunity of making a considerable profit by engaging in another venture; E. M. would, in this case, advise him to sit still, and let the opportunity slip. I, on the contrary, assert it to be justifiable in him to borrow and make use of credit, if he can. Let him apply, for the money he wants, to some rich Landholder, who has a large sum lying idle at his Banker's; if it is not *idle*, the Banker has lent it to some other to trade with, which supports my argument equally well; but supposing the Landholder's money to be entirely unemployed, and he lends it to the Merchant in want; he must certainly know that this money is to be employed in trade, and he therefore willingly risks it on the industry, honesty, and success of the Merchant, at the interest of five per cent. If the venture does not succeed, the lender and the borrower of the money may both suffer in the loss; yet many laborious hands will have been employed (as by the particulars of the invoice and account-sale will be seen) in the circulation of this money, which otherwise might have been locked up useless in an iron chest. But should the venture succeed to the Merchant's wish, besides the having employed and fed a number of industrious people, he has the satisfaction of returning his Friend the money he borrowed, with profit and advantage to them both.

Suppose,

Suppose again, that a Merchant has his whole stock invested in goods sent to a foreign market or in goods brought from abroad to sell at home, and that the prices of his goods have fallen, so that he cannot possibly dispose of them without a loss; he lets them lie in the Warehouse in the expectation of a better sale; mean while he has parted with all his money, to answer the purchase of those goods, and the prices still continue to fall—will E. M in this case, oblige him either to sell with loss, or to sit idle till the markets rise, rather than make use of his credit to undertake any thing else, in which he foresees some advantage may be gained?—If E. M. will allow a Merchant neither of the liberties I have cited, he certainly understands little of the subject on which he writes. A considerable part of the rents of the landed Gentry, and much of the monied property of these kingdoms, are circulated in methods similar to those above mentioned, and are thus made subservient to the general benefit of the community in which we live.

Other instances of trust or credit might be given, that would, with their explanations, fill a book; but a column of your paper, Sir, is all that is allowed me, and I must be brief.—Every Bill of Exchange that is drawn, and every Bill that is discounted, are credits given to the drawer, the accepter and indorser of those bills, 'till they are actually paid. Every Cargo that is ordered from Russia and the Baltic, is paid for by the credit which our Merchants must ask of their Friends at Hamburgh or Amsterdam. The Merchants of those places, by accepting the bills for the purchase of goods in the Baltic, confide in the honesty of the British Merchants for their reimbursement at the time those bills are due; would E. M. by his reasoning, destroy that confidence, and at this critical

critical juncture diftrefs our trade? I again aver it, he is a traitor to the ftate. But in detecting the fallacy of his reafoning on the national credit, I fhall produce againft him ftill ftronger proofs.—We have only an *ideal poffeffion*, fays he, of one hundred and thirty millions; and he brings in other affertions to terrify the Stock-holders out of their property, and to frighten the monied people from lending on government-fecurity in future. Whatever revolutions may hereafter happen in the government of this Country, it will certainly be for the intereft and fecurity of our rulers, to regard as facredly inviolable the national funds; for thereon will chiefly depend the faith and confidence of the people at home, and the credit to be given them by the inhabitants of the neighbouring ftates. Money or notes may be feized on as plunder, by the different Competitors for power, in the cafe of a civil war; but the debt due by the Nation to fo many individuals, will find protection from the interference of fome of thofe individuals themfelves. Too many of the leaders of the oppofite parties will be creditors of the ftate, ever to think of expunging the national debt; they *muft* protect it and keep their property fecure.

Whilft therefore Government-fecurity remains, this Sum of one hundred and thirty millions is as much a *real poffeffion* as any property in filver or in gold. Its value is founded on the opinion of mankind, and on the difficulty of it's acquifition, which alone make Gold and Silver of more eftimation than Copper or Tin. Nor is that large fum abfolutely loft to the Nation, as E. M. would have us believe. The greater part of its value remains among us; I fay of its value, for that fum never exifted in thefe kingdoms in fpecie: It has been paid and expended at different

ferent times, and circulated in the manner following;—Suppose the Administration (A. A.) have occasion for 1000 l. To raise it on the public in general would distress the industrious Merchants and Mechanics (M. M.) who have occasion for their money: A. A. therefore apply to several Landholders and rich Dowagers (L. D.) to lend them the money, and only demand of M. M. their proportion of the interest on the 1000 l. instead of the capital sum. Excepting what is expended in purchasing our naval stores, and in the supporting our forces abroad, the sum borrowed by Government is circulated by our army and navy among our husbandmen and manufacturers at home. Our soldiers, indeed, are, to appearance, drones in the State, because they do no labour for the wages they are paid; but they protect the industrious in their work, and are therefore useful to the community at large.

Let not then E. M. so much lament the enormous amount of the national debt, as the deplorable state of human nature, that we cannot all inhabit this world in peace. War is, at one time or other, unavoidable; and the most easy and convenient method of carrying it on, is, by raising the supplies in loans, from those who have a superfluity of money, and think it is safer to trust it to government-security, than to venture it with a merchant's trade. Those loans have certainly occasioned a scarcity of money among the trading part of the nation, because, if we had been at peace, I take it for granted, much of their amount would have been lent out in trade; but then I consider, that raising the supplies within the year would bring on the trading people considerable more distress. By the first means you only detain

from

from them what they never obtained; by the second you deprive them of what they actually possessed.

As I have mentioned the disproportionate quantity of money to the increasing trade and manufactures of this country, I cannot help communicating to E. M. a conceit of mine, that, I believe, with his notions of public credit, will make him stare. It is briefly this: That I have long wished all the one hundred and thirty millions of national debt were owing to the Dutch, and our other good neighbours abroad; not because I would erase the account, or commit the Bank-books to the flames; but because, with this sum employed in our national trade, which would be so much more money brought into the kingdom, we should make a profit of eight or ten per cent. ourselves, and could very well afford to pay three one half per cent. to foreign states*. This will seem a little absurd to them who only view the interest of the money owing to Foreigners, as so much money lost to the kingdom; but by them who have any knowledge of our general and extensive Trade, I flatter myself I shall be perfectly understood. At all events, I will not attempt at present to add any thing by way of illustration. I have already exceeded the extent of the Column you allow me; but, if you like my reasoning, I may perhaps continue this subject another Time. Before I conclude, however, indulge me with a few words more to your correspondent E. M.

I would not have him imagine that the extraordinary fall of the Stocks during the war, was owing to

---

* Since these Letters were first published, the legislature has adopted the same idea, in passing an act which empowers the proprietors of lands, in some of the West-India Islands, to borrow money, on mortgages to the subjects of foreign states.

to a diffidence of government security: It proceeded entirely from the increase of the Funds or national debt, which at every subscription brought annually so many more sellers of Stock to market; and as idle money became scarce, and the Purchasers decreased in number, the prices proportionately fell. Add to this the number of timid Stock-holders, who, at every occasional fall of the Stocks, will, at all hazards, sell out, and realize their share of the Public Funds, through the dread of a greater fall. These temporary falls in the prices of Stocks are certainly injurious to the fortunes of them who, by contracts or agreements previous to the falls, are necessitated to sell; but, on the other hand, they who bought in, during the low prices of the Stocks, now reap the benefit of their rise; they enjoy perhaps five per cent. for their money, besides the certainty of a great profit on their capital, when they chuse to sell out of the Funds. It was the prospect of this high profit and interest; that tempted so many Foreigners to buy into our Funds during the war; and their continuing since to sell out, has acted upon the prices like so much new subscription brought to market, for which there has not been a proportionate demand. But when the increase of our wealth, by commerce, shall have exceeded the amount of the Stocks so forced into the market by the Foreigners' precipitate sale, we have great reason to expect, that the prices of the Stocks will rise as high as ever they were at any past time.

Tedious as I have been, I cannot quit my subject without dropping a hint, which, if adopted by Government, might hereafter prevent much public confusion and distress. In case of the Books of the Bank being destroyed, how are the Creditors of the State to prove their claims? That confideration I know prevents many monied people abroad from invefting their property in our Funds, and I therefore humbly conceive, it would add confiderably to the public credit, if, inftead of the Receipts now delivered at the Transfer Office, (which are of little ufe. as being never called in) Certificates, Bonds or Receipts were delivered to the Purchafers, which fhould be produced and exchanged for others at every new Transfer. This additional fecurity from Government, to the Proprietors of our funds, would, I confefs, be attended with its inconveniences, which it would be impoffible to prevent. It would make the transferring of Stock more tedious and formal, which of courfe would be a great lofs of time to our induftrious Stock-jobbers, and would at the Bank occafion an expence of falaries to many additional clerks. But both E. M. and I have proved, that, fooner or later, the inconveniencies confequent on war, every Man muft feel.

LETTER

LETTER III.

On CREDIT.

To the PRINTER of the PUBLIC ADVERTISER.

SIR,

IT is a Duty incumbent on every one, to be useful, in some shape or other, to the Community in which he lives. As he, who follows any profession or trade, is benefiting the public at the time he is earning his bread; so he, whom Fortune has placed above the necessity of gaining a livelihood by his own labour, ought to dedicate his time to the Service of the State. With this view, Sir, I have occasionally troubled you with my correspondence: Tho' placed not in the last-mentioned situation of life, I have leisure enough to allot some hours to the service of my neighbours, if there is any thing in my reflections that can be of use. The uprightness of my intentions, which I believe you can sufficiently attest, and the national importance of the subject on which I write, ought to gain me the *attention* of my readers. Their *confidence* I would not ask: Let their own judgments enquire if my reasoning is right. I proceed to some explanation of what I wrote you last.

I have said, that as war is at one time or other unavoidable, it is less distressful to carry it on, by borrowing money of them who have abundance to lend, than by raising the supplies on them who have occasion for their money in trade. This led me next to assert, that as, by these frequent loans to the public, much money had been with-held from the trade of these kingdoms, which otherwise might have been lent to the merchant or manufacturer, it would have been for the general interest of this country, if the whole of the national debt had been owing to the inhabitants of other states. The Government for example, instead of accepting the loan of 1000 l. from a landholder in Lancashire, borrows that sum from a gentleman at Antwerp or Amsterdam. The gentleman in Lancashire, disappointed of the government-security, lends his 1000 l. to a merchant at Liverpool, who immediately gives employment to the manufacturer, by investing it in goods for the coast of Africa. Those goods are sold, or rather, at a prodigious advantage, exchanged for slaves; the slaves again, are sent to the West Indies where they are sold for bills of exchange on London. And thus a chain of traffic has been carried on, at a considerable profit, which the Liverpool merchant could not else have undertaken, for want of the necessary funds.—Suppose, on the whole, he has made a profit but of ten per cent. deduct the interest of the 1000 l. borrowed of the Fleming or Dutchman, and the remainder is so much gained to Great-Britain. But the gain may possibly be more; for, observe, the bills given on London are for the proceeds of sugar, coffee, cotton, and other products of our islands sent to London, which, without the purchase of those slaves, would never have been cultivated, and great part of which products are exported again to foreign ports, are there sold, and are paid for by specie or remittances from abroad.—Should another 1000 l. wanted by government,

ment, be borrowed abroad, and another landholder, instead of lending to the supplies, should lend that sum to a proprietor of lands in one of our new islands; with that money the proprietor buys slaves, stocks his plantation, and cultivates a tract of land that would otherwise have lain waste. The maintenance of these slaves adds to the consumption of the salt-beef and butter of Ireland: their slight clothing, and little list of household furniture, are supplied by the British manufacturers; and the produce of their labour is advantageously disposed of, as already mentioned. The same use would be made of 1000l. lent to a Carolina or Virginia planter. Much of the rice or tobacco, cultivated by him, would be sold in foreign ports, and the remittances for the neat proceeds would be so much profit to the nation, after deducting the interest of the 1000l. borrowed by Government of the Gentleman or Merchant abroad. Again, if another 1000l. were lent by a landholder to a merchant trading to Quebec; the merchant, with that money, purchases an assortment of goods of our manufacturers at home; those goods are sent by the merchants of Quebec into the inland parts of North-America, and are bartered for furs with the natives, or are paid for by corn sent to foreign ports. This exportation of corn from Quebec, being but an infant trade, deserves but cursory notice: the furs, however, are mostly exported after they come to England, and are sold for the money of the inhabitants of other states. In support of my argument, I need produce no more examples;

"For when one's proofs are aptly chosen,
"Four are as valid as four dozen."
PRIOR's ALMA.

From the above I believe it will be sufficiently plain, that whatever sum of money is lent to our Government, by Foreigners, is so much money lent to the nation to trade with, for which we can afford to pay a reasonable interest, with great profit, and advantage to ourselves.

It is also evident, that, as the national debt has not been so borrowed of foreign states, it has been borrowed of our monied people at home, and has been with held from our manufactures and trade. This has naturally occasioned a scarcity of money among our merchants and manufacturers; and that scarcity of money, again, has naturally caused all credit to stretch. By straining the cord it will sometimes break; but let us not reason against the use of a thing from its occasional abuse. Every man is a judge with himself of its proper use; he is to determine if the paper that is offered him is good; he is to remember not to throw too much of his stock into one channel; and he ought to be provided against disappointment of payment in case of need.

Among the several causes of the extension of credit in these kingdoms, I have omitted one, that, I think, does particular honour to the generous and unsuspicious minds of the natives:—They are, of all nations, the least difficult to treat with, and the most averse, through motives of personal interest, from distressing their neighbours; and thence partly their unbounded trust to one another.

I intended next to shew, that, excepting what fictitious bills or notes are discounted, there is a real property, *somewhere*, for the value of all the paper-currency of the kingdom; but this, in the language of the pulpit, I defer to another opportunity.

LETTER

LETTER IV.

On CREDIT.

To the PRINTER of the PUBLIC ADVERTISER.

SIR,

WHEN Mr. Locke sat down to write his Essay on the Human Understanding, he tells us, he imagined he should have comprehended his subject in a few sheets. But an Essay-writer is in the state of a traveller in a wood. If his aim should be to get thro' his subject with the most ease and conveniency to himself, he will be contented to follow the *beaten* track, as knowing *that* path must soon come to an end;—if, on the contrary, his journey be in the search of truth, he must be careful that he does not pass it in his way; and, in this his search after truth, he will have so many bushes to beat, so many briars to remove, and so many sloughs to wade through, that it will be impossible for him to guess when he shall reach the plain. Happy, if he does not bewilder himself, or impatiently leave truth behind!

With this apology for being so troublesome to you, Sir, and so tiresome to your readers, I continue the subject of my Letter of last Week.

I said in my last, that, excepting for *fictitious* draughts, promissory notes, or bills of exchange, there
was

was a *real property* for all the paper currency in the Kingdom. Before I proceed to the proof of this assertion, it will not be improper to define, to those not conversant in trade, what is meant by *fictitious paper*.—If A. gives his note to B. at 12 days date, in exchange for B.'s note, payable at 14 days date, and goes with this note of B.'s to discount it, or get money for it from C.—*that* is a fictitious transaction between A. and B. neither of whom may have property wherewith to repay C. his money; and so far it is of *fictitious value*; but if C. a man of real property, pays this note to D. for goods bought of him, it is then of *real value*; for C. in case of A. and B.'s failure, can take up the note with *his* money.—In like manner, A may make a draught on B. payable to himself, or order; B. to serve his friend, accepts it, though he has no property of A.'s in his possession; A indorses it to C. and discounts it with him for money. *That* again is *fictitious* paper. So likewise is a bill of exchange which A. draws upon himself in the feigned name of a merchant at Edinburgh; he makes it payable to his friend B. and, after accepting it, he gives it to B. to get it discounted with C. and to bring him the money for his or their common use.

Those are three cases of *fictitious* paper, by which persons of real property may be defrauded out of their money; but if the security of either A. or B. be good, any one of those transactions I regard in the light of a loan on a man's promissory note; for which, if it should go through a hundred hands, there is a *real* value, as long as there is a property subsisting to answer the note when it is due; however, law and form and equity require, that, for every paper given in payment, value shall have been received; and that when

when C. lends his money on the security of *two* or *three* persons, he shall not find he has lent it on the security but of *one*.

Such *fictitious* paper has been of late but too much circulated and it is certainly a great abuse of *credit*; but, from the dread of that *abuse* to want to abolish the use of credit, is little less than to desire to stop the circulation of the coin current in the Kingdom, from an apprehension, *that* coin may be counterfeited by some of our Birmingham coiners.

I come now to that paper currency of this Kingdom, for the value of which there is, somewhere or other, a real property existing; I mean not all in specie or money, but in money, lands, products, manufactures, and all kinds of saleable commodities. I begin with a Bank Note.

A. brings 100 l. to the bank in specie, for which he receives a note of that value, No. 1 : C. brings a bill of exchange to be discounted at the bank (B) who having already discounted to the amount of its capital, gives him nearly the whole sum received of A. Thus the value of the note, No. 1, remains no longer with B. in specie; it is in the hands of C. or of them to whom he has paid the money. Another Merchant D. brings a bill of 100 l. to discount with B. for which, instead of money, he receives a note, No. 2; where is the real property lodged for the value of this note? Not in the bank, B. for we have supposed it to be nearly run out of specie, but in products and manufactures, in the possession of E. who had bought them of D. and for the value of which he had given a draught on F. or else the value is in F. who trusts E with the amount of the draught till he sells the goods and remits the money. But if the 100 l. which D. discounted should only have been

E.'s

E.'s promissory note, then the real property for the bank note, No. 2. is in the goods sold to E. or ultimately in money paid by D. to his labourers (if the goods should have been products of the Country) or to his manufacturers, and the sellers of the raw materials, if the goods were manufactured. This money, again, paid to the labourer or manufacturer, is ultimately repaid by the purchaser and consumer; and who ever views the harvests of our fields, the flocks of our meadows, and the rich stores of manufactures in our opulent cities, can never doubt the real value of our current paper. He will indeed from the above case perceive, that the bank itself, from imprudence, might happen to stop payment; but that would be but a temporary inconvenience, which other conveniences abundantly repay. I say a *temporary inconvenience;* for though the bank might stop payment, from the Directors having been so imprudent as to have issued too many notes of the nature of note No. 2, and from a run being made upon it for the payment of those and other notes which they had issued; yet, I take it for granted, it will ever be in possession of real property, though not of specie, sufficient to answer all claims that can be made upon it.

We see, then, the Bank of England, by being possessed of the confidence, and much of the property of the nation, is become a kind of intermediate agent between the purchaser and manufacturer, and between the labourer and consumer; supplying the manufacturer with money to proceed in his business, till he can find a ready sale for his goods; and providing the labourer, landholder, or cultivator of the land, with the means of improving and cultivating his estate, until it can produce wherewithal to repay
the

the debt. Of this laſt nature, chiefly, is the buſineſs of the banks in Scotland, which I meant to conſider next; but my plan is broke in upon by two of your correſpondents, who deſerve ſome anſwer before I finiſh this letter.

E. M. miſtakes me when he ſuppoſes, I looked down on him with pity and contempt, becauſe only he differed in opinion with me.——Grateful to my Creator for the reaſon he has given me, I aſſume no merit to myſelf, nor do I deſpiſe any man for differing in his judgment with mine.

It was the ſelf-ſufficient manner in which E. M. delivered his thoughts, that made me behold him with ſome pity and contempt. As he now ſays, he will not oppoſe me in the field of credit; I retract my charge (which he ſo ſeriouſly takes up) of his being a traitor to the State. I will even join my forces to his, to attack luxury, ſo far as it conſiſts in extravagance, diſſipation, and waſte, which the abuſe of credit greatly ſupplies.

E. M. will not allow, that any landholder will, now-a-days, truſt a merchant or manufacturer with money. From many inſtances, within my knowledge, I am certain of the contrary. But ſuppoſe the landholder himſelf will not lend the money, his banker will do it for him; elſe little would be got by his banking buſineſs.

Your correſpondent H. L. is very much ſurpriſed I ſhould affirm, "that the opinion of mankind, and the difficulty of their acquiſition, make gold and ſilver of more eſtimation than copper or tin."—He would certainly have been more amazed, if, inſtead of the word *opinion*, I had made uſe of *certain knowledge;* and, inſtead of *eſtimation*, I had written *intrinſic worth*. But he will be pleaſed to recollect, that every man, who receives a guinea or a shilling, is not a gold-refiner or silversmith. He takes the money, through an opinion he has formed of its value, from the knowledge and judgment of other people. Impress him with a belief that the metal or coin is base, and that he may get any quantity for a few apples, and the estimation of it will be no longer high in his opinion. By difficulty of acquisition I meant, that a man must do so much labour, or part with such a quantity of goods, to obtain the possession of a certain piece of metal in exchange.

Not considering, then, in this received opinion of gold and silver, the *certain knowledge* of their superior uses to copper and tin, I believe my comparison, with regard to the public funds, will be allowed to hold good.

As long as we have an opinion of the good Faith and security of government, a share in any public fund is a real property, because convertible, at our will, into any other property or possession, which, by sale, we can receive of our neighbours. In like manner are bank stock and bank-notes real properties, as long as they are currently sold; from the opinion universally received of the solidity of the bank, which none but the bank-directors can certainly know. I have said a real property, in opposition to an imaginary worth; for I have shewn, that the value of bank-paper, though founded on opinion, has, in reality, a property in the kingdom to answer it, which, as much as gold and silver, makes that value good.

LETTER

LETTER V.

On CREDIT.

To the PRINTER of the PUBLIC ADVERTISER.

SIR,

THERE is one great inducement to a Writer, to communicate his thoughts to the Public, thro' the channel of your Paper, rather than in any Publication of his own;—the certainty of having Readers, or at least of being in the way of being read. But this manner of publication, I find, has also its inconveniences, which render perodical Essays, on the same subject, not so easily understood.

Some Readers have neither attention nor memory sufficient to retain the reasoning on any argument, continued from week to week; others, again, are possessed of so little patience, to follow out the reasoning themselves, or so little candour to allow the Writer has capacity enough to do it for them, that if he should assert any thing beyond their immediate conception, they confidently affirm it to be false, because he has not instantly produced his proof.— A Writer in this situation must be pardoned repetitions; for, without them, he would be too liable to be misrepresented or misunderstood.

By my last Letter it will have appeared, I admitted that the circulation, exchange, or transfer of property

perty in bills, or in notes, may be greatly abufed; but, excepting in thofe abufes, which amongſt a trading people it is impoffible to prevent, I affirmed, that a real property exiſted, fomewhere, equivalent to all the paper currency of the Kingdom; and this affertion I began to prove in the inſtance of the circulation of a Bank Note. It will have alfo appeared, that I did not mean, the real property above-mentioned exiſted *all* in fpecie, but in money, lands, products, manufactures, and all kinds of faleable goods; but I will make myfelf ſtill better underſtood by the following proof:—A Farmer of Norfolk, F. fends a cargo of wheat to Rotterdam, and orders his correfpondent there, R. to remit the neat proceeds of it to his friend L. at London; when the remittances come, L. difcounts the bills at the bank for which he gets bank notes, with which notes he anfwers F.'s draughts on him for the remittance for the wheat. There is therefore a circulation of notes, fuppofe to the amount of 1000 l. for the value of which no fpecie appears until R.'s remittances become due; M. the Merchant on whom the bills from Rotterdam were drawn, muſt then find the fpecie to pay the draughts on him in the hands of the bank; but inſtead of fpecie he has only bills remitted to him by R. being draughts from A. at Amſterdam, on H. at London, for a cargo of hemp ordered from Ruffia, and paid for by A. Their bills in the hands of M. being not yet due at the time he muſt pay R.'s draughts, he gets them difcounted at the bank, who give him notes for them, and with thofe notes he difcharges R.'s draughts;—thus 1000 l. of bank notes ſtill remain in circulation, for which no fpecie has been paid, and the only property to anfwer them is A.'s draughts on H. in the poffeffion of the bank; if H. has fpecie, with that

that he will discharge A.'s bills on him, but if he has not, the cash must be raised by a new circulation, which will last for several months, as the credit given at the sale of hemp is so long, and he will not receive, till the expiration of that credit, the payment for its sale. During this new circulation, the hemp remains the ultimate real property to answer the paper current on that account; or else, if we must have specie, we must look for it from the purchasers of the cordage or sail cloth, into which it was worked. We see, however, by this transaction, that specie has neither gone out nor come into the Kingdom. The exportation of the wheat, paid for the importation of the hemp; but as that exportation of wheat is now become a trade but little practised, we must expect specie from another quarter; we must expect it from Spain, in return for our woollen manufactures; and we must give time for our rice, tobacco, and other products of our plantations to come to market, and be sold and exported again to Europe (all which is an extension of credit) until payment is actually made in specie.

In this account I do not include the exportation of our lead and tin, and of our steel manufacture; for our importation of wine, flax, hemp, timber, &c. perhaps exceeds the amount of all that is demanded, in the produce and manufactures of this country, from most states of Europe, excepting Spain. My present design is to enquire no farther into the balance of our national trade, than to shew from whence we must expect the ultimate payment, or return, for our manufactures in specie; and by this and my former Letter, I think, it has been sufficiently shewn, that we must expect that ultimate payment from Spain, at the returns of her bullion-ships from America; or

from

from the products of our colonies and plantations, after they are sold here, and exported to other parts of Europe.

These returns, every one will perceive, must take up some time in compleating, and the necessary trade to obtain them, must be carried on with an *extensive credit*, as there is not sufficient specie in the Kingdom.

A question here will naturally be asked me, Why is there not sufficient specie in the Kingdom? If the reader will recollect, I allowed in a former Letter, that though the whole of the national debt was not so much money lost to the Nation, yet part of it had been paid away in supplying ourselves with naval stores, and in supporting our troops that were on service out of the country. As the sum so paid away must have, for several years, considerably exceeded the balance due to Britain from the rest of Europe, it must ultimately have been remitted from this country in specie or in bullion, which, as I have before observed, must take several years in returning. I do not add, to this account, the share of our Funds, which Foreigners have sold out since the peace, and which would appear to have been also paid in specie or in bullion. *That* is not so much cash spent out of the Kingdom. It was money lent us, and all of it that exceeded the amount of our remittances for our troops and naval stores, must have been formerly brought into this country in specie or in bullion. This we must suppose to have been the case, from the variation in the course of exchange between London and Holland; at the latter end of the war it was considerably in our favour, notwithstanding the sums we had to pay to Germany and the Baltic; but since the peace it has fallen against us, altho' we have no

unusual

unusual expences on the Continent. I may, however, add another cause of the scarcity of specie—the sums that have been exported to India; but we must expect to see them soon return to us, since if not the trade, the revenue of that country is in our favour. I might also add, the specie that is exported to Holland for the sake of the profits on our gold and silver coin; but as the quantity, so exported, which exceeds the balance owing to Holland, and other countries, paid by the exchange to Holland, must return to England in bullion, to be coin'd again; or, according as the exchange may vary, will perhaps be sent back to England in the same identical coin,—I state, to the account of the specie lost to the Nation, only the *Profits* on this last exported money.

Having traced the circulation or transfer of property, in a note of the Bank of England, I need not enlarge on the indispensible use of credit, in the circulation of property, by means of the notes of other banks, and other trading companies, in this country. I shall only observe, that the notes of each of them are as current as gold and silver, within that particular circle where their respective solidity is known, by some, or, through belief, received in the opinion of others.—I come now to the consideration of the paper-currency of the Banks of Scotland.—Having admitted that there was not a property, in specie, equivalent to all the paper-currency of England, no one can be so unreasonable as to expect it, in the poor and barren country of Scotland. No such property, in specie, can there possibly exist. Though the balance of trade, between England and Scotland, is supposed to be in favour of the latter, yet other causes drain that country of its money. Much specie must originally have come from Scotland, for the

purchase

purchase of many estates in the New Islands, paid for on the 'Change of London. The grand undertaking of buildings at the Adelphi must have swallowed up another considerable sum. The Sixteen Peers, and Forty-five Members of Parliament, are not all placed or pensioned; the expences, therefore, of their annual journey to London must principally be defrayed by the income of their own estates.——— Other noblemen and gentlemen of that country, who come to England, or go to the continent, for their amusement or improvement, must have their incomes remitted, for the expences of their journies; and so much of the taxes of the country, as exceeds the payment of the civil and military expences of it, must also be remitted to England; so that, on the whole, the course of exchange is constantly against that country. But this is not all: It is fallacious to suppose, that when the premium given for a bill on London (deducting the merchant's commission) is remitted in specie to England, the account between the two nations is entirely settled; *that Premium* is only a standard by which is shewn what passes, *in bills,* among the commercial people. It remains to know, whether the cash collected in Scotland, by the English Riders, in payment of the debts due to their masters, (the English grocers, manufacturers, and the like) does not amount to a sum, larger than what is carried out of England by the Drovers, in payment for the Scotch cattle. I would also have the landed gentlemen of Scotland consider, that all the cash they bring up in their pockets to England, is so much money entirely lost to their country. It no where appears in the account between the two nations, the balance of which has, hitherto, so erroneously been calculated by the premium, or course of exchange.

They

They give no value for this cash; they levy it on their tenants, who, by that means, become tributary to England, as much as if they were a conquered people. The same reflection is applicable to the journies of our English travellers through Europe. What is spent in the improvement of their minds may be regained to their country; but the sums that are squandered in pleasures, being much more considerable, I ought to have included them in the account of specie exported, and to this kingdom totally lost. England, however, has resources which Scotland has not. Scotland has neither produce nor manufactures sufficient to feed and clothe, for any long duration of time, the inhabitants of other States. It is already drained of specie; thus a *real property* to answer the Scotch bank-notes, we must seek for in lands and effects. The effects, by which I understand all kinds of saleable goods, may be found as we traced them in the English notes. The lands appear answerable to the notes, in a practice which England has not. Some landed gentlemen, of unintailed estates, by binding that property, join with a few monied people in forming a bank. They issue notes in the common course of business, similar to those in England, and of which, therefore, we need not treat; but they also issue notes to persons, who have a credit or permission given them to draw on the bank, to a certain extent beyond the balance due to them on their accounts. As one man may have money in the bank while another draws out, this, well-directed, might be of general use; but it remains with the directors to tell if this is the whole state of the case. May we not suppose, they have issued so many notes above the balance of specie in their hands, and so many people have failed to whom they had advanced money on credit, that they have brought themselves into distress. In such a situation, the notes cannot be immediately paid; the ultimate payment must be expected from the sale of their manufactures, and of some of their landed estates. In the mean while, a number of the noblemen and gentlemen agree to receive those notes in payment, and, by the concurrence of the people, they pass every where in the country as before. Here we see but an instant inconvenience, for the want of specie, in the internal commerce of Scotland. After the first disappointment, every thing goes on as it usually did. Certain pieces of paper, authenticated and registered at a public office, to have their value in the land and estates of the country, are by the farmers received, in payment of corn or cattle, from the miller and grazier, because their landlord had promised to accept them in payment of their rent; the miller and grazier received the notes from the baker and butcher, because they knew the farmers would accept them; the baker and butcher received them of the shopkeeper or manufacturer, because they knew the miller and grazier would accept them, or the notes could be given in payment for goods to the manufacturer and shopkeeper again, who are under the necessity of accepting them of their customers, or of wanting the provisions of life. As long, then, as the trade of a country is confined within itself, we see no great inconvenience in substituting paper-currency instead of gold or silver coin*; but that is not the case with Scotland; for, though the balance of trade be not against her, yet we have seen that, from other causes, the balance on the importation and exportation of specie must be considerably

* Since this was written, the paper-currency in North-America has proved the possibility of the case.

ably in favour of England; and supposing the specie to be now almost entirely exported from Scotland, how is the friendly or commercial intercourse hereafter to be carried on between the two nations? No man can carry Scotch notes to England (at least not farther than Newcastle), because they are not current there; and yet many gentlemen will be travelling up to London, who will want money to bear their expences, and many English riders will come with notes to the banks of Scotland, to receive payment for them, and carry the cash to England. Thus, tho' no immediate distress is felt in that country, an universal stop of payment must in the end ensue, if some precautions are not taken, and every man has not a little patience with his neighbour; and if this stop of payment should take place, the estates of some of the landed gentry must come to sale, to answer the payment of their current paper; and the estates of others must also come to market, if their banks must call in the credits given them, and which the gentlemen made use of to improve their lands. If the money is also called in, which the banks lent on credits to the merchants and manufacturers, it will bring on the latter immediate distress, without bringing to the former any relief till the merchants and manufacturers have sold their effects.

Thus, tho' the failing of one link is likely to bring the whole chain of credit to the ground, we shall find the original cause of its fall in the negligence of the workmen, who had undertaken to keep it in repair, not in the badness of the materials of which that chain was made.

I shall now sum up the argument and conclude. I have allowed that *Credit* has been abused; but I have also shewn that the use of credit cannot, in this

kingdom

Kingdom, be abolished, as long as it proceeds from a scarcity of specie; our large exportation of manufactures to our Colonies; and the income of many of our purchasers and consumers, at home, consisting in rents received at periodical payments. If, aiming at brevity, I have expressed myself in a manner not to be thoroughly understood, I hope the following comparison will secure my meaning from all misrepresentation. *Credit* is to this Nation, at present, what a crutch is to a Soldier crippled in the wars; part of the money, which he earned in the service, he has spent abroad; the rest is in the hands of the butcher, baker, shoemaker, and taylor, to whom he paid it since his return from war, for the provisions or common necessaries of life; he is lame of one leg, but still he has the entire use of his hands, with which he can earn his bread; if you deprive him of his crutch (because a drunken fellow of an impostor may make use of the same artificial support to lead a lazy life and beg) the poor honest veteran will fall to the ground at once; you rob him of the means of supporting himself till he recovers his former strength; you rob him of his present livelihood, and the prospect of recovering the fortune he has spent; he may never be cured of his lameness as long as he crawls on the earth; he is liable to be trod upon by every passenger in the street; he cannot defend himself; he can never defend his country, or stand against its enemies again while he lives.

LETTER

LETTER VI.

On CREDIT.

To the PRINTER of the PUBLIC ADVERTISER.

SIR,

GIVE me leave to trouble you with a few lines, in anſwer to a very proper queſtion, put to me by your correſpondent J. S. in your Paper of the 23d inſtant. "How I could prove that a real property, ſomewhere exiſted, to anſwer all the paper currency of the Kingdom, without I knew the exact quantity of that paper?"—Though I have already given ſome examples applicable to the ſubject, yet I ſhould have made it more clear, by making a diſtinction between property to anſwer a note, or bill, by which every one recovers what is his due, and property to anſwer a note, or bill, by which ſome one muſt ſuffer a loſs in the tranſaction. By excepting fictitious notes and bills in my former Letters, I certainly did not mean to include them in the firſt claſs of paper, although I might then have made the remark, that as ſoon as value has been received for a note, and it has paſſed current, there is ſomewhere a property to anſwer it, even if the perſon who gave the note was not worth a ſhilling. For inſtance: A gives a note to B, and when it becomes due A is found to be inſolvent; B then loſes the amount

amount of the note; but the value of it, or the property to anfwer it, remains in the hands of thofe to whom A has paid the money away; if, on the contrary, A had only ftopped payment when the note was due, and has debts to fhew, which are owing to him, for a fum above the amount of that note, then the property is in the hands of thofe debtors to A; and B fuffers but a temporary inconvenience, by the payment of the note being delayed.

Thus it will be feen, that though the great quantity of paper currency is a certain mark of the fcarcity of fpecie, and fome individuals may lofe their property in its circulation; yet is it alfo a fign of the general opulence of the Kingdom in lands, manufactures, and all kinds of faleable commodities; for no paper can pafs in that circulation without a real property having been exchanged for it, and a real property muft therefore fomewhere exift, equal to the amount of all the paper currency in the Kingdom.

MISCELLANEOUS

MISCELLANEOUS POETRY.

An EPISTLE to Dr. * * * * * *, on his changing the Fashion of his WIG.

Dear Doctor,

 'TIS with great concern,
With much regret I've chanc'd to learn,
That you are dubb'd an arrant prig,
Because—you've cast your bulky Wig.—
The *Wise*, indeed, put no great stress
On Man's appearance, or his dress;
They hold, a Priest could say a pray'r
Without his gown, in elbow-chair;
Or read a Sermon in his shirt;
For what is man but dust or dirt?
And, deck him o'er as well's you can,
Before the Lord but *such* is Man.—
They hold a justice, on the Bench,
Would be as wise in garb of wench,
And, in an apron and a cap,
With as much ease could take a nap,
As in his robe and lion-wig,
Which puff him up so wond'rous big.—
The *Honour'd Speaker* of the *House*
Makes *them* but recollect the Mouse,

That

That from a Mountain came forth squeaking;
When *Ay*'s and *No*'s are all *his* speaking,
Which he could utter, in his jacket,
With much more ease and much less racket,
Than when, from robe, he surly roars
In concert with the jarring doors.—
They hold, a Counsel, at the Bar,
In Law and Sense would go as far,
And have of *Brass* sufficient stock,
Tho' *he* should plead in fustian frock.—
They hold, *that* man may know a science
Who puts formal'ty at defiance:
They think, good Doctor, *you* cou'd write
Prescriptions just, and fit, and right,
To any patient that wou'd fee you,
Tho' with bald noddle he shou'd see you.—

But small the number of the *wise*
To them who wear but *Wisdom*'s guise;
To these (whose wisdom's all pretence)
You give, alas! severe offence:
Should you succeed in your *new mode*,
You'll drag them o'er a rugged road,
(For Robes and Perriwigs, I wot,
Than learned store are sooner got,)
Each *fool* must study o'er his books,
To be as wise as now he looks;
The *wise* ev'n wear a *wiser* face;
If Wigs are brought into disgrace,
And, all formality thrown down,
You strip the robe or learned gown.—
When used to ornaments, descry
How much *plain Nature* hurts the eye:
Lay bare, for once, great *Camden*'s skull,
I dread, he'd look confounded dull;
And, shou'd you give *his* Wig a pull,
Wise *Mansfield*, too, wou'd seem a fool;

Mild

Mild *George* himself appears not wise,
When stript of all his regal guise;
He smiles a mere *good-natured Man!*
(For *King* discern him, if you can;)
And but his Royal Robes and Crown
Now make us heed his laugh or frown.—
   In *Blackstone's Commentaries* look,
You'll find it said, in his fourth Book:
A man may whore, and lie, and drink,
'Till into hell his soul he sink;
Provided always, no offence
Be given to his neighbour's sense;
And, of his life, no *public* sample
Shall set the world a bad example.
So, had you turn'd it inside out,
(This Wig we've heard so much about,)
And worn it, Doctor, in your House,
No creature would have car'd a louse;
You might have made a night-cap o' it,
Or, puking, spit your phlegm into it;
For any such as *private* use
Had saved you, Doctor, much abuse.
But, no;—in spite of all I say,
You wear it in the face of day;
You wear it in the public street,
And trample *form* beneath your feet.
Now, who contemns old forms, will find
Few partisans among mankind;
Forms are but cheats, (thou unbeliever!)
Which please *deceived* and *deceiver;*
So, thou, disturbing *other's* pleasure,
Art meted with *thy meddling* measure:—
Sly *Caution* sneers,—mean *Prejudice* will rail,
When *learned Doctor* struts in spruce *pigtail.*

           K k   An

An EPISTLE concerning TATLERS;— especially Those in a Country Town.

THAT I, who liv'd so chaste in Town,
  Should for a Rake be, here, run down;
That I, who ne'er, in all my Life,
With love attack'd Another's Wife;
That I, who ne'er debauch'd a Virgin,
Should now be rank'd with *Major Sturgeon*,—
Is hard;—dear Tom, you'll think it odd;
You do,—by that assenting Nod.
Then listen, Tom, while I rehearse
The cause, in *Hudibrastic* Verse;
And, should you at my folly smile,
Yet own, at least, my want of guile.
  I, who have liv'd so long abroad,
Am us'd to travel ev'ry Road;
Am us'd to cast my Eyes about,
To find each *curious* Object out;
But none so fine in curious *Art*,
Like *nat'ral* Objects touch *my* Heart;
And, Tom, of all those Things in *Nature*,
None please me like a *Woman-Creature*.
Now, when a comely One I meet,
By Day, or in the open Street,
Tho' prim She be as any Quaker,
I've e'er some civil speech to make her.
This honour to the Sex is shewn
In every Nation, but our own;
Address but, here, a Female Stranger,
You're look'd on as a second *Ranger;*
Tho' not the *Virtuous*, but the *Prude*
Repulse you most, or think you rude.

This mode of mine t' accost a Dame,
Put half our good Town in a Flame;
From Youth to narrative Old-Age,
Put ev'ry Gossip in a rage;—
" A rage, egad! and who, so stern?"——
Be still, dear Tom, and you shall learn.——
Intending me some wicked harm,
'Twas *Prattle* sounded the alarm;——
Prattle, (whose eyes are staring wide
In search of sights on ev'ry side,
Whose lips and tongue, with talking big,
Out-do in Dirt, his dirty Wig,)
To see the plainer all things pass,
Hath got a House where two Streets cross;
And thence, he said, in all his Bile,
He saw me on a Maiden smile!
Address her with familiar Air,
In words that made e'en *Prattle* stare;
(What rais'd suspicion still the more,
I've learnt this Damsel was a ———;)
All this he saw, with good intent,
To give me, as a Friend, a hint;
All this he saw, (he'll roundly swear)
But whisper'd in *Another*'s ear;
Another's, and Another's still;—
Now, *Prattle*, tattle out thy fill,
Thou Clapper to a Water-Mill!
Since thou forgot'st that I, the first,
Should, with thy tattle, have been curs'd;—
If for *my Honour* was thy fear,
Thou should'st have whisper'd in *my* ear.

This Story, Tom, and twenty more,
Flew thro' the Town, from door to door.
Each *Gull*, who kept a little Doxy,
Now quak'd lest I should prove his Proxy;

To spoil *my* sport, proclaim'd me, to her,
A dang'rous, fickle, gen'ral Wooer;
Each *Husband*, to appease his Wife,
In praise of chaste, and holy life,
Describ'd me as a *filthy Beast*,
That kept *nine* Mistresses at least;
Tho' well they know, I am so poor,
I can't afford to pay a ———;
And then, ye Fair, so great's my pride,
I hate to give a Lass a bribe:—
No charms for me, without the heart,
The fairest Form's most beauteous part!
And sure I am, as God's above,
Where *Int'rest* sways there's little *Love*.

   The *Tabbies* next began to tattle,
Full faster than my neighbour *Prattle*;
They purs'd their lips, turn'd up their noses,
Like parch'd Tea-leaves, or Cabbage-roses;
Held up their Fans, as I did pass 'em,
As if afraid I should harrass 'em;
Declar'd to each that had a Daughter,
To trust her with me was *Maid-slaughter*;
For that I had, with artful wooing,
Of thousand Virgins been th' undoing.
" All this, my friend, you'd better sink;
" Some Pots, when stirr'd, the stronger stink."
If stink I must, before I rot,
Some *Tabby*, too, shall stir a pot.
For, 'mong these Maids of holy life,
Who scorn the raptures of a Wife,
I'm most provok'd at *Ranter*'s airs;—
Ranter,—to manage her affairs,
Do Fam'ly-duty, as—read pray'rs,
Et cætera—(dear Tom, remark.)
Keeps in her house a *bouncing Clerk*,

And

And brawny Footman, on occasion,
To give his Clerkship a vacation.
I say not, Tom, there's any harm
In keeping *Clerk* or *Valet* warm;
(They're fed for service, or protection)
I only mean to hint correction:———
Who *bawl* for *Virtue* and *Decorum*,
Should e'er have *Decency* before 'em;
And ere abroad for Scandal roam,
They surely ought to look at home.
But what gives hypocrites a price,
Like railing loud at Neighbour's vice?
What turns the eyes of Folk from *You*,
Like pointing out what Others do?
Who will suppose that e'er *you* know,
One sin, you thus, lamenting, shew?
Or, from your soul, you do not hate
The deeds you blame at bitter rate;
Say, Tom,——but no;—you'd make it long;
E'en sing, in chorus to *my* song:—
Old Women! prattle while you can;
Ye Young! but think me a *good Man!*

The DISCONSOLATE WIDOW.

A Christmas Tale.

THE shock I hardly can sustain
To see my Neighbour suffer pain;
I could not bear that ev'n my Foe
Should live in misery and woe;

But him, I view, who loses life,
As freed from trouble, freed from strife;
At least from mortal care at rest,
If number'd not among the bless'd.
  So, when I mourn, in sable clad,
'Tis but my *loss* that makes me sad:
A *Patron*, dead! whose firm support
Secur'd me sinecures at Court;
A *Friend!* whose soothing speech and smile
Could well the hapless hour beguile;
A *Mistress!* or a *loving Wife!*
" Who was the comfort of my life."
In short, 'tis on a *selfish* score,
That folks the death of friends deplore;
And this I fairly mean to shew,
In story of a widow's woe.———
  A buxom Widow of Ampthill,
Who e'er was us'd to have her will,
A notion took into her head,
That, tho' her *Dear* was surely dead,
At Husband's loss the less she'd grieve,
Nay, some delight would still receive,
(Sweet comfort!) if she only cou'd
Get *Tommy*'s image cut in wood.
The image got, she dress'd it out
With shirt, and cap, and tooth-ach clout;
In bed then laid it; and, undress'd,
She hugg'd the image to her breast.
  For two long months, as gossips say,
She, constant, with this image lay;
And to her maid, young *Betty*, swore,
Her *Tommy*'s death she'd e'er deplore.
  Now *Bet* (a blab as ever breath'd,
In whom no secret could be sheath'd,

But

But out it flew like Quixote-fword)
Unto her *Serjeant* gave the word;
To him fhe told her lady's fancy;
He told it to his fav'rite *Nancy;*
This, *Nancy,* with the tidings fraught,
Unto her Love, the *Corp'ral,* brought;
(No French or Spanifh foul difafter,
Thro' Britifh corps, e'er travel'd fafter;)
The *Corp'ral,* for his very life,
Could not with-hold it from his *Wife;*
His *faithful Wife* the *Captain* told it,
And *he* the myft'ry foon unfolded.
   The Captain, vers'd in widows' cant,
Guefs'd all this buxom Widow's want;
With rev'rence due, and low fubmiffion,
To *Bet* he thus preferr'd petition:
That fhe, moft gracious, would allow
The cap, pull'd off from Tommy's brow,
To be transferr'd unto his head;
Then lay him gently in the bed,
(Said Captain meant) in *Tommy's* ftead.
As lovers' fuits are often gain'd,
He, with a bribe, *his* fuit obtain'd;
Straight to the chamber was convey'd,
And fnug beneath the blankets laid;
On pillow grac'd the very fpot
Of Tommy's nightcap and its knot;
And panting lay,—but clofe and ftill
As any thief could in a mill.
   Whereas fome Critic-wits may think,
We wrote that line to fill a chink,
(For Critics oft are curfed bitter)
We'll give a fimile that's fitter:
By which they'll fee, our own free will
Here introduc'd both thief and mill;

Not

Not dearth of rhime,—for, on occasion,
We *can embellish* our narration.
   * Have you ne'er seen a hungry Cat,
Forbear, for once, her wonted squat;
Lie all along, and seeming dead,
Till Bird hopp'd near, in little dread;
When up sprang Puss, poor Sparrow seiz'd;
With riot-paw its bosom squeez'd;
Plagu'd it with tossing and with tumbling;
Then stopp'd its pipe with fairly mumbling?
So Captain lay;—but, you shall hear,
Not so quite ended Widow's fear.
   At last, into her chamber came
The long-expected blooming Dame.
O! how the Captain's courage rose,
As, gradual, she unpinn'd her clo'es!
Struck was the Hero with delight,
When he beheld the beauteous sight!
A sight, ye Gods, what words can tell?
A bosom! shap'd in gentle swell!
A coral lip! a sparkling eye!
An arm!—but soft, the minute's nigh,
We pass her *other* beauties by.
   As into bed the Widow crope,
She strait for *Tom* began to grope;
Then gave, with circling arms, a clasp
So tight, it made the Captain gasp.
" In life again, my pride and boast;
(The Widow scream'd) a ghost! a ghost!"
For soon she fully understood,
The Captain was not made of wood.

Our

* To do justice to this simile, thou wilt be pleased, kind Reader, to rehearse it in the most *tragical* Manner.

Our Widow's heart was not so harden'd,
But *greater* crimes could well be pardon'd.
On marriage-vow, then made 'fore Heav'n,
His bold intrusion was forgiven;
" With this proviso (cry'd the Prude)
" You shall lie still, and not be rude;"
Yet, here the wits have shrewdly guess'd,
The Captain was compleatly bless'd.

 The morning dawn'd, when *Bet* arose,
And, hasty, huddled on her clo'es;
Curious, she, to know the fate
Of Widow, with her loving Mate;
(For much it would have eas'd her mind,
T' have known the Widow had been kind;)
She lightly tript along the floor,
To listen at the chamber-door.
But, hush'd was all, not stirr'd a mouse,
Dull silence reign'd throughout the house;
So, to the key-hole she apply'd
Her mouth, and to her Mistress cry'd:
(But truth must here narrate the whole,
Her eager *eye* first try'd the hole:)
" O Madam! such a fall of snow,
" No mortal, sure, did ever know!
" I saw it, as below I stood,
" Full five feet thick upon our wood;
" I swept till I did fume and fret,
" But not one faggot could I get;
" The patience of a Job to tire,
" I've nought, alas! to light a fire."
" O! *Bet*, (cry'd Dame, and bit her lips,)
" Take *Tommy*;—cut him into chips;—
" Some better comfort I require,
" So *Tommy* now may light your fire."

L l   A BROIL,

A BROIL, between some Men offended,
That was BEGUN, but never ENDED.

YOU ask me, Tom, what cursed spleen,
   Infects the Members of our *Green?
And why, instead of social life,
Nought rules the Club but hellish strife?—
To please a Friend, I'll free rehearse
Dry, storied facts, in crabbed verse;
Although the task will tire, indeed,
For *I* must *write* what *you* must *read*.
  Now, lest my tale should prove deficient,
(For ev'ry fact hath *Cause efficient*)
I must, in this poetic sinning,
Sing all th' affray, from the beginning.——
  Duces (I mean the *Gentry*) sat
In judgment o'er their Ven'son fat †,
Condemning, as a *horrid Treat*,
What they had most devoutly eat;
But " Vulgi stanti *non* Corona,"
For fruit was sent by fair Pomona;
And all the waiters were retir'd,—
When discord fell the council fir'd.——
Old *Customs*, strong as *Statutes*, bind,
In wholesome laws, the human kind;
And not *unwholesome* Those, I wot,
Which certain jolly folk have got:
Such as,—a bumper to the King,
(While moves the bottle round the ring;)

A second

---

* A Bowling-green Club; where a little 'fray happened, which I thought the parties ought to turn into mirth. The story, I confess, is local; but I have given it a republication, because it contains some admonition to our clubs of *jolly fellows*, and because, too, our politicians may find in it some truths.
  † 'Twas the Ven'son-feast Day.

A *second* to his royal Dame;
A *third* to ev'ry fellow's flame;
The President (grand Monarch!)'s lafs,
Next claims another bumper-glafs;
All which we drink, and grow the fatter,
Or elfe are drench'd with falt-and-water.*
Now Some, who ftill deny'd their fault,
Drank Water, here, without the Salt,
Nor would acknowledge, nor obey,
The Prefident's defpotic fway;
Whom ev'ry Club, that we have feen,
Submiffive view as King or Queen.——

The *Colonifts* firft kick'd and fpurn'd
Becaufe *Old Cuftoms* were o'erturn'd;
But thefe obftrep'rous Sons of Water,
In *their* revolt, revers'd the matter;
O'erturning Cuftom's ancient Rule,
That Each commands to play the Fool;
To fire his brain till madnefs border,
And drink,—as Prefidents fhall order.——

To numbers *four*, I think I hinted,
The bumper-toafts fhould e'er be ftinted;
And had the rebels drank them all,
I fhould efteem their fault but fmall;
(Since fov'reign rule, by bounteous Heav'n,
For purpofe *good* was folely giv'n†;)
But they refus'd to drink the *four*,
Which made our Monarch wond'rous fore;
He argu'd, reafon'd, jeer'd or jok'd,
Was nettled firft, and then provok'd;
Till words arofe, which caus'd the breach,
And, moft of all, *Bob Lucid*'s fpeech.

* The common punifhment for mutiny, in thefe Cafes, is a Bumper of Salt-and-water.
† See a moft excellent Sermon, preached before the Univerfity of Cambridge, by Dr. Watfon.

Now *Frank*,* supposing It to mean,
That *He* should be expell'd the Green,
Discharg'd, forthwith, the total mess
Of Negus red,—in Robert's face;—
Such was th' *Intent*;—but Fate commanded
To sing on *whom* the liquor landed;
And much we feel—when we must note,
It spotted all poor *Percy's* coat;
(But let not *Percy* make a pother,
He can afford to buy another;)—
Bob us'd his *hands*;—but *most* his *tongue*,
In using which I deem it wrong;
(Foul language only stains the *Speaker*,
Nor makes the *taker* worse, nor weaker;)—
But Robert thought, as I did think,
The *bowl* had follow'd fast the *drink*;
Now, bowl or bottle, at his head,
Might maim a Man, or lay him dead;
And though " a Man was mad with anger,"
Makes not, in *law*, his guilt the stronger,
A gen'rous soul, howe'er in rage,
Shou'd warn defence, ere war it wage.———
So, 'stead of giving nose a twitch,
Or using vulgar kick o' breech,
Bold *Frank* on honour's law relied,
And with the Negus but *defied*.
What sooner to defiance led,
Frank's black coat formerly was *red*;
He was to *swords* (ill-luck to heap on!)
More us'd than to the *Parson's Weapon*.
He had not read sly *Jenyns'* creed,
That makes of *valour* little need†;

No†

---

* The President of the Day.

† See his *Internal Evidence of the Christian Religion*.

Nor had good Robert great affurance
In *paſſive courage*, or *endurance;*
Nor can they yet, perhaps, agree,
That *friendſhip* may not always be
A *chriſtian* virtue, when, with heat,
One makes a neighbour's broil compleat.
Yet, I muſt chooſe to give applauſe,
Ere I eſpouſe Another's cauſe;
And, till I found the cauſe was *good*,
I'd ſcruple much to ſpill my blood.

Now, let us take another look,
Before we ſhut ſly *Jenyns'* book;
And let him note, for winter's ſeſſion,
My ſhrewd remarks in this digreſſion.
In Parliament, a tedious year,
I next him ſat, and thought it queer,
He e'er obey'd the *Treas'rer's* nod;
But now it ſeems no longer odd;
For here thou ſay'ſt, my little quiz!
(How could I read it in thy phiz?)
" *A Patriot-deed no Virtue is*."
'Twas this that made thee ne'er divide
With *Savile*, on thy Country's ſide;
But, right or wrong, give firm ſupport
To ev'ry meaſure of the Court.
Yet, *paſſing wiſe!* the Men may be
With whom you ever did agree;
Or, elſe, this inference I draw:—
You neither *heard* nor ever *ſaw*,
Save when the " *Queſtion!*" rous'd to vote;
And then,—you held by *Cooper's* * Coat.——

The

---

* Secretary to the Treaſury.—It is to be feared, there are many indolent, well-meaning Members of both Houſes of Parliament, who make little uſe of their own underſtanding, but follow (like blind Beggars) thoſe Leaders in whom they have put their truſt.

The Men I sing, were men of *spirit*,
Tho, *Christians*, both, of *modern* merit;
They both were warm;—but why should others,
Who calm beheld, not live like Brothers?
Why should, on this, the Club divide?
Let reason cool the cause decide:—
In all this *mighty great* affair,
(Tho' *Percy* at his coat may stare)
Nought suffer'd but the *earthen-ware*;
For, 'tis with sorrow, we must say,
The *bowl* return'd to *mother-clay*;—
Frank paid the *bowl*; and, for the liquor,
Let's scorn it,—till he's made a Vicar.

* * * * * * * *

Our *Tale* has such a *Moral* in't,
We need but close it with a *hint*;—
Of *Britain*'s *broils*, then, be it said:—
We wish the costs as ready paid!

The

NOTE. I should not have taken notice of Mr. J——'s parliamentary conduct, were it not to make a distinction, which, in his *Internal Evidence of the Christian Religion*, he has unluckily forgotten. I join with him in blaming that *ambitious Patriotism*, which prompts us to wish the prosperity of our own Countrymen, at the expence of the prosperity and happiness of other Nations. But I must ever praise that generous Patriotism, proceeding from a motive of universal benevolence, which fires us into a resistance against the *Few*, in their tyranny, or oppression of the *Many*. In this last kind of Patriotism, our Author seemed a little defective.—For the rest,—*Valour*, *Friendship* and *Patriotism* are certainly not Virtues inculcated by Christianity, to the exclusion of an universal good-will towards our fellow-creatures. And when they are employed *offensively*, in a War of Depredation, they act totally against the Spirit of our Religion.—But as this Globe is not inhabited by perfect, *inoffensive* Creatures, we must presume that these *pagan* Virtues (as he calls them) were implanted in our breasts, for the wise purpose of *Defence*, in the many unavoidable encounters with sublunary Evil.

(263)

The PROVOKED STEED*.

THE Man that plann'd the Chariot-pin†,
   Of praise I would not strip;
He saves the necks of them, within,
   Who wildly wield the whip.

Yet, equal praise to them, I give,
   Who Pins need never use;
Who kindly with their cattle live,
   Nor *Nat'ral Rights* abuse.

To Him still greater praises be,
   Who first contriv'd the art
To scratch a brute, (where bit a flea)
   And taught it not to start.

By maddest Bull that ever roar'd,
   Or leapt o'er fence of thorn,
He dreads no danger to be gor'd;
   But leads him by the horn.

A country-

---

* These Lines allude to the Defection in America, occasioned by our wrong management.—The *Steed* (America) carried his *Rider* (the King) very well, in the old *beaten* track of accustomed Government, till the unusual appearance of the *Paper-Kite* (composed of Stamp Act, Resolutions, &c.) startled him.—Instead, then, of soothing him to go on, the unlucky Boys of Ministers, with their *coercive Measures*, provoked him to bring his Rider to his sad Catastrophe. The Americans threw off their Allegiance a few Months after that Event was here prophecied.

† A new-invented Pin, to detach the Horses from a Carriage when they run away with it;—alluding to Dean Tucker's Plan for emancipating our American Colonies.

A country-wight *, of gen'rous foul,
    Thus bears a mild command:
First courts his herd with friendly pole,
    Then feeds them from the hand.

Of him a stately Steed I bought,
    And mounted on his back;
On way, no *untry'd* path I sought,
    But kept the *beaten* track.

We travell'd long both safe and quick,
    Till, sudden, in a fright,
Started my Steed, and aim'd a kick
    At *stooping Paper-kite*.

I strok'd his neck, and scratch'd his ear;
    So! so'd! him well, of course;
For that curs'd Kite had caus'd his fear;
    No fault was in the Horse.

No rider, sure, (unless in spite)
    Would lash a startled steed;
Mine calm'd so soon, and fac'd the Kite,
    I could its papers read:——

Some *Resolutions of the House*,
    Some *Acts* of a blind nation,
Down, in the swamp, some *Stamps* fell soufe!
    And eke a *Proclamation*.

For,

---

* An eminent Grazier in Leicestershire, who tames all his Cattle by the means of a long Pole, with which he scratches them; and, by shortening it gradually, he comes at length to feel them with his hand.

For, lo! 'twas but a puff of wind
   That gave this kite support;
Now *puffs* deceive, as oft we find,
   And spoil the gazer's sport.

The youths, to whom this kite belong'd,
   Came running up soon after;
First, round me, in a circle, throng'd,
   And, next, began their laughter:

" What frightens, Sir, that nag of thine?
   " The kite can do no harm;
" In dreadful hue though it may shine,
   " 'Tis but a *False Alarm*.

" Are you, great Sir, afraid to chide;
   " To use your whip or spur?
" Come, we shall teach you how to ride,
   " And soon shall make him stir.

" He kick'd our kite,—and there's for that;—
   " By Jove! he shall leap o'er it;
" Rare fun, my lads!—now, t'other pat;"—
   Not long my proud steed bore it;

The imps their switches ply'd so well,
   My horse grew furious quite;
Then plung'd, and threw me (sad to tell!)
   In dirt, with *Paper-kite*.

Now prosper long our noble King!
   Our lives and safeties all!
And grant, that GEORGE regain his seat,
   Should *He* get such a Fall!

To the Honourable Miss SEYMOUR, with the Present of a NOSEGAY.

GAY flowers, fair Seymour, oft convey,
    This moral to some maid:
The days of youth must pass away;
    Like flowers all beauty fade.

But thee I need not thus remind
    Of beauty's fading state;
Tho' Heav'n to thee has been full kind,
    Thy heart is not elate.

Thy parents form'd thy mind to prize
    What lasts when beauty's gone;——
With these few flowers, in simple guise
    I teach thee *this* alone:——

The swain that steals too near thy heart,
    (Let these poor sprigs now rest,)
With soft surprise will make it start,
    And flutter in thy breast.

Ah! gay his look and sweet his smile,
    When first that swain appears;
His heart thou'lt think, is void of guile;——
    But try * him a few years;

A second try;—another, too;
    The bad will keep but ill;
The *constant bloom* must prove *him* true,
    To whom thou yield'st thy will.

* The Author would not here be understood to recommend Coquetry. A lady may *try* and ascertain the tempers and dispositions of *several* lovers, without encouraging the addresses of *any*.

LINES sent to a YOUNG LADY, with the Present of a Pocket-book, and some genuine Court Plaister to heal a Cut in her Finger.

WHILE you, *Maria*, here inclose
    My scrolls, with cautious look,
Your secrets in *your breast* repose,
  But *mine*—within *this book*.

Now tell, sweet balm! so kindly spread
  On this soft silk I lend,
How I would heal, (tho' each vein bled)
  The sorrows of my friend.

Yet, may she ne'er a thought conceive
  She would from me conceal!
Maria ne'er one pain aggrieve,
  Should give me pain to heal!

SEMPER EADEM.

LINES written on the Canvas of a half-finished PORTRAIT of Mrs. CREW.*

SURE, lovely maid! no ills of life
  To you were ever known;
No loss of friends, nor wedlock's strife,
  Yet caus'd you e'er to moan.

* The Lady, whose countenance expresses the most perfect serenity of mind, was drawn with her head resting on her hand, and her eyes fixed attentively on the ground.

Then eye not, with that thoughtful look,
   The duſt from whence you ſprung;
With pangs of woe, too ill to brook,
   Your heart was never wrung.

An ANSWER to ELIZA's Choice of a Huſband, and of the Manner in which ſhe would paſs her Life.

THY choice, ELIZA, proves thy mind,
   To be for tender Love,
For Friendſhip form'd of pureſt kind,
   Chaſte as the ſpotleſs Dove.

But vain thy choice!—for, here below
   There is no *laſting* peace;
And bliſs, once known, imbitters woe,
   If e'er that bliſs ſhould ceaſe.

Thy *firſt* fond wiſh * ſhould'ſt thou obtain,
   And Heaven deny to laſt;
The Huſband gone!—alas! the pain,
   To ſigh for bleſſings paſt!

Then pray not for a mortal mate;
   Be happy as thou art;
Contentment's known in ev'ry ſtate,
   If grateful be the heart.

* For a Huſband.

Praise Heaven for all thy days of peace;
  But should that peace be small,
Pray Heaven thy virtues to encrease,
  And Heaven may grant 'em all.

If more thou ask, thou canst not know
  What evils may ensue;
Thy boon might end in deepest woe,
  And ever make thee rue.

The truths I sing are not less strong,
  Howe'er my numbers fail;
More precept yet conveys my song:
  O! hear my own sad Tale!

Three years I lov'd; three years I sigh'd
  For fair *Maria*'s hand;
Three years my bliss she still denied,
  By Parents dread command.

Till threaten'd, by their tyrant will,
  To † prostitute her charms,—
(To shun a certain, future ill)—
  She fled into my arms.

Five years of sweet delight did roll,
  Such!—such thou hast not sung!
To tell the joy possess'd my soul,
  Exceeds all human tongue.

Three

---

† All the Sentimental Poets agree, that the woman who marries without a proper friendship and affection for the man whom she weds, is but a prostitute licenced by the Church.
 As the Manner of MARIA's death is generally known, I imagined it would do no injury to her memory, the disclosing the motives that urged her to her last desperate deed.

Three blooming boys, with cherub face,
    Were offspring of our love;
But, ah! she fear'd a num'rous race
    A weight on me should prove.

She fear'd some dark Misfortune's storm,
    Should wreck me in its fall;
In virtuous mind and beauteous form
    She'd brought to me her All.

Her generous soul it suited ill,
    That Heaven denied the power
My coffers with her wealth to fill,——
    To gild the golden hour.

She bad me,—" live; be happy still;"—
    She said, " I die ere long;
" Forgive, my friend, forgive this ill;
" My infants can no wrong."

Then, from me sprung with frantic start,
    With dauntless fury fir'd,
She plung'd a dagger to her heart;
    Repented, and expir'd.

* * * * * * * *

Her EPITAPH;

Inscribed on a plain Marble Slab, between the Duke of ARGYLE's and Mr. HANDEL's Monuments, in WESTMINSTER Abbey.

THO' low in earth, her beauteous Form decay'd,
    My faithful Wife, my lov'd *Maria*'s laid,

                  In

In sad remembrance the Afflicted raise
No pompous tomb, inscrib'd with venal praise.
To Statesmen, Warriors, and to Kings belong
The trophied sculpture and the Poet's song;
And these the Proud, expiring, often claim,
Their wealth bequeathing to record their name;
But humble Virtue, stealing to the dust,
Heeds not our lays or monumental bust.

   To name her virtues, ill befits my grief;
What *was* my Bliss can *now* give no relief;
A Husband mourns!—the rest let Friendship tell;
Fame! spread her worth! a Husband *knew* it well.

ELEGY on the Death of a favourite TURTLE-DOVE.

BE hush'd, ye winds!—ye billows! cease to roar;
   Ye white-crown'd lilies! droop your gaudy heads;
And all ye flow'rs! that bloom on Forth's sad shore:
   For fair Eliza mourns her turtle dead.

" O Julia! Julia! lovely Julia! hear;
   " Hear the known sound of thy Eliza's voice;
" Come, pick thy meal;—thy little bill draw near;
   " Swell thy full crest, with flutt'ring wing rejoice.

" Where art thou, trifler?—soft-plum'd fav'rite!
   " where?
   " Why tarry thus at fond Eliza's call?
" At first-pip'd note thou us'd, ere now, t'appears,
   " Fly to my arm, or on my bosom fall.

                         " Alas!

" Alas! what fight! my Julia dead and cold!
" What hand prophane hath done the murd'rous
" deed!
" Oh! no!—no villain, harden'd, fierce, or bold,
" In wanton malice could make Julia bleed.

" 'Twas *Nature* dragg'd her to the shades of death,
" In spite of constancy, in spite of love;
" No chaste desires could here prolong her breath,
" Nor life as pure as angels boast above.

" Ye infants! weep;—ye spotless virgins! mourn;
" Of what avail your innocence, your worth!
" Since, soon, too soon! you must to dust return!—
" Virtue insures no residence on earth.

" Yet, in a heav'nly and immortal state,
" A sure reward awaits your virtuous deeds;
" That hope is *your's*, tho' short should be your date;
" But where the comfort when my Julia bleeds?"

A Consolatory ELEGY, addressed to a YOUNG LADY,
on the Death of her favourite TURTLE-DOVE.

TIR'D with the dance, the gay and crouded ball,
  To peaceful home *Maria* now retires;
Tho' oft she follows fickle Fashion's call,
  Great,—great Ambition all her bosom fires.

She pants for ev'ry language, ev'ry tongue;
  She burns to study ev'ry Science thro':

But

But say, *Maria*, shall it e'er be sung,
   Thou hast forgot thy harder self to know?

Thou wert not born to rule a stubborn state,
   Or on the Bench explain the doubtful Law;
Or at the Bar (its rigour to abate)
   Plead for the Guilty, resting on a flaw.

To live by Traffic, thou wert ne'er design'd;
   To steer the vessel to each distant coast;
To wage fell war against thy fellow-kind;
   To raise a Bulwark, or command a Host.

Heav'n has not form'd thee, with *Hygean* bowl,
   To cure or comfort each corporeal ill;
Nor must thou, teaching Physic for the Soul,
   High from the Pulpit preach th' Almighty will.

Then, wherefore all that study, all that pain,
   To learn each science, and each language read?
From these, *Maria!* lo, what little gain!
   Thy mind is ruffled at a Turtle dead!

Thou weep'st, fond maid! with tears bedew thy Dove!
   Now wring thy hands; and tear thy auburn hair!
Thy heart is feeling, and unfeign'd thy love;
   But all thy soul is sadden'd by despair.

If such thy sorrow at *imagin'd* ill,
   O may'st thou never love a thankless Swain!
A Lover lost!—(what could thy passions still?)
   Pride, grief, or fury, then would wreck thy brain.

VERSES

VERSES sent to a Young Lady, with the Present of a Landskip-drawing.

DEPICTED, here, Contentment's* cot behold!
  With lowly roof of mean thatch cover'd o'er;
Where, jarring loud, no costly gates unfold,
  But *Meekness* stoops to ope its humble door.

Next, imag'd, see the stream of human care;
  In which some, angling, earn their scanty bread;
(Who, hardy, try to wade, no better fare;
  † For Rocks and Cat'racts, thwart their vent'rous tread.)

Some, musing, stand aloof,—and view the shore
  Where vainer mortals think sure bliss to find;
They, prudent, shun the rapid torrent's roar;
  Heav'n's doom receiving with an *even mind*.

Others, again, with wealth and princely pow'r,
  An ample arch, high, o'er the torrent throw;
And soft they roll, in golden, giddy hour;
  But where they'll end, alas! they little know:

A wood obscure, perchance, they have to pass,
  † Where no broad path admits proud grandeur's car;
Their wheels may stop, ingulpht in deep morass;
  Their steeds may stumble o'er some traverse bar;
    Full

---

* In the Landskip to which these lines allude, was a river in front, on the left-hand bank of which was a Hermitage or Cottage; on the right-hand bank stood an Angler, and a statue of Contemplation; and, farther removed, was a Bridge with a Post-chariot driving along it.

† Excuse a *rumbling* line or two. When I think the sound is expressive of the sense, I take no exception against the *snarling R*, or any other letter of the alphabet.

Full many a prickly thorn and bramble tall
　Obstruct their passage, like an armed foe;
The arch may crack,—then headlong down they fall;
　Plung'd in the flood, they're swept to seas of woe.

A

NORTHERN PASTORAL.

On the Death of the Earl and Countess of
SUTHERLAND.

Address'd to the Reverend Mr. ANDREW KINROSS,† at whose Academy, at Enfield, the late Earl and the Author of this Pastoral pass'd some years, very happily, together.

Fortunati ambo! si quid mea Carmina possunt,
Nulla dies unquam memori vos eximet ævo.
　　　　　　　　　VIRG. Æn. Lib. IX.

THE sun was sunk beneath the * western hill;
　Fall'n was the breeze; the chilling ev'ning still;
No leaf now rustled on the tallest tree;
No fly was seen; nor heard the humming bee;

† Much honour is due to this Gentleman for the share he has had in my son Charles's education; tho' he may gain little by the productions of my brain.—

* The season is supposed to be the Autumnal Equinox.

But still a murmur, from the neighb'ring shore,
Disturb'd the ear with harsh-resounding roar; †
Tho' calm the wind, the waves yet heav'd on high,
And, with their foaming, pleas'd the shepherd's eye;
Their foam alone was to the vision free,
For hazy twilight blended sky and sea;
But, when the sun shone bright upon the tide,
Blue seem'd the billows from the mountain's side;
The azure sky reflected, then, was seen,
And, as it ice, obscur'd the ocean's green.
The buzzing beetle, wing'd now with his shield,
Through dewy vapour, skims along the field;
And, here and there, regardless of his course,
The slumb'ring sheep he strikes, or startled horse.
Up bounds the timid sheep, and stamps the ground;
His wak'ning mates, all wond'ring, rise around;
Then as a host, with dastard panic struck,
Within the * fold runs, scar'd, the num'rous flock.

 The oxen, loosen'd from the clay-shod plough,
Cropt their green food beside the favour'd cow;
The cow, indulg'd, because to man she yields,
In milky store, the pasture of his fields,
Was, by *Corinna*, guided to the mead,
And left to wander where she list to feed:—
When old *Menalcas*, wearied with the day,
Sat by his fire, and doz'd the hours away.
Young *Colin*, wont to practise to his sheep,
Play'd on his pipe, and lull'd his sire asleep;
Whilst fair *Corinna* deck'd the scanty board,
And spread such fare as cottagers afford;

         Then,

---

 † As the most beautiful Landskips, in the north, are in the neighbourhood of the sea, the Author will be forgiven for giving a peep of it in his pastoral.—

 * The folds in the north are large enough to admit of such a race.

Then, all impatient, from the neighb'ring town,
Awaits gay *Damon* with her bridal gown.
But good *Menalcas*, in his antient chair,
Repos'd not long his mind from worldly care;
For soon he started in his sleep, and cried,
With voice of horror:—" See how swift they glide,
" Pale spectres both!—ah! trace them as they fly;"
With that he breath'd, and gave a deep-heav'd sigh.
Colin, appall'd, his pipe dropt on the floor,
Then ghastly star'd, and shun'd the half-shut door.
The scar'd *Corinna*, trembling, totter'd near,
And sought, in light, a vain relief from fear.
Menalcas woke:

MENALCAS.

   My children, did you see
Two spectres pass?—but, fool? it cannot be;
It was a vision fear'd me, in my dream;
And what I thought I *saw*, did surely *seem*.

COLIN.

Nought have we seen; but grant, ye pow'rs who know!
No ills may fill our father's house with woe;
For when, last night, I led my sheep to fold,
Stiff stood my dog, as chill'd with frost and cold;
I call'd him to me; foreward still he star'd;
Stopt was my flock, and seem'd at something scar'd.
Some sight, portentous, they did sure descry;
Some sight impervious to the human eye.*

CORINNA.

O father! hear what I have to relate;
(I dread there's something, darkn'ing, in our fate,)
         I told

---

* Some of the country people have a notion, that brutes see many strange things which the human eye can not discover.

I told it not; for, when of ghosts I speak,
You gravely chide me, for a mind so weak:—
As, late last night, I left our neighbour's door,
And crofs'd the yard*thick-stock'd with all your store,
Pale shone the moon, and, awful! to my sight
Expos'd a figure, or a stalking spright;
I stood aghast; when, lo! another came,
In white apparell'd, and in shape, the same;
It look'd around; and, with a wond'ring air,
A gesture made expressive of despair;
It paus'd and listen'd; sudden, looking back,
It view'd its mate turn round the wheaten stack;
But, ere its mate slow-glided from my sight,
It stopp'd and beckon'd to its sister spright;
With solemn step the second follow'd near,
And wrung its hands and wip'd a falling tear.—
Ha! *Damon* comes; my brother, welcome home;
But why so sad? and why that dismal gloom!
Why on that front, so smooth of late, a frown?
Is *Pie-ball* dead?—or have you lost my gown?

DAMON.

Alas! my sister, what I have to mourn
Exceeds all losses you or I have borne;
The cause of sorrow, which you read so well,
Exceeds your guess,—almost my pow'r to tell:—
Our chieftain's dead!—but, first, his gentle mate
Fled to the skies, resolv'd to share his fate.†

CORINNA.

---

* The monopolizing of farms being not yet so general in the North-Country, as it is in the South, it is no uncommon thing, in Scotland, to see a cottager. possess'd of a very comfortable farm-yard.

† The Earl died a few hours after his Countess, who was brought to her grave by a long and tender attendance on him during his last illness.

CORINNA.

Fidelia dead! my lov'd, my honour'd friend!
Then, farewell peace;—contentment's at an end.
My *friend* she was: she gave me e'er that name,
As to our cot, with gifts, she daily came;
Yet not with these *Corinna*'s love she won;
With female counsels, with her smiles alone.
When oft, at eve, I fed my feather'd flock,
She by me sat and held her little *Jock*;
Reprov'd him, gently, if he dar'd to bark;
Each rarest chicken, by its curious mark,
She told me next; then, from my wooden bowl
A handful took, to feed her fav'rite fowl;—
Even such small gifts denote a generous soul.

COLIN.

Fidelia gain'd my rev'rence and esteem;
So sweet her voice! so mild her eyes did beam!
She sooth'd my music, when she listen'd near;
My pipe was softer, and its notes more clear.
Then, how she smil'd! when oft my lambkins stray'd,
And skipp'd around her, as they wanton play'd,
Of her light step, nor little *Jock* afraid.
But her lov'd lord!—for him a tear must flow;
Courage forgives such weakness in our woe;
Courage, unmov'd, its own misfortune bears,
Tho' for a friend it drop some trickling tears.
Beneath my woe my mind, alas! must bend:
I've lost a chieftain, and a noble friend;
A second sire;—he promis'd such to be,
If you, my father, luckless, died 'fore me.
When † *Constance* led his men to Britain's war,
I too, tho' young, his standard follow'd far;

Peace

---

† The Earl was Colonel of the Sutherland fencible men.

Peace bless'd our isle ere we had seen a foe;
The band dismiss'd,—home tides of shepherd's flow;
Constance, in friendship, as in judgment, ripe,
Call'd as I went,—"Here, *Colin*, take this pipe;
" With notes melodious cheer our native shore,
" And glad your soul, when I shall be no more."

DAMON.

That pledge, dear *Colin*, of our chieftain's love,
Must now your pastime and our comfort prove.
Sound it aloft, while I forget my grief,
And in its music seek a short relief.
O stun the horrid billows of that shore,
That sink my spirit with their hollow roar;
All notes, now sounding in a solemn tone,
Awake my woe, and move me but to moan.
That roar was wont to glad our mountain's side;
But, now, more grateful is the distant tide;
When loud the surge in waves came rolling in,
Large gifts it floated * for our soil so thin;
But could it halt, and e'er at low-tide roar,
I'd shun the rock;—nor sea-weed gather more.

MENALCAS.

Your grief, my children, I, too well, approve,
For *much* to grieve arraigns the God above;
Yet, when, in dust, a long-lov'd friend is laid,
By sudden impulse nature's well obey'd;
A tear will start; the firmest soul will feel;
Each heart must bleed, that is not hard as steel.
Alas! they're gone; by heav'n's high will they sped;
Just is that doom by which they, dying, bled.

But

---

* The sea-weeds, which the tide throws upon the shore, afford the farmers, along the coast, a rich manure for their land.

But dry your tears; we're not of hope bereft:—
A child they had, an *infant* they have left;
That helpless orphan now demands our care,
Demands the love we to each other bear;
The parents dead, be all the joy we have
To save the daughter from a greedy grave;
Our past regard, for them, we best shall prove,
Their infant tending with our fondest love.
 Corinna! you (for now the winds blow cold)
Shall work a cloak, her tender limbs t'infold;
With flowing stream, from fullest udder prest
Of fav'rite ewe, supply the mother's breast;
Soon as, with shouts and far-resounding horn,
The jolly huntsmen hail the ruddy morn,
(Your daily gift supporting on your head)
With cautious step to yonder city tread.
 And you, my sons! each day you trudge to town,
Soft lamb-wool carry; (healthier far than down!)
Be that her bed, with that her, cradle line;
A healthful bed exceeds a golden mine!—
Cull, too, at morn, the fragrant herbs, that grow
Where feeds your flock upon the mountain's brow;
Their juice, to babes, more pleasing far must be
Than Indian coffee, or than Chinese tea.—
Be mine the task, as at the hearth I sit,
The softest mittens, for her arms, to knit†;
Or, if you'll strip some willow-twigs, with care,
I'll work a cradle and a wicker-chair.—
 Pleas'd with the thought, the old man gave a bound,
And with his staff, transported, struck the ground.
With that he cheer'd his children to their meal;
Then kneel'd to God to bless the common-weal,
To bless the orphan, and their board to bless;
And pray'd t'avert, in grief or joy, Excess.

† Knitting is a common employment among the shepherds in

An EPITAPH intended for MICHAEL UTTELY, of ENDFIELD;

Who having, by the Benefaction of Friends, purchased his Tombstone, and laid it in the Church-yard of that Place, continued to pay a daily Visit to the Spot of his future Abode.

UNthinking mortals! stop, and mark this stone;
   No darling son, no daughter, lost, I moan;
No bones of a dead father, claim a tear;
No honour'd reliques of a monarch, here;
In this dark vault, his debt to nature paid,
Michael, a poor, but honest man, is laid;
Michael still liv'd when friendship laid this stone;
A Friend inscribes it *now*,—a friend unknown;
Who means, of all his worth, alone to tell
One goodly practice: ere by age he fell,
Serenely sad, he courted oft the dead,
And, to his tomb, a daily visit made.
Ye great, ye proud, ye rich, ye poor, attend;
This lesson follow: fearless view your end.

On the DEATH of the Reverend Mr. L. STERNE, Author of the SENTIMENTAL JOURNEY, &c.

MOURN, Britons! mourn; your fatal loss deplore;
Mirth's fled your isle, for *Sterne* is now no more;
Sterne, who, to man, this lesson left below:
He most is blest, whose *feelings* overflow.

EPITAPH

EPITAPH for an old SERVANT at HOPETOUN HOUSE.

PASS not, proud mortals! thus unmindful by;
 Here moulders one, who never told a lie;
Who ne'er detracted from another's fame;
Nor e'er, by scandal, brought a man to shame;
In life's uneven path, contented, trod;
Curs'd not his neighbour, nor blasphem'd his God;
To converse private gave no list'ning ear;
Nor was, one slander, ever known to hear;
Who, silent to his friends as to his foes,
His master's secrets never would disclose;
But faithful, sober, pious, good, and just,
Serv'd him obedient, and fulfill'd his trust;
More *virtuous*, none, in boastful Greece or Rome;
More *great* could be,—* for *deaf* he was and *dumb*.

In Memory of ROBERT COX,

Who died on the 26th of March 1777, in the 78th Year of his Age;

Having long and faithfully served, in the Office of Common-Crier, the Town and Corporation of Northampton.

THEN silenced, by the voice of Death,
 Tall *Robin* fell—whose mighty breath

---

* I don't know if I have made myself perfectly understood; but I meant that it was impossible for him to *shine* like a man who possessed all his faculties.

Gave vent to speech, in stronger strain
Than Mortal e'er shall speak again;
Who words, in tidings, never spared,
But freely with his neighbours shared;
Who news of * *wanton murder* bore,
With sound of bell, to ev'ry door;
And oft, in honour of the *dead*,
Such fervent praises sang, or said,
So he were (he'd vow with little thinking)
Return'd to *life*, † when they were *stinking*;
Who loud proclaim'd, to foe and friend,
The *losses* which misfortunes send;
Who told of *robberies* and *theft*,
And men of goods, by *fraud*, bereft.—

Such were the services, of late,
One noisy Man perform'd the state!
And now *another*, with *his* bell,
Attempts to toll the warning knell;
Attempts the praises of the dead;
O! may ye profit by his trade!
Each time his bell alarms the street,
Remember,—life is short and fleet!
Think on the hours (to your sad cost)
Which time hath *stol'n*, and ye have *lost*;
Reflect how oft ye heedless *stray*
From honour's path, from virtue's way;
O! let *its sound* supply your *sense*,
And think—ye'll soon be *summon'd* hence!

An

---

* Dead rabbits, turkeys, and geese;—fresh salmon, cod, and all kinds of fish,—† eke live lobsters and oysters, are advertised for sale by the town-crier.

An OCCASIONAL PROLOGUE, spoken at the Opening of a Country Theatre.

[Spoken from behind the Scenes.

PRAY, let me go;—pray do, good brother Tom,
Let's see our barn, now these fine folk are come,
[Enters in the character of a Farmer.
Zooks! what a change! I vow I should not know it!
The droll Contriver, surely, was a Poet,
Or some Improver, (both alike their brains!)
Who else would change plain Nature with such pains?
But, *hocus'd-pocus'd* All, with so much art!
That Juggler, *Jonas*, must have play'd a part.
Where all the *skins* that hung on yonder beam?
Vanish'd they are, like visions of a dream!
Unless, perhaps, (I'd tell if I were near 'em)
In gloves, the Fair on *whiter* skins now wear 'em.
The late black *cobwebs*, by some witch's paws,
Are conjur'd all to—Ladies' lace and gauze!
Here dwell'd some *lambs;* and still, I trust, they're found
Sitting, transform'd, in innocence around.
Our *oats* no more!—yet, if the truth were known,
There, in their stead, a few *wild oats* are sown.
Our *chaff* and *straw* are also stol'n or fled,
But soon return in—Players, poorly fed!
And short their stay,—(I must 'em friendly warn)
For harvest's near,—and I shall—clear the barn.
My *flail* I see converted to a cane;
A Critic's stick!—to *thresh* out what they mean.
The *sacks* that held our little stock of grain,
Now turn'd to *silks*, more *precious stores* contain.
Zounds! now I think;—in this same place, I'm told,
They've dug a Pit—that can an hundred hold!

Who

Who knows, the Play'rs—(the speedy way to thrive)
Mean to inter their Landlord, here, alive;
Be that their game?—Then, by the setting Sun,
My worthy Friends, 'tis time for me to run!
                           [*Seems to go, and returns.*
Soft!—ere I go,—I hope I've not offended;
                               [*Assumes the Actor.*
No Peasant I;—my manners must be mended;
With aught I said I meant not to offend;
For *each to please* is every Being's end;
That point in view, why speak not as we can?
If not the *Actor*,—sure, you'll praise the *Man*.

A PROLOGUE, spoken to some favourite Passages, from the most celebrated ENGLISH AUTHORS, rehearsed, to a numerous Audience, by the Young Gentlemen educated at a public Academy.

WHO studies Nature, thinks not, sure, to find
    A close attention in a giddy mind.
To hear dull precepts can we Youngsters sit?
No;—mix your maxims with some fun or wit;
Such keep us fix'd.—In *Sermons* would you teach?
Snore then we must, tho' *Stonehouse?*self should preach.
Treat us with *travels*, or some new dress'd *fable*—
All nail'd you'll find us 'round the desk or table!
At *tales* of woe, too, we can give an ear,
And learn to drop, at others' grief, a tear;
Can learn from *story*, as we greedy read,
How best the paths of rugged life to tread;
To shun oppression; aid the meek and mild;
Befriend the widow, or the orphan-child.

So giddy youth, by Moralists we're told,
Are cast to goodness in a cunning mold;
Are fashion'd into any shape you lay;—
Amuse our minds,—we're work'd like Potter's clay.
 Our Master, thus, with kind intention fraught,
Meant, with a Play, t' have *pleas'd* as well as *taught;*
" To raise the Genius and to mend the heart," (1)
Cato was nam'd, and each assign'd his part.
Fir'd at the name, I gave *my* hearty vote;
But none so tame, to wear the petticoat!
" To wake the soul by tender strokes of art," (2)
No hardy youth would play the *woman's part.*
" Mount *Me,* quoth Tom, upon their wooden pegs!
" Lud! I shou'd trip,† and break my spindle legs."—
" *My* head, quoth Dick, is worth their's all together;
" It ne'er shall noddle with an *Ostrich Feather.*
" Mayhap, hereafter, they may ornament it;
" But, by their leave, they shall not *now* torment it;—
" Dress it, like bull or ram, with curling force;
" Or give it Blinkers,‡ like a vicious horse;
" With grease and powder bake it to a crust,
" While iron pins stick in it,—till they rust;
" Force o'er my nose their sulky hat,—and then
" Cock up my pecker,§ like a tippling hen!"
" Shall I, cried Jack, expose my tawny breast?
" First, with fat feeding swell my scraggy chest;
" With beef and pudding plump me up at pleasure;
" In acting, then, you'll find me quite a treasure!
                           " *Falstaff,*

(1 & 2) Lines from Pope's Prologue to the Tragedy of Cato.
† Imitating on tip-toe a Lady's step.
‡ Drawing his handkerchief over his head into the shape of a French night-cap.
§ Forcing a round hat over his nose, and imitating a hen drinking.

" *Falstaff*, or *Scrub*, or any part but lass's;—
" In woman's clothes!—I'd fright the very glasses."—
 The Drama, thus, was partly laid aside;
Since none would act the widow, wife, or bride;
Some speeches yet, from *Shakespeare*, we retain,
And, here and there, a thought from *Milton* gain;
Pope's Chaplet, too, and those of other Bards
We've robb'd,—t'amuse you with, instead of cards.—
Spadille, Manille, and Basto, swift be gone!
The Muses here shall drag you from your throne:
A milder rule the Fair have chosen now;
Sparkled each eye, and smooth'd is every brow;
While dimpled cheeks the bosom's peace proclaim;
A softer sway succeeds your tyrant-reign!
 But should the agents of the Muses' will
Their high behests *imperfectly* fulfill;
Aw'd by your presence, Ladies, should we fail,
We trust your candour will us here avail;
We trust you'll judge us as you would your Swains;
Who faulter most as most they feel their pains.—
Smile on us, *now*, and, if we meet when older,
Plainer we'll speak, I warrant you, and *bolder*.

An OCCASIONAL EPILOGUE to the MOURNING BRIDE. Spoken by ALMERIA, at the Theatre at NORTHAMPTON.

A Gothic taste hath reign'd, in latter Age,
 To raise the dead, to—spout upon the Stage;
Here murder'd Kings, stabb'd Wives, and poison'd
 Maids,
Start up to life,—and hail you from the shades.
          Thus,

Thus, *We tame* Players, when our Authors bid,
Tho' slain must rise,—(*our* Coffin has no lid!)
                         [*Pointing to the floor*.
And, courting praise, but dreading more offence,
With *ghostly speech* oft shock all common sense.
   But *Me* the Bard, by favour and protection,
Hath here exempted from a *Resurrection*;
He kill'd not *Me*; and meant by that to tell,
A *Mourning Bride* hath seen nor *Heav'n* nor *Hell*;
Unknown the joys of Matrimonial life!
To her unknown, its troubles and its strife!
Yet, tho' I'm left a Bride, I know full well
Where, on this earth, is plac'd my Heav'n or Hell;
If you but *smile*, I think my faults forgiven,
And blessed then! *my soul is all* in Heaven!——
But should you *frown*, I need no deeper go,
To feel the torments of the *Damn'd* below.
   No more behold me, tho' in sable gown,
A *Mourning* Bride,—I'm wedded to your Town;
I'm pledg'd to please you, and my little charms
Are all to win you.—Take me to your arms;
Protect me, cheer me, place me by your side;
If *you applaud*, I am a *Happy* Bride.

The SAILORS and the STONE IMAGES; a Parable.

QUOTH tarr'd *Jack* unto *Tom*, as passing St. Paul,
   They were viewing the statues* plac'd high on
      its wall:
                                 "But

---

* On the North side of the church, where there are five statues; and the one on the corner of the front makes the sixth apostle in view.

"But six 'poftles I fee, blaft the builder! he's out."
Quoth Tom: "the reft fleep;—watch and watch,
   mate! about."
My tale has a meaning;—you'll guefs it;—'tis fhort:
You need but to name our divifions at Court;—
Sleep *half* of our Rulers, as owls in old walls,
The *reft*, they keep watch,—like th' *Apoftles* on Paul's.

CONTENTMENT within the common Reach; or,
   a PICTURE of MY FAMILY.—Written in the Year
   1767.

> O mille volte fortunato, e mille,
> Chi fa por meta a' fuoi penfieri. in tanto,
> Che, per vana fperanza immoderata,
> Di moderato Ben non perde il frutto!
>   Il PASTOR FIDO.

WHEN, daub'd and befpatter'd with mud and
         with mire,
In riding from town to my own country fire,
I enter the houfe, (in like dirty condition
As was fatty *Slop*, the Shandyan phyfician,
When he fell from his poney, with projectile force,
At the terrible fight of *Ob'diah*'s coach-horfe)—
My two ftouteft lads, with a thundering din,
Come galloping to me, to welcome me in.—
In each hand a pratler, I march to the parlour;
There madam fits fuckling her dear little fnarler;
The youngeft, I mean, who's got fnuffling his nofe,
Where I my dull noddle would, gladly, repofe.
                                             Tho'

Tho' dirty I look'd as the doctor 'foresaid,
Pray, let not the simile farther be read;
For, in grandeur, I seem'd as the arms of this land,
That 'tween two supporters, illustriously, stand:
A fierce, noble lion, and his unicorn mate,
Prance, proudly erect, and attend them in state.
A kind kiss having had, (a sweet welcome to home!)
I forthwith begin to disorder the room.
I pull off my boots;—but not *such* as sly Trim,
To please uncle Toby, in humorous whim,
Converted to mortars;—but *such* as he might
Make field-pieces of,—full as dread in a fight.
Yet not *such* as Hudibras stuff'd bread and cheese in,
The rats and the mice with the scent so well pleasing,
That oft they their noses attempted to squeeze in;
But, not with comparisons longer to tire,
These boots, as they are, I set up at the fire.
Quick, arch looking John pops the dog into one,
As the dwarf thrust Gulliver into the bone;
And Charles, who is ever as keen at a joke,
With matter combustible makes t'other smoke.
Having, farther, my surtout thrown down on a chair,
And haul'd out my slippers from under the stair,
I'm challeng'd by madam, to walk out and play
With the *sweet, little Cupids*, while yet it is day.
Then out we all sally, with loud-shouting noise
And joyful acclaim from the two elder boys;
With her suckling Maria trips lightly along;
Leads, smiling, the van, as she hums us a song.
Next follows the kitten, pursu'd by the dog,
(For teazing poor kitten there's ne'er such a rogue,)
She squalling and mewing, *he* barking before us,
Assist, in our music, to fill up the chorus.
But how you would laugh, to behold, in the rear,
The scene we exhibit,—(a scene the most queer!)

In Holland, I doubt not, with wonder you've seen,
Trail'd on by one nag, needy doctor's machine;
A carriage have we, full as light to the feel,
That runs without horse, and that has but one wheel;
With pompous, big phrase I e'er scorn'd to beguile:
A *barrow* 'tis called in plain, vulgar style;
In which having stowed my two shouting boys,
And fill'd up the bottom with hay and with toys,
I put to my hand, and, on wheeling the barrow,
Cry,—" who'll buy my puddings? nice puddings of marrow!"
As the children then chuckle, I surely am pleas'd:
Thus see, by how little from care I am eas'd;
Hence learn to contain, in a space full as narrow,
And carry your wishes all—in a *wheel-barrow.*

THE NEW BRIGHTHELMSTONE DIRECTORY.

ADVERTISEMENT.

It was the custom at Brighthelmstone, some years ago, for the Gentlemen and Ladies to go into the water at the same place of dipping. The Parson of the Parish at last remonstrated against the indelicacy (not to say indecency) of this custom; for, tho' the Ladies dipt in their lannel gowns, the Gentlemen bathed all naked, and might consequently be viewed at the Women's discretion. He accordingly prevailed on the Guides, to assign to each Sex a separate bathing-place. However, when I arrived at Brighthelmstone, I found the whole Association of Guides ripe for rebellion, and threatening to bring the Men and Women together again, even in despite of the honest Parson. The *Gentlemen*, to be sure, could have no objections to the alteration; but as the Ladies seem'd to be rather neutral in the question, I was really apprehensive it would have been carrid against him. It was, therefore, principally to laugh the Company into the Doctor's opinion, that I scribbled the following Letters. They first appared in a Pamphlet, now out of print, and too slovenly written

to

to undergo a second Impression; but, having corrected them as much as my time would admit, I here present then to my Readers, as, to some of them, my little ridicule on the Subject may still be of service. The custom of promiscuous bathing, I understand, is still continued at Scarborough. Being not blessed with either a Wife or a Daughter, I am not swayed, in this matter, by motives of self-interest. But I profess myself to be a sincere friend to the Fair Sex; and, as Such, I ever considered that, next to the fear of God, the chief guard on a Woman's *Virtue* is her *Modesty*. We daily see the Chatity of a Woman subdued, whilst her Modesty remains unconquer'd; but when once the Latter is overcome, the Former must fall in the conquest.

INTRODUCTORY

INTRODUCTORY LETTER.

From London, July 22, 1765.

I'M told, my dear friend, you continue to lave,
   For the fake of your health, in the *Brighthlm-
    ftone* wave;
Any int'reft had I with thofe half-fifhy legions,
Who ramble below in fubaquean regions,
I'd not fail to indite a poetical treatife,
To *Neptune* addrefs'd, and his wife, Madam *Theis*
Who, deep twenty fathom the fubmarine gulph in,
Keep the fign of—(as poets have told us) the Dolpin
And who furnifh their cuftomers, as they can beait
With fea-water bumpers, inftead of good claret
I'd call upon them, as juft now I was faying,
That for *you* a large ftock of good health they wak
    lay in;
By fending their Nymphs, and their Nereids fo gren,
(Cookwenches and chambermaids of the faid inn)
With Triton their oftler, who, as old *Homer* fays,
Blows his horn too as poftboy, and drives the poft-
    chaife,
I'd get them to cull all the fimples that grow
In the valleys and coral plantations below;
To impregnate the waters, above we refer to,
With quantity double of fanative virtue;
That my friend I might meet when returned, as I wifh,
As bonny and plump, as a brifk healthy fifh;—
But int'reft, alas! in thefe realms having none,
I muft hope that, without it, your job will be done.
    Mean time, my dear friend, when you take your
        fea lotion,
Without *draw'rs* ne'er venture to dip in the ocean;
                                   For,

or, as *Virgil*, and all the old poets affirm,
The Nereids like fury, will bite at a worm;
And, truly, deplorable would be your fate,
Should they snatch at, and then run away with your bait;
In such a sad plight, you'd look blank as December,
And your house * be depriv'd of a very good member.
Give the same good advice to your friend, jolly *Mills*,
To guard himself well 'gainst such terrible ills;
(To the wise, faith the proverb, sufficient's a word,)
For what is a soldier, depriv'd of his sword?
How dismally sad would his hardship be reckon'd,
When, the *first* being lost, he could ne'er get a *second*.
In your absence I join'd an agreeable band,
And rambled half over the south of the land;
A fortnight ago I return'd in good case
To this great, noisy, smoaky, delectable place;
Whence, with fervour that friendship suggests and secures,
I give it you under my hand, I am Your's.

B. S.

LETTER II.

Saturday, from Brighthelmstone.

SINCE then, my good friend, you've provok'd me to write,
I'll take up the pen, and will scribble thro' spite;

I'll

---

* House of Commons.

I'll plague you with rhime, and will teaze you with
  letters,
To wish both my fingers and fists were in fetters.
Yet, now you're from home, and have nothing to do,
'Twill doubtless amuse you to read something *new;*
And *new* things, to write *you,* are not hard to light
  on,
As you ne'er was to dip in the water at *Brighton.*
So call'd they this town of *Brighthelmstone* of old,
'Tis here fit to tell, lest the critics might scold;
A well-written book,—('tis a rule they would quote,)
Should be understood without comment or note.
Digressions are granted;—and those, when there's
  need,
I'll use at discretion;—and so, I proceed;—
Proceed in my *Letter*, but not in my *Story;*
For *that*, in due time, shall be laid down before ye.
I hate the *old* mode of beginning a tale,
By which facts that follow are render'd quite stale;
With which epic poets, in stories so rare,
Present you in front, with a bill of their fare:—
Arma virumque cano Trojæ qui primis ab oris,
So Virgil begins, and foretels what's before us;
And Dan Pope, I find,—(for I never read Greek;)—
With as little caution makes *Homer* to speak;
For pray note in *Iliad*, where *passions* prevail,
Thus learned translator commences his tale:
" Achilles' wrath, to Greece the direful spring
" Of woes unnumber'd, heavenly Goddess! sing."
In *Odyssey* too, as begins the translation,
Ulysses's feats are forestall'd in narration:
" The man, for wisdom's various arts renown'd,
" Long exercis'd in woes, O Muse! resound."
  To said bill of fare I should make no objection;
('Twould certainly save both my sight and reflection;)

Q q
Provided

Provided the author would tell me what's *good*,
And what he had dress'd as my *best* mental food;
For my dish I could choose at the very first look,
Then skip o'er the *Trifles*, and shut up the book.
　　Perhaps now you wish,—(and 'twould give you
　　　　no pain,)—
I'd skim off the cream from my poor, shallow brain;
And dishing it up, in one good, solid mess,
Shou'd feast you at once, without fear of excess,
Or cloy to your stomach, by swallowing of trash,
Prepar'd by the pen of a rhimer so rash.
But I,—in my letters thus hobbling in verse,
Because I foresee that true wit will be scarce,
And would fain make a shew at small cost of reflec-
　　tion,—
Shall oft write you trifles,—by way of connection,—
To fill up the spaces 'twixt humour and wit,
The two standing dishes of comical writ.
As when, at Lord's dinner, roast-mutton is serv'd,
To side-board 'tis sent, and there left to be carv'd;
You may thank your kind stars, I shall not set aside,
My small dish of wit to be wishfully ey'd :—
You might perhaps find, 'twas not easy to reach it;
So, rather than trouble your person to fetch it,
Contented you'd dine on nonsensical trash,
That cost me, in writing, as cheap as a—dash.
Yet dashes, my worthy, good Sir, I must tell ye,
Help often to furnish a hungry man's belly;
My friend *Tristram Shandy* would cut a sad figure,
If, from his Opinions, with critical rigour,
We lopt off the dashes, which lengthen his chapters,
And serve to prolong his digressive, odd raptures.
His book of those dashes we must not curtail;
They fed the droll author, by helping its sale;

　　　　　　　　　　　　　　　　　　　　His

His bookfellers too, have been blefs'd with paunch fuller,
Than if, from his judgment, he had written cooler,
Or lefs he had drawn of thofe lines without ruler.
   Allow me then dafhes;—allow me digreffion;—
Forgive my bad metre, and want of expreffion;—
I warrant I'll give you,—in procefs of time,—
With *matters of fact*,—a full volume of *rhyme*.——
But now, I fhall follow rhetorical laws,
And, as other great orators,—*here make a paufe.*
For this proverb thofe orators well underftood:
" Too much of a thing is for nothing thought good."
So, true as my pen e'er to fingers and hand,
Your fervant I am, Sir, at ev'ry command.

LETTER III.

Monday.

WITH fea and fea-bathing, dear Sir, in my head,
This morning I rofe in good time from my bed:
Perceiving machines with fome people go in,
I ran to the Creek at the end of the *Stene*;
I ran in fuch hurry to be at the fea, man,
I was, ere I wot, among all the fine women.
'Gad! how lucky, thought I, to time it fo pat!
So, making a bow, as I took off my hat,
I begg'd an old Beldam that ftood dripping there,
(While fhe and the women all gave me a ftare)

To shew me a water machine that was empty;
"What Dæmon, quoth she, brought you hither to
    tempt ye?
What business expect ye? What thing seek ye a'ter?
'Tis here that the *Ladies* refresh in the water.
Devoted, this place, to *their* innocent pleasure!
You cannot dip *here*, tho' you offer'd a treasure;
So take yourself off, for I have no more leisure."
I thought myself happy she did her speech break off,
For the women, provok'd, might have twisted my
    neck off;
So, making the ladies another low bow,
I put ship about, and I follow'd her prow.

  I coasted the land to the West of the town,
Where men I perceiv'd, in their slippers, walk down;
Their footsteps I follow'd, when soon I descried
The Carts, in which *Gentlemen* to the sea ride;
But so snug!—and so close!—(admiring them much)
How many to Tyburn would gladly have such!
For holes are in these (tho' above cover'd in)
Thro' which you can *see*, and can never *be seen*.
And that is the cause, as I afterwards heard,
From bathing the *Men*, by the *Women* were fear'd;—
For in plung'd the *former* as naked as born;
But in wool dipp'd the *latter*, like sheep when they're
    shorn.
It therefore did frighten some few *modest* men,
T'have women so near them in flannel so thin;
And some lik'd as little the Ladies shou'd peep,
Whilst *they* all *their* beauties so hidden did keep.—

  I ask'd for a Cart, and a good civil Guide
Handed *me* into one, as he would do a Bride;
Or e.se a Bridegroom that came there to be wedded,
(Like Venice's Doge) and to Thetis be bedded.

                        Impress'd

Impress'd with late danger, and narrow escape
From barbarous maiming, or merciless rape,
I ask'd of the Guide, (as the minutes did pass,
While he stood at the door to await my undress,)
What man first advis'd 'em, and who was that rash one
Bade the Ladies to dip it in lonely queer fashion?
Who bade them to lave, in those waves clear as crystal,
With all the prude airs of a Nun or a Vestal?
For the men all in buff, but the women in sacks,
Did bathe once together—like hounds in full packs.
" Alas! my good master, no great revolution
E'er bred in a kingdom such horrid confusion,
As hath, in our town, this late curs'd innovation;—
What good, Sir, at best, can it bring to the Nation?
My three Fellow-guides, there, and I (to our cost,)
Experience what sums, by this change, here are lost;
For Storks thin as you, and decrepit old age,
Are now all the Birds that e'er hop to our Cage;
For one that dips *now*, there us'd once to dip *ten*,
And most of them too, stout, strong, able men.
It did my heart good, (tho' it made my teeth chatter,)
To see them flounce, tumble, and kick in the water;
To swim 'fore the women they were all so willing,
A pint they oft gave me along with my * shilling!
The old women, too, at the East of the Town,
(The Guides you saw dripping, each in her rough gown;)
Have loudly complain'd that their salt-dipping trade,
Since the late innovation, is greatly decay'd.
The Parson, of whom we suspected the least,
(For where there is mischief shou'd ne'er be a Priest)
'Twas

* A shilling is the common fare of a bathing machine, and a Guide to attend it, at Brighthelmstone.

'Twas *He* first propounded this curs'd innovation;
He went to the Doctor, on deep consultation:—
Quoth he, 'My good Doctor, I find that my health,
And strength of my limbs are departed by stealth;
When first I did dip, or did dive in the sea,
I stood brisk and hearty, and stiff as a tree;
A pleasure to see me! I lik'd to be seen;
I car'd not if thousands beheld me go in.
Lamentable change!—In my gait I now stoop;
Tho' often I dip it, (my head) it will droop;
No more the huge parson! whose diving all prais'd,
At whose flouncing and plunging the women so gaz'd!
The worst of the matter,—the older I'm grown,
Their glee is the greater to have my tricks shewn;
They want, in my strokes, at the age that I be,
The same feats of flouncing and plunging to see:
With children by dozens†, (all by the same woman)
In me they expect the great strength of a Roman.
Now, worthy, good friend, I confess to my shame,
I dread to outlive—(as some Heroes) my fame;
Then give me advice—(you've the best in the nation)
Till death, to preserve this my great reputation.'—

"The advice, quoth the Doctor, is easy to give;
I'll tell you, my friend, how your fame may still live:
We'll counsel (tho' some it should grieve to the heart)
The men and the women to dip it *apart;*
Then laving unseen by the eyes of the Fair,
Tho' you dip as old Gaffer, no mortal will care.'

" So planning the separate baths that you've seen,
They banish'd the men from the end of the *Stene.*

But

† The Parson was certainly an excellent swimmer, and the legal father of many children. For the rest, though but a maker of rhymes, I claim the Poet's privilege of decorating my story with fiction.

But Parson and Doctor their trade have mistaken,
For Brighton the dippers have mostly forsaken;
Thence all the confusion of which I complain,
And greater confusion I'll ne'er see again."
    Enough, my good fellow;—'twould make a Saint scold;
Enough of your tale;—for I'm shiv'ring with cold.—
    With that he retir'd, and return'd with a horse,
To drag my machine to the ocean, per force;
He bade me sit fast; and then shutting the door,
He tugg'd me along, as the billows did roar;
He tugg'd me along, with such noise and such clatter,
(While prated the people all round in the water)
I could not but think of the wonderful knocks
Which Gulliver heard on his great, wooden box,
When dropt in the sea by the eagles in fight,
He was haul'd by a cable, and by a ship-wright
So stunn'd above hatches, he could not guess where
The tumult would end that erected his hair.——
    Now, having a simile just at my hand,
My friend, I will use it, and then make a stand:—
Take me, in my cart, for—*the brain in your head*;
The guide and his horse for—*these rhymes you have read*;
They have lugg'd it on slow, in a pace that did creep,
Into a sea frothy, and not very deep;
But trust me, dear Sir, as your slave or dog-keeper,
I wish you to dip in some thing that is *deeper*.

LETTER

LETTER IV.

Tuesday.

I Found, (as to Sermon one morning I went,)
  The Church, on a hill of an easy ascent;
Yet not quite so easy, but, ere reach'd the top,
To breathe, your fat people, must, now and then, stop,
This makes folk the temple so eagerly fill,—
(All claiming great merit in climbing this hill,)
And I, tho' my carcase is sparing and thin,
With th' utmost exertion did squeeze myself in;
But, once *in*, I protest I would lose my best blood,
Than not see the people, at *Brighton*, so good,
So civil, so kind, and withal so polite!
When enters a person, attracting their sight,
They pause in their pray'r,—or they stop in their
    vow;
Then make a low courtesy, or still lower bow —
They think it is pleasing, perhaps, to their God,
Whilst praying, to deign a poor mortal a nod.
From this civil custom, at least, we descry,
They're humble *'fore God*,—and their minds are not
    high.—

My mind on a walk being fully intent,
To the *Stene*, after breakfast, this morning I went;
This *Stene*, or this green, I found cover'd with nets,
Round which sate the ladies in parties, or sets.
Oft having discover'd the wiles and the arts,
Made use of by women t' entrap people's hearts,
Quoth I to myself, who can tell but those snares
By women are laid, to catch men unawares?
So, shunning the nets, I went round to a stand;—
The high, wooden stage of our musical band;

Such,

Such, rev'rend, dear Sir, as you've seen in the North,
From which, as from pulpit, the parson holds forth,
When his kirk is too little;—the good, worthy people
Then cough in the wind, 'round his thin, wooden
  steeple.
But when to this white-painted stand I drew near,
Notes warlike, loud-sounding, were blown to my ear;
Instead of the voice of proud parson, pronouncing
Paul's sermons to mortals, and hell-fire denouncing,—
Bassoons, clarinets, with flute, hautboy, and horn,—
(Their like have not pleas'd me since e'er I was born)
Play'd a march, Sir, that made me to strut on the
  green;
With the air and the step of theatrical queen.
I marvell'd to hear, from this musical stand,
No scraping of cat-gut, to strengthen the band;
So, asking a friend the good cause there was none,
And why the *wind-music* thus pip'd it alone,—
He told me, the ladies thought none but a brute
Preferr'd a dry bit of a gut to a flute;
Them, therefore, to please, ev'ry pipe, from its throat,
Emits its soft music in rapturous note.
Those hogs, replied I, grunting loud in the corn
Round the stand,—I suppose, are to aid the French-
  horn:
Those pigs and those children, all trotting before us,
Assist, with their squeaking, to fill up the chorus;
Those greyhounds and petts, skipping round with
  blithe heart,
T' enliven our music, each barks out his part.
Let the dice, which from yonder small houses rough
  rattle,
For kettle-drums sound in a march to a battle;
Whilst that Switzer cur, (with his visage demure,
Attending his master in sea-dipping cure,

Rr   And,

And, following his Lordship, you never saw fail,
On the ladies' clean garments, to wipe his fox-tail,)--
Shall beat with his paw,—nod his head at his leisure,
Of each novel tune to denote us the measure.—
Such a band, I defy, now, both *Abel* and *Bach*,
Of noisy musicians together to pack.

 Of all the true things, my dear friend, I do write on,
In rhiming Epistles from this town of *Brighton*,
I like best the subject of eating and drinking,
Because 'tis a topic that costs me no thinking;
No thinking to *write of*, but much *to enjoy*,
For eating and drinking is, here, my employ.—
My breakfast, made after young widow's receipt,
Is nicer than ever weak dipper did eat:—
Pray take a neat's foot, friend, or else a fat calf's,
And cut it in bits, when you've split it in halves;
In four quarts of milk then well boil'd let it be,
Till the four quarts of milk are boil'd down into
   three.
Whilst you boil it, remember to skim off the fat;
Each scullion can give you his reasons for that:
It cloys the best stomach, with fat to be fed;
Fat cumbers the members, and weakens the head,
And makes one do nothing,—but sleep,—in his bed.
And thence, the sly Frenchmen this consequence
   draw:
Bons cocs,—(and keen dippers,)—*ne sont jamais gras.*
With my *soupe a la veuve*, (clean'd well with a skim,)
I'm frisky, awake,—and awake when I dream.
Each morn, after dipping, I make it then smart;
With bread in proportion, I eat up a quart;
Now, friend, as you wish to look big in your clo'es,
I beg, for your breakfast, you'll take the same dose.—
 On ending my meal, with some horsemen I troop,
And take a long ride, to digest *widow's soupe.*

          So

So pleasant the ride on a turf that's so green!
Refreshing the breeze! and the air is so keen!
To fill my void stomach, I never can wait
Till dinner-bell tingles,—my hunger's so great;
So, lighting from horse, as the clock has struck one,
To bait at the Ship, Sir, I instantly run.—
A proof of the justice of this antient saying,
" The looks of the phyz are not, always, betraying."
At the *Old Ship*, in Ship-street, is now to be seen
In the face of the Lady who keeps the said inn;—
I vow Mrs. Hicks is a lump of good nature,
Tho' not to be notic'd in any one feature.
From the looks of her daughters, alas! I must own,
Are inward sensations, Sir, as little known;
Tho' pretty, and civil in *outward* behaviour,
They ne'er granted, *inward*, one complaisant favour;
They've fed me with coffee, with bread and with
    butter,
With choc'late and jellies,—and more I could utter;
Yet all from their hands, only forc'd me to mutter:—
" Your smiles, my sweet fair! are but semblance
  " and art;
" And so are your *gifts*,--if you give not your heart."
At *Shergold's* I dine with a club, or a meeting
Of *damn'd honest fellows*, who deal in *short eating;*
That name they but give to some delicate dish;
For, *in fact*, they eat *long*, and they drink like dry
    fish.
But not for their eating or drinking, I swear,
When e'er I make one, I am glad to be there;
Their good-sense and breeding brings me to their
    table,
To share in their dinner as oft as I'm able;
Their affable tempers have gain'd my esteem;
Their gay conversation has banish'd my spleen;—

For, tho' for the vapours I came to be dipt,
(For loss of *Maria*, you know, I was hipt,)
To *their* conversation, I think it is sure,
And not to the bathing, I owe my late cure.—

   As from dinner till supper's a long time to fast,
I treat myself oft with an interim-repast:
For cards in the rooms when the weather's too hot,
Some evenings, on horseback, to *Shoreham* I trot:
Regale myself their, Sir, as any dry drunkard,
With the scent of the shore, and a *spicy cool-tankard*;
At *Rottendean* often, with loving intent,
Drink tea with the ladies fair under the tent;
But oft'ner I trip it with some laughing maid,
To *Preston*'s green grove;—there partake, in cool shade,
Of the coolest refreshment I ever shall see,—
A sweet frothy syllabub under the tree!—

The SYLLABUB under the Tree.

A NEW SONG.

I.

FLOW joy to the souls of my friends, in full tide;
Sit each merry swain with a nymph at his side,
With smiles on their cheeks to betoken their glee,
While I sing of my syllabub, under the tree!

II.

The wit of the beau, and the flights of the belle;
The gay conversations, in which they excel;

The *smart things* they say, and their *solidity*,
Compare with my syllabub under the tree.

III.

The joys of a court, and the bliss of a king;
The star on his breast, with its ribbon, or string;
Though solid they seem,—alas! if you see,
They're too like my syllabub under the tree.

IV.

Most speeches we hear, so sonorous and strong,
In the senate declaim'd by the patriot throng,
(What lurks at the *bottom?*—the *froth* we but see,)
Are too like my syllabub under the tree.

V.

The priest when he talks of his piety most;
When soldier and sailor their feats often boast;
Merchant and lawyer, vaunting loud honesty,
Compare with my syllabub under the tree.

VI.

Hard words of the scholar, in Latin or Greek,
Seeking thoughts of the *learn'd*, when his *own* he
    should speak,
(His thoughts should seek words, critics all must
    agree,)
Compare with my syllabub under the tree.

VII.

When fops count us vainly the fair they have won,
How many they've kiss'd since the last setting sun;
Snorting praises, the prude, of her own chastity,
Compare with my syllabub under the tree.

VIII.

When John kisses Margery in guise of true love,
And vows, as he kisses, he'll constant e'er prove;
His vows and his kisses from froth are not free,—
They form but a syllabub, under the tree.

SUPPLEMENT

SUPPLEMENT
TO THE
LEVELLER's Cursory THOUGHTS.

The two following Fragments were in the hands of a distant friend, at the time the Cursory Thoughts went to the Press. I cannot, however, omit them in this Publication. My political readers, having already seen how truly a cool, dispassionate man could divine the Event of the American Taxes, will not, perhaps, be displeased to read his Sentiments on some Subjects, agitated in the late Petitions, as he published them nine years ago in the Public Advertiser. —The quotation from Mr. Macpherson will have its proper weight, tho' he has not drawn the parallel I have wrote to it.

* * * * * * *

' When the Julian Family reduced the Roman Re-
' public into an Empire for themselves, they did
' not change, in appearance, the ancient form
' of government. Though a new power started
' up in the State, all the old offices remained.
' Despotism had the decency to cover oppression
' with

' with a mask, and to execute its most rigorous
' plans thro' channels neither unknown nor formi-
' dable in the days of freedom. *The power of the
' first Cæsars consisted in* INFLUENCE; *and an over-
' awed and* VENAL SENATE *were the obvious in-
' struments of their Tyranny.*'

  Macpherson's Introduction to the History of
   Great-Britain, page 281.

SO likewise shall fall the fabric of our British constitution. When some future King shall aspire at ruling the Nation according to his sovereign will and pleasure, he shall effect his purposes of despotism, through the means of a *venal Senate*. He shall bribe a majority, in both Houses of Parliament, with money, which they shall vote him unaccounted for by the Keepers of the public treasure. That majority of votes being secured, they shall, by *ex post facto* resolutions, expel whatever Member shall become offensive to the King; they shall for ever exclude that Member from the house, and in his place admit another against the voice of the people; against the written laws of the land. They shall behold their Countrymen butchered, by the military in the hands of the executive power, and shall suppress all inquiry into the cause of that bloody massacre; they shall with vengeance seize upon and commit to prison whoever shall give information of their Debates, or their secret Proceedings; they shall also imprison whatever Magistrate shall presume to act agreeable with the law, in opposition to their senatorial resolutions; they shall avail themselves of the privileges, first assumed to protect them from the power of the Crown, in order to oppress their Constituents, the People. In short, the King shall have but to issue his Royal
             Mandates

Mandates from the mouth of his Minister, and he shall find a Parliament *willing*, and an Army *able*, to enforce his commands throughout his kingdoms; and when these things shall come to pass, and the people shall see that "every wanton and causeless restraint of the will of the subject, whether practised by a Monarch, a Nobility, or a popular Assembly, is a degree of tyranny," they shall lose all respect for their Representatives; they shall revile them, abuse them, and wish them to be no more; they will suffer the King, in his turn, to tread on their Senate as on a footstool, which, deprived of its support, will be trodden like a rotten plank to the ground. All these shall come to pass; but the time is not at hand. Virtue and Independence is yet with the People; and great must be the struggle before they will submit to the tyranny of a nobility and gentry, so vicious, profligate, and abandoned!

April, 1771.

' As for Parliaments, they are but the Shadows of
' what they were, or rather worse; by which I
' mean that they are now become the Instruments
' of that Power they were instituted to restrain.'
Present State of Europe, 3d Edit. P. 290.

WHOEVER reflects on the past and present state of France, must tremble for the liberties of Great Britain. Our present Sovereign is a good man, and, in all his speeches, seems to wish well to the British Constitution; but if ever a wicked enterprising Prince should ascend the Throne of these kingdoms,

Kingdoms, either a revolution muſt take place, or the conſtitution will be entirely altered. A violent convulſion, however, muſt precede. The body of the Nobility, the bench of Biſhops, and the majority of the landed Gentry, will adhere to the Crown.—The Nobility, becauſe needy, profligate, or abandoned, will expect their loyal attachment to be rewarded with places and penſions; the Biſhops and the generality of the Clergy, from principle, will admoniſh us to ſubmiſſion and obedience to the will of him, whom Providence hath appointed to rule over us; and the majority of the Gentlemen of landed property will naturally pay their court to the head of the executive power, as being poſſeſſed of the beſt means of providing for the neceſſities of their younger children; for as the law of inheritance now ſtands, what readier proviſion is left for the younger ſprouts of the nobility and gentry, than the employments in the army, the navy, and the different departments of government.

But, on the other hand, the ancient conſtitution will be contended for by all the trading and manufacturing cities in the kingdom; by the whole monied intereſt in the nation; and by thoſe gentlemen of landed property who ſtill retain a ſpirit of independence. Thus, while ſome, from intereſt or principle, will ſupport the arbitrary will of the King; others, from the ſame motives, will contend that every law and every meaſure of government ſhould be formed from the ſenſe, or for the benefit of the people.—The King's Friends, not daring openly to diſavow this poſition, will attempt to bribe a majority of votes in the Parliament of Great-Britain; they will then maintain that every act is, in reality, the act of the people, tho' perhaps under the ſanction of

that

that venal Parliament, the will of the King alone shall rule the nation. The free and independent part of the people, however, will behold this farce with a noble indignation; and, from foreseeing their resentment of it, proceeds, too, my apprehension of a revolution.

That, indeed, may happen in some future reign. But our present gracious Sovereign, intending nothing against the interests of his kingdoms, will never meet but with obedience and affection from all his people. He has no occasion to employ the means of bribery and corruption to influence a Senate in his favour; and should his favourite counsellors advise him to it, they would bring upon him much unneceſſary trouble. Had I his Majesty's confidence, I should direct him a far different conduct. I should advise him to begin his first speech to his Parliament in the following manner:

' *My Lords and Gentlemen,*

' Having no private purpose of my own to serve,
' in the assent I shall give to any bills you may pre-
' sent for my approbation, I desire you will, in all
' your deliberations, have nothing in view but the
' immediate good of my people. Sufficient to me is
' my prerogative of refusing my assent to any law,
' you might propose, contrary to *their* interest; and
' should you meditate any act contrary to *mine*, I
' shall refuse my assent to that also; being confident
' I shall ever meet with the support of my loyal and
' affectionate people. As you have already settled
' a revenue sufficient for the expences of my family,
' I will not have the debt of the civil list increased,
' to the oppression of my poorer subjects. I mean
' not to influence the deliberations of Parliament
' with

'with a long lift of finecure places and penfions, by which the induftrious are burthened with the fupport of the indolent and abandoned. In thefe fentiments I am happy to find I am fupported by the votes and refolutions of my faithful Commons of Ireland; and I doubt not you will alfo concur with their opinion, when I declare I mean to leave you, as you have ever been, *free Agents*, to act for the welfare of my people. I fhall look on none as enemies to my family and government, who confult not my will in the fentiments which they fhall think proper to deliver. I fhall regard none as *my Friends*, who are enemies to our noble conftitution.'

January, 1772.

LETTERS

LETTERS

ON THE
CUSTOM of IMPRESSING SEAMEN.

ADVERTISEMENT.

The following Letters were first published at the time, when the affair of Falkland's Island threatened us with a war with Spain. The sarcastical *Junius* then took notice of them in a Letter addressed to their Author; and, tho' I pretend not to say that *Junius* thought himself in the argument foiled, certain it is, he deemed them not equally deserving of a republication with the Letters of *Sir William Draper*, and the *Reverend Mr. Horne*.—Yet, however inferior in composition, or how much soever beneath the *entertainment* of the Public, they may be esteemed, their *subject* deserves its *attention;* it merits the notice of every man who to Humanity has any claim.

LETTER

LETTER I.

To the PRINTER of the PUBLIC ADVERTISER.

SIR,

WHEN the dreadful apprehension of any danger is past, we are often surprised, if not diverted, at the effects of our fear. When, therefore, the present alarm shall have subsided, and the Navy shall be sufficiently manned for our national safety, I hope my countrymen will be in a temper to give the *Press Warrants* all due and attentive consideration.—Impressing seamen into his Majesty's service, by a Warrant from the King, or his Commissioners of the Admiralty, has been practised so long, that the memory of man runneth not to the contrary; and having been received as a custom by the tacit consent of our forefathers, it is therefore in a manner become one of the *Leges non scriptæ* of these realms. But (*malus usus abolendus est*) if it be not a good custom, it ought to be no longer used; it ought to be abolished; the Legislature ought to declare it *not to be the law of the land*. And such a declaration ought to be passed, before we can truly call ourselves a free people; for the natives of that country can never be called free, where one innocent man, maintaining himself by his own industry, can be imprisoned or restrained by the arbitrary will of a few.

The Liberties of a Briton consist in the right of personal security; the right of personal liberty; and
the

the right of private property. All these are wantonly violated in the execution of a Press-Warrant. An honest industrious man is attacked in the public street by a Press-gang; if he resist, he is maimed, wounded, or killed; his personal security is then gone: if he is overpowered, he is dragged on board a tender, is hurried away to sea, and is perhaps never heard of more.—Adieu then to his personal Liberty! it travels with him to the bottom of the sea. But how can his personal property be affected? What property can a low mechanic, or a day-labourer have? What hardship, pray, on him, to make him change his trade for a good birth on board of a man of war? I answer, that the wages of his labour are his property, and they ought to be as much at his disposal, as the great house in Bloomsbury-square is at the disposal of the most noble and most puissant Duke of Bedford. They are dearer to him, for they are his all. Set fire to the Duke of Bedford's house, and you burn but one of a thousand houses he is master of; His Grace can put his head into another the very next moment; but drag a labouring man from his work, and you leave his family exposed to misery and want, or to become a burden on their parish, than which nothing can be a greater hardship to a truly British mind. It may perhaps be called pride; but it is a noble and a commendable pride: The same man that disdains to take alms of his neighbour, would, in the station of Peer, scorn to receive a pension out of the revenue of this indebted State. 'Tis the soul that makes the free man in whatsoever degree. The same noble spirit of Independence, which has brought our Liberties to what they now are, burns in the breast of the mechanic as much as in that of the Lord. Have we not seen a Peer of

the

the realm, shot dead by Mungo Campbell, for offering to disarm him of his gun? And have we not heard of the undaunted behaviour of a sailor on board of an East-India ship, who, rather than be pressed into a service that he abhorred, singly opposed himself to the force of a whole Press-gang, and in the unequal conflict met with his untimely end? Think, Sir, what these men must have suffered, at the thoughts of having their inclinations forced, contrary to the natural Liberties of mankind, limited by no determinate law.

Agreeable then to the dictates of humanity, agreeable to the principles of civil Liberty, the practice of Press-warrants cannot be continued in this country. In what manner, without them, to man our navy, I do not presume to prescribe. I shall only remark, that notwithstanding the late incessant use of them for these six weeks past, there are not found seamen enough to man twenty ships of the line. This circumstance ought to be a sufficient hint to Government, to propose some plan for keeping up a *standing navy*. Every argument is for it that can be used in favour of a *standing army*, and with so much the greater force, as our enemies must first cross the seas, and encounter our navy, before their landing in this Island can render the army of material service; and because too, much longer time and experience is requisite to train an able seaman, than to make a common soldier complete. Many are the duties of the former; the latter needs but to have a natural courage and strength of body, and his trade is then learnt in the firing of a Gun. The Highlanders in the year 1745, and General Elliot's light-horse in the last war, have shewn us what raw soldiers can do that have but Officers to lead them to slaughter. The last

defeat

defeat of the French fleet by Sir Edward Hawke, has, on the contrary, shewn of what little use a sailor is that has not been taught his business at sea.

AN ADVOCATE IN THE CAUSE OF THE PEOPLE.

LETTER II.

SIR,

WHEN I troubled you last on the subject of Press Warrants, little did I imagine I should have three such able lawyers as Mr. Glynn, Mr. Dunning, and Mr. Wedderburn, to agree with me in opinion, that the custom of impressing men for his Majesty's Navy was, by long usage, and the tacit consent of the people, become part of the law of the land. I own it is very flattering to my vanity, to find my sentiments have so far coincided with those of the three learned Gentlemen.—But, at the same time, it greatly mortifies me, as a Briton, to think what foreign nations will say of the freedom of our glorious Constitution, when they read the opinion of those Gentlemen on the legality of pressing, as it is delivered to us in your Paper. They have been told by the great Montesquieu, in his Essay on the British Constitution, (Esprit des Loix, Lib II. Ch. 5.)

"Il y a auſſi une Nation dans le monde, qui a
"pour objet direct de ſa Conſtitution la Liberté
"politique;"—and again, at the end of Chap. 6.
of the ſame Book, "Ce n'eſt point à moi à exami-
"ner ſi les Anglois jouiſſent actuellement de cette
"Liberté, ou non. Il me ſuffit de dire, qu'elle eſt
"etablie par leur Loix, et je n'en cherche pas d'avan-
"tage." They are there aſſured by that great Lawyer, that Civil Liberty is eſtabliſhed in England by
its laws.—They are now informed by three of our
firſt Civilians, that the perſonal liberty of a Briton
is ſtill left, on the old plea of State neceſſity, at the
arbitrary Will of the King. Will foreign Nations,
with reaſon, not exclaim, "Where, Britons! is your
boaſted Freedom? In what is it greater than our's,
when the rich and the powerful are only to be free?
Where, your ſo much vaunted patriotiſm, that formerly oppoſed the arbitrary taxation of ſhip-money,
and aboliſhed the Star-Chamber, and but lately declared General Warrants illegal? Shall we ſay that
ſelf intereſt alone animated your Patriots to thoſe
noble deeds? Yes, 'twas nought but vile ſelf-intereſt
that moved them to oppoſe the will of their Kings:
The ſhip money affected the purſes of the rich as well
as the poor; and the Star-Chamber and the uſe of
General Warrants endangered the life and property
of the Peer, alike with thoſe of the common man.
If it be a love for the natural rights of mankind that
fires the breaſts of your Patriots, Why do they not
ſtand forth? Why do they not now raiſe their voices
in the Senate againſt the inhuman oppreſſion of the
poor—againſt the cruel, unconſtitutional cuſtom of
preſſing men? No, it is ſordid ſelf-intereſt or ambition that animates them to action; for the rights of
their fellow-creatures they can have but little regard.
They

They are, on the contrary, making daily sacrifices of them to their own ambitious designs, by enacting laws, which declare actions, in their nature inoffensive, to be crimes, and which direct the persons offending against such laws, to be tried otherwise than by a jury of their Peers. Ye short sighted generation of men! your own avarice and ambition will bring you to slavery in the end. You are daily depopulating the country by raising your rents, and enlarging your farms. You will thereby lose that weight in the State which accompanies a body of tenants, attached, by affection or dependence, to the interests of their Lords. These ties on the common people gone, which ensured you their support, how will you withstand the power of any arbitrary King? Self-interest and self-preservation (if a veneration for the natural rights of mankind guides you no more) ought to instruct you, to make it the interest of the poorest member of the community, to contend for the general good, and to support, with his life, the Liberties of his Country, and the safety of the Common-wealth.

" The same spirit which invigorated the armies of Rome, ought to animate the people of a free State. The Great Montesquieu makes this remark on the difference of a Roman army, from a modern band of mercenary troops: Each Roman trusted to the strength of his own arm, and put little confidence in the assistance of his neighbour; a modern soldier confides in the number and bravery of his companions, and the experience of his leaders. The first conquered; the latter is ignominiously put to flight. Then take not from your common people, by unnecessary oppression, the power and inclination to stand in the support of Freedom. Remember the fate of Denmark: The Commons, rather than submit to the tyranny of the Great, surrendered their liberties to the the King. Such may too soon be the case in Britain. But you will say, this custom of pressing men is only practised in case of necessity; in the time of war, when our enemies come unexpectedly upon us. And who cause that necessity but you, the very inhuman oppressors of whom we complain? You deal out places and pensions among yourselves, and plunder the State of that revenue which ought to be employed in its defence. Nay, some of your vile pensioners are not ashamed publicly to assert the legality and necessity of oppressing the poor. They openly declare, that the public safety depends on the continued custom of impressing men: But they should have considered, how many serviceable seamen, a pension of two or three thousand pounds a year could have maintained! how many brave men, for that sum, would have fought for the liberties of the State! They should have considered too, how much money could be saved, and the number of men that could be spared to the Navy, by disbanding part of that army that serves chiefly to garrison your territories abroad; and may hereafter be employed to awe the people into an obedience to laws, enacted against their real welfare by a corrupt Legislature, that shall be bribed into a compliance with the will of their King."

Such may be the sentiments of foreign Nations with regard to the boasted Liberty of the British Constitution; and with an envious and malignant satisfaction, they will behold the Britons fall from that Freedom, to which they themselves could never attain.

Junius

Junius having expressed himself, on the subject of Press-Warrants, in the following terms, drew from me the Letter addressed to him:

"I REGARD the legal liberty of the meanest man in Britain, as much as my own, and would defend it with the same zeal. I know we must stand or fall together. But I never can doubt, that the community has a right to command, as well as to purchase the service of its members. *I see that right founded originally upon a necessity, which supersedes all argument. I see it established by usage immemorial, and admitted by more than a tacit assent of the legislature. I conclude there is no remedy, in the nature of things, for the grievance complained of; for, if there were, it must long since have been redressed.* Though numberless opportunities have presented themselves, highly favourable to public liberty, no successful attempt has ever been made for the relief of the subject in this article. Yet it has been felt and complained of, ever since England had a navy."*

* See Junius's Letters Vol. ii. page 269.

LETTER

LETTER III.

To JUNIUS.

SIR,

THERE is a bigotry in Politics as well as in Religion. Precepts which, on examination, we should have found to be erroneous, are often implicitly received by us, because we have formed an opinion of the integrity and sound judgment of those by whom they were penned; but the majority of the people are biassed by those principles entirely which they have imbibed in their youth, and pay deference to those persons and things which their parents instructed them to revere. The greater, therefore, the reputation of a writer, the stricter guard I must keep over my belief; for the easier he might lead my judgment astray. I even think it my duty, when such a writer errs, to sound the alarm, lest my fellow-citizens be unwarily misled.—Junius is their favourite political guide; but shall they follow him blindfold, because he affirms it to be dark? No; let them walk with their eyes open, and see if there be not a ray of light.——Credulity and superstitious veneration have ever held in darkness the human mind. It was not till the Pope and his Priests had forfeited their character of Holiness and Infallibility, that the Reformation took place in Religion, and mankind began to think for themselves; the Scriptures began to be understood in their original meaning; though many

to this day interpret them, not as they have considered them in their own minds, but as, by their Priest or their Parents, they are taught to believe. It was not till the Prerogative of the Crown was abused by the House of Stuart, that the Revolution succeeded in the Government of Britain. Men then lost that fear and reverence with which they used to behold their King; and they began to imagine it would be better for the Common-weal, that his power and prerogative were curtailed. The authority of Monarchical Law-writers became also disregarded; and customs which, before that period, were peaceably received as the laws of the land, were then found to be illegal and inconsistent with the rights of a free man.——Our minds are becoming still daily more enlightened: General Warrants have lately been abolished as illegal; and you, Junius, have publicly arraigned the conduct of our Chief Magistrate, with a freedom hitherto unknown. A few years ago, a Jury of your own countrymen would have perused your sentiments of their King, with almost the same horror and detestation as they would have read blasphemy against their God. You have, indeed, Sir, been the greatest reformer of our Political Creed, and I revere you for your enlarged mind; (not that I approve of any disrespectful language to the King, or of any personal satire on Ministers, beyond their actions in a public character;) yet what you have written on the subject of Press Warrants does not become your pen.———I wish, Sir, for your own honour, you would give that matter a second consideration.— You say, " I see the right (of pressing men into the sea-service) founded originally upon a necessity which supersedes all argument. I see it established by usage immemorial, and admitted by more than a tacit

‘cit affent of the Legiflature. I *conclude* there is no remedy, in the nature of things, for the grievance complained of; for, if there were, it muft long fince have been redreffed." Now really, Sir, this *conclufion* is more like the argument of a bigotted Prieft of the Church of Rome, than the found reafoning of a Proteftant Divine. You might as well have told us to reverence the Pope, to believe in Tranfubftantiation, and to kneel to all the images of the Popifh Saints; becaufe, if it were not proper fo to do, our anceftors would not have done fo before us. Would you not have been laughed at, if, in the debate on the legality of General Warrants, you had declared there was no remedy againft them, becaufe, if there were, they muft long fince have been declared illegal? Were not General Warrants as much eftablifhed by ufage immemorial, as is the arbitrary cuftom of preffing men? And were they not as anciently admitted by the tacit affent of the Legiflature? Surely, Sir, if you had been ferioufly difpofed to inveftigate the truth, you would have delivered yourfelf in a more rational ftile.

A man of your *fertile* imagination could eafily have thought of a remedy againft the grievance complained of, in the cuftom of preffing men. You could have fhewn us, that a body of feamen, kept in conftant pay, was much more neceffary for the defence of their country than a ftanding army. You could, during the peace, have found employment for thofe feamen in the Dock-yards, in the Herring-fifhery, in the Cuftomhoufe-cutters, and in fully manning thofe inactive men of war now moft improperly called Guardfhips, tho' originally intended to guard our ifle. In fhort, Sir, if thofe feamen were to do *nothing* during the peace, they would ftill be more requifite than an army in peace, frequently employed to add force to the prerogative of the Crown. But Junius was not in earnest. He is perhaps one of our discarded Ministers (or rather one of their Secretaries, for Ministers seldom write so well). He expects to be employed again; and as he may then have occasion for men suddenly to put a fleet to sea, he must not deliver his opinion *against* Press Warrants; for, if it were received, he might hereafter find a difficulty to equip his fleet; the remedy, though found by him, being not yet applied to the grievances of which the nation would complain.

To an ADVOCATE in the CAUSE of the PEOPLE.

SIR, 18. *October*, 1771.

YOU do not treat *Junius* fairly. You would not have condemned him so hastily, if you had ever read *Judge Foster's* argument upon the legality of pressing seamen. A man who has not read that argument is not qualified to speak accurately upon the subject. In answer to strong facts and fair reasoning, you produce nothing but a vague comparison between two things, which have little or no resemblance to each other. *General Warrants*, it is true, had been often issued, but they had never been regularly questioned or resisted, until the case of *Mr. Wilkes*. He brought them to trial, and the moment they were tried, they were declared *illegal*. This is not the case of *Press Warrants*. They have been complained of, questioned, and resisted in a thousand instances; but still the legislature have never interposed nor has there ever been a formal decision against them in any of the superior courts. On the contrary, they have been frequently recognized and admitted by Parliament, and there are judicial opinions given in their favour, by Judges of the first character. Under the various circumstances, stated by *Junius*, he has a right to conclude, *for himself*, that there is no remedy. If you have a good one to propose, you may depend upon the assistance and applause of *Junius*. The magistrate, who guards the liberty of the individual, deserves to be commended. But let him remember that it is also his duty to provide for, or at least not to hazard, the safety of the community. If, in case of a foreign war and the expectation of an invasion, you would rather keep your fleet in harbour, than man it by pressing seamen, who refuse the bounty, I have done.

You talk of disbanding the army with wonderful ease and indifference. If a wiser man held such language, I should be apt to suspect his sincerity.

As for keeping up a *much greater* number of seamen in time of peace, it is not to be done. You will oppress the merchant, you will distress trade, and destroy the nursery of your seamen. He must be a miserable statesman, who, voluntarily, by the same act increases the public expence, and lessens the means of supporting it.

PHILO JUNIUS.*

LETTER

* See Junius's Letters, Vol. ii. page 290.

LETTER IV.

To JUNIUS.

SIR,

SINCE you have confessed yourself to be the writer of Philo Junius, I shall make no apology for addressing you again.—You accuse me with treating you unfairly. I shall retort the accusation, and prove your want of candour to me.——It was the *necessity* of a Press Warrant, and *not* its *legality*, which I denied.

I never called in question the *legality* of pressing seamen; on the contrary, I have in a former letter admitted the custom, as now become, by usage immemorial, part of the common law of the land. I had therefore nothing to do with Judge Foster's argument upon the legality of pressing seamen, unless Junius, in his former Letter, had thus expressed himself: "I have read Judge Foster's argument on the
" legality of pressing seamen; and I am so much con-
" vinced by it of the legality of the custom, and the
" inexpediency of abolishing it, that I conclude there
" is no remedy, in the nature of things, for the
" grievance complained of." Had you delivered yourself to that effect, you might, for your justification, have referred me to Judge Foster: but you reasoned in a far different manner; you said. "I see the
" right founded on a necessity, which supersedes all
" argument,

" argument. I see it established by usage immemo-
" rial, and admitted by more than a tacit assent of
" the legislature. I conclude there is no remedy, in
" the nature of things, for the grievance complained
" of; for, if there were, it must long since have been
" redressed."

It was in answer to these words that I affirmed, you did not mean to investigate the truth. You ought to have shewn the necessity was *real*, and could not be prevented; you ought to have proved, that *no customs*, transmitted to us from the ancient arbitrary government of our kings, had been lately declared illegal—before you made your hasty conclusion.

I agree with you, Sir, in your assertion, that General Warrants and Press Warrants have little or no resemblance to each other. The *first* affected the persons and property of the rich, as well as of the poor; every Member of the House of Commons brought the case of Mr. Wilkes home to himself; and General Warrants were consequently, on the resistance, declared illegal. But the case of a Press Warrant is entirely different;—*that* affects but the personal liberty of a poor mechanic, or the very *Scum of the Earth*:—and it is supported by the rich, on two principles; the first is, that if they do not raise men by force, they must procure them by pecuniary means, and pay a bounty out of their purse; the second is, that no rich man foresees in the custom any danger to himself; and, therefore, though Press Warrants have been, as you say, complained of, questioned, and resisted, in a thousand instances, it does not follow, that they have ever met with a fair trial. No pressed man was ever tried by his Peers: I mean by free men, equal to him in his station of life; he is tried and condemned by Justices, Judges,

Judges, and Senators, who can have no feelings for his state. I except, however, some truly patriotic Magistrates of London, who lately and so nobly stood forth the defenders of the liberties of their fellow-citizens.—*Their* conduct proved, that Press Warrants can be effectually resisted, by those who are willing to grant protection to the injured and oppressed. If then we admit the use of them, from ancient custom, to be legal; we must also acknowledge, it is repugnant to the *modern* notions of the rights of man. Our *modern*, and I may add, our *just* ideas of liberty, do not admit of force or violence to be used against the meanest of our fellow-subjects, to detain him, but by the express declaration of the written law of the land, or by customs received as laws, by the long continued assent and non resistance of the people. We cannot say that Press Warrants have entirely that sanction *now*.—

A man, detained by a Press Warrant, has not forfeited his liberty, by the commission of any crime: he has transgressed against no rule of conduct laid down to him; he is a prisoner at the arbitrary will of the king;—but he is *poor*, and that is accounted to him a sufficient crime. The legislature, at least, overlook him as unworthy of attention; no declaratory law is made for his relief; and the Oppression of an ancient arbitrary government is continued to these times. How then shall he hope for protection? —A discontinuance and resistance of the custom, such as were practised by the patriotic Magistrates of London, would protect him, and would soon render a Press Warrant both ineffectual and illegal.

But Junius will tell me, this is all but idle declamation, unless I propose to him some remedy against the grievance complained of, or a preventive for the

necessity

necessity of the case. I should propose it to him, if a Newspaper scheme was the most ready to meet with countenance and support. But Junius must know, how averse Ministers are to adopt any scheme, that does not come forth as if projected by themselves. Does any proposed law, even in the Senate, meet with success, until it be first approved of by a nod of ministerial assent? And to obtain that too, it must be countenanced and supported by some great man. —I cannot, however, conclude, without observing, (in reply to the last paragraph of your letter) that a body of seamen, kept in constant pay, would oppress the merchants, and distress trade, far less, than does the occasional sudden press of all their sailors, when their ships are ready to put to sea.

In the first instance; the burthen on trade, towards defraying the expence, would, in this opulent kingdom, be but small; and, in a very short time, the *first* demand for seamen for the royal fleet, would not be felt by the mercantile ships at all.

In the second instance; the stroke is unexpected, and relief unprovided for. The ships are then detained in port at an extraordinary, unforeseen expence; their cargoes, by that expence, are raised in their original cost; the market, for the sale of those cargoes, is perhaps lost by the detention of the ships; and if those ships are bound to parts, to which they can sail only at particular seasons of the year, their voyages are entirely lost; and both the ships and their cargoes, with the interest on their prime cost, remain dead weights in the merchant's hands.

A few Words more, Sir, and I have done.—You misrepresent me again, when you say, I talk with wonderful indifference about disbanding the army. I only affirmed, that a body of seamen, kept in constant ftant pay, was more neceffary than a ftanding army, for the defence of our ifle; except what is abfolutely requifite for our garrifons abroad, and to guard the body of our king, the reft of the army, I ftill maintain, might give place to an additional number of men for our fleet. I truft in our militia as much as in raw recruits, or in foldiers unaccuftomed to action. What better, after a long peace, would the regular troops be found? Their fuperiority would exift but in the experience of their vetran officers; and in the advantage of that experience the militia might be made to participate; as, at fome future opportuniy, fhall (in our *theory*,) be fufficiently fhewn.

Three LETTERS

From a MERCHANT in LONDON, to his FRIEND at AMSTERDAM; containing a Sketch of BRITISH POLITICS in the Year 1779.

LETTER I.

My dear Friend,

I AM happy to learn, you are returned in good health to Amsterdam. It was so long since I had any accounts of you, that I was really apprehensive some misfortune had prevented you from writing; but how agreeably was I surprized to find, you had at last settled your affairs at Batavia, and were come to pass the remainder of your days in your native country!—You tell me, I have been most punctual in acknowledging the receipt of your remittances, and in my advices about the execution of your orders; yet you cannot help reproaching me for my total omission of public occurrences, and particularly for my unpardonable silence on the subject of British Politics. For what purpose, my dear friend, was I to trouble you, on the other side of the Globe, with the vile, despicable deeds of your antipodes? As long as their High Mightinesses, your States, preserved their neutrality, and lived in Christian peace and

charity

charity with the reſt of mankind, you had no more to do with the Politics of Europe than an inhabitant of the Moon. But you will tell me, *Homo ſum*, &c. that you are a Man, and that nothing, which concerns the happineſs of mankind, can be unintereſting to you. Conſidering the matter in that light, I muſt own myſelf to blame; for ſurely nothing, in the hiſtory of mankind, has ever happened more intereſting to a generous mind, than this cruel and unnatural War with our American Colonies. What man of feeling, what friend to freedom can, without emotion, behold thouſands of lives ſacrificed, to deprive fellow citizens of their liberties, and erect a dominion of the ſword * ?

I ſpeak as a *Citizen of the World*, which you know I have ever conſidered myſelf to be, ſince thoſe ſeven years of my youth I ſo pleaſantly paſſed on the Continent. An early and long reſidence abroad, will generally ſtrip a man of all prejudice in favour of his native country. The ſpot where he was born muſt, in time, be forgotten for the place where he has formed his connections. But a man, guided by the true ſpirit of the Chriſtian Religion, though he had never ſet his foot out of Britain, will regard all mankind as his kindred, to whom no injury muſt be done, even for the benefit of himſelf or his children. I ſhall perhaps be told, the ſcripture has particularly enjoined us to provide for our off-ſpring. True; but though a man with a numerous family be ſtarving, he is in no ſhape permitted to ſteal from his neighbour, in order to ſupport them. If then an individual is not

---

* Such was certainly the object of the War at the beginning of it, and one ſucceſsful Campaign would make us haughtily avow it again.

not allowed to mantain his family by theft or robbery, why should we suppose it lawful for one Nation to rob and plunder another, with a view to aggrandize itself, and debase its rival?

In the eye of the Almighty, the one deed must be as sinful as the other, although custom, with mankind, has not rendered them equally criminal. The number of associates, in guilt, tends to diminish the consciousness of it; but, were we to be early and generally instructed in the principles of universal benevolence, — peace, justice and industry would reign on the earth, nor would barbarous War sweep off to death so many of its inhabitants. The fault lies not in our Religion, as some Authors have insinuated; the blame of those massacres is with us, who do not follow its instructions. Observe, my friend, the people called Quakers; observe your own Nation, who, next to them, live nearest to the pure principles of our Religion: Are they not more temperate, sober, industrious, peaceable and just than the rest of mankind? And are they, on that account the less happy and contented with their present earthly condition? The misfortune then is, that all Nations are not Christians; and War is become at times unavoidable, on the justifiable plea of self-defence, or resistance.

I am making a sermon of a letter; but to prove that I am tolerably well qualified to give you an impartial account of our American dispute, it was not improper to express these sentiments of universal benevolence.

I shall not take up your time in arguing, which Party has justice on its side; for that question is now lost in the natural rancour, or bitter hatred, consequent on a long contest. I shall endeavour to trace
out

out the expediency, or inexpediency of the measures pursued to subjugate America, and the probable advantages or disadvantages that would accrue to this country from such a conquest. In the mean time, the means employed to obtain the end, strongly remind me of a story I have heard of one of your Countrymen, which, though it be not new, I cannot but relate to you, as you have never heard it.

" A Dutch Merchant, on a visit to his Friend in Yorkshire, was taken out one morning on horseback to shew him the diversion of hunting. He saw a very fine run with some excellent Harriers, and the Hare at last was killed. But when he got in at the death, instead of demonstrating any satisfaction at the sport, (of which he had not the least conception), he gravely asked the Master of the Pack, how much each Horse cost him? What were the wages he paid to his Huntsman and Whippers-in? And what was the charge of keeping so many Horses and Hounds? On being told the exorbitant sum.—What! cried he, so much money spent in killing a poor animal of a Hare! Why, give me an order, my friend, and I will send you from Holland as many Hares as you please, and they shall cost you no more than a shilling a-piece, delivered at your own house in town."

If the glory of hunting and worrying our fellow-creatures be our *sport*, thirty millions of money has been properly expended; if, on the contrary, our real object be to *fill the pot*, I think I shall make it appear, that instead of a *substantial* dish, we are providing for ourselves a very dear and a very bitter, but intoxicating Cup of Comfort.

I am, &c.

May 13, 1779.

LETTER II.

Go‍d loves from Whole to Parts; but human soul
Must rise from Individual to the Whole.
Self-love but serves the virtuous mind to wake,
As the small pebble stirs the peaceful lake:
The center mov'd, a circle strait succeeds,
Another still, and still another spreads;
Friend, parent, neighbour, first it will embrace;
His country next; and next all human race.—
        Pope's *Essay on Man*, Ep. 4th.

YOU see, my friend, I have not yet done with my favourite theme of Universal Benevolence. I cannot help dwelling on it; for, to me, Benevolence appears to be the most God-like of Virtues; and it is certainly the virtue that, of all others, the most distinguishes a Christian from a Jew, a Heathen, or a Turk —But let us not misinterpret our poet in the lines I have quoted. He did not surely mean to recommend it as a virtue in mankind, to act contrary to one of the great attributes of God. He only meant to say, that, according to the *imperfection* of our nature, the human soul, in its benevolence, must rise from individual to the whole; for it is a weakness, and not a virtue, in us, to mete out our love according to friendship and consanguinity, and not according to the respect due to merit where-ever to be found.——Agreeable to my notion, then, I would compare the influence of benevolence on the human mind, to the touch of the finger on a musical glass, the tone of which is full in proportion as its circumference is wide; and whose sound gradually decreases as the stroke is given nearer the center, till, at last, the vibration becomes totally dead. The selfish man, with his narrow, contracted mind, may be industrious, may be an affectionate husband, a tender parent, and, as an individual, a most useful member of the community; but it is impossible that he should ever make an upright minister of state. He can have no political opinion that will not be biassed by an attention to his own private interest. The public good is but a second consideration; his first concern will be to keep himself in place.—Mr. Pitt, who paid little attention to the œconomy of his family, had his mind wholly occupied with national affairs; and Great-Britain, under him, rose to the summit of her greatness. Other ministers have been accumulating wealth, or enriching their relations, while the kingdom has declined to a most despicable state. In abilities we may grant them to be equal, but in independence they surely were not. The one would have an opinion of his own, and acted of himself; the others are guided by a *Cabinet*, and must submissively do as they are bid.——But, though Pitt, as a *Patriot*, deserves the highest commendation, as a *Christian* he was liable to blame. His benevolence did not extend to the *outermost* circle; for, in the very last words he uttered, he breathed against the French a spirit of hatred and revenge.

I have said, that universal benevolence is the distinguishing characteristic of a Christian; I may also add, it is the most striking feature in the character of a Whig. As, in the government of these kingdoms in particular, a Whig is distinguished from a Tory, by supporting the rights of the People against the arbitrary encroachments of the Crown; so is he also to be known by his mild and benevolent conduct

to

to mankind in general, in oppofition to that haughty, tyrannical fpirit of government, by which a Tory, if he had his will, would rule the whole nations of the globe. That this fpirit has been too prevalent in the caufes and conduct of the American War, I fhall hereafter demonftrate to you in a fummary account of it. But my attention is at prefent drawn off, by fome late occurrences, which you will naturally be more anxious to be informed of.

Since my laft letter, an account is arrived from Georgia of great fuccefs attending the Britifh arms in that colony. As, however, we are referred for fome particulars to a verbal report to be delivered by Col. Campbell, and as it is uncertain whether the whole of that report has been publifhed, we are left to believe that fome fecret diftreffes (fuch as we read of in the Howe papers) have followed the detachment in Georgia.

By fuch arts as thefe, my friend, has the nation been led on from one campaign to another, fince firft they were told to advance, becaufe they had paffed the Rubicon; a reafon for proceeding, which logically meant but this—Becaufe you have plunged into the river, my lads, you muft attempt to fwim over, although certain to perifh in the middle of it.

We have had much talk of the mediation of Spain to make up matters between France and us. But I very much doubt thefe appearances of friendfhip are but blinds to cover fome approaching attack *.——— Men are willing to believe what they fervently wifh to happen; and well do the French know, our Miniftry wifh for a peace.

You

---

* The Spanifh Manifefto appeared foon after this was written.

You will have heard of the Debates which have happened about turning out one of our Ministers, for misapplying the public money. It was shewn in Parliament, that the sum, voted for the Navy for the last seven years, exceeded the sum, voted for the same term of years last war, by near seven millions.

But the Minister, in his defence, affirmed, that he had now in the Dock-Yards materials to last for three years; which, on a moderate computation, we ought to allow to amount in value to the above sum of seven millions; for which the Minister will shortly produce seventy good ships of the line, each ship only valued at 100,000 l. sterling: Then where is there any embezzlement? Like the Miser in Moliere's Play who reckoned all the enjoyments of life as already in his possession, because he had wherewithal to purchase them safely locked up in his strong box, our Ministers, wisely considering that ships are liable to decay, to be taken, sunk or lost, have carefully hoarded up those seven millions—equivalent to some grand fleet to be hereafter at their pleasure produced.

Notwithstanding this formidable fleet we are flattered with, I perceive our Minister at the Hague has delivered a Memorial to your State, or rather a Prohibition to their Subjects, against the transporting to France any naval or military stores in your neutral vessels. This is now openly anulling the treaty, on the faith of which you traded, and the benefit of which we ourselves enjoyed at the time it was made, when *we* were at Peace, and *you* were at War with the French Nation. Do you, then, observe it at your peril. You must acknowledge, my friend, that your States have long been guided by a false œconomy; for, instead of being provided with a powerful fleet, to throw into the scale as you should think proper, to keep the balance even,—your ships have been idly rotting in their harbours; and, instead of being courted and respected by both Parties, you are insulted as being useful to neither.

LETTER III.

IF I were to write for a newspaper, and wished to gratify the curiosity of the people, I would treat of nothing but temporary subjects, or the mere idle talk of the day. But writing to you, my friend, who are desirous to form an opinion of what is likely to happen, from your judgment of what has already past, I will refer you, for *recent* occurrences, to *other* informants, and will endeavour to give you a little abridged account, or *Histoire raisonnee*, of some past events connected with our American affairs. Nor would this be altogether useless in any of our public papers; for, since the commencement of this American war, thousands of my fellow-subjects are grown up to manhood, and are entered into life, who can have no other conception of the original dispute, than what they were taught, by their parents or teachers, implicitly to believe. Add to this, the English are a people who, in public as well as in private concerns, are universally allowed to be too generally guided by the caprice of the day. It is therefore become requisite, frequently to remind them of their true interests, and as earnestly to persuade them to a

deliberate

deliberate review of every occurrence in their national affairs. To rouse the *passions* of the people is but to wish to break the windows of a Minister;—to convince their *reason*, is to raise an effectual opposition to his wicked measures.

If you were to cast your eye, my friend, over the list of our privy counsellors, you would be astonished to think that our affairs have, for some years past, been so very unfortunate. But your surprise will cease, when I tell you, that every matter of national importance is first canvassed in a *secret cabinet* of *King's Friends*, who suffer none to be summoned to the privy council, but such as are known to be well affected to *their* government.—I must further inform you, that these *King's Friends* are *Tories* to a man; and you will remember, in my last letter, my definition of a Tory, to be a person who not only elevates the prerogative of his King, to the debasement of the rights of the people, but who would willingly enslave the whole human race, and make them to be subservient to his own will and pleasure. These men stick faithfully together; and whatever is done by any of them, is acknowledged only as the act of the whole council. The King can do no wrong; so sayeth the law, and *he* must not be censured. Nay, for so much as falls under his immediate inspection, his Majesty is greatly to be commended. I mean for the regulation of the army, which, in no reign, has had more attention paid to it. We have it under the hand of one of his Majesty's *Tory* Ministers, that " every officer who distinguishes himself, and is the " means of advancing the *glory of his Majesty's arms*, " may be certain that his services will not pass un- " noticed by his most gracious master *." To teach an

---

* See Lord George Germaine's Letter to Sir William Howe, March 3, 1777, in the Parliamentary Register, for 1779, p. 393.

an army to maſſacre at the will of their Sovereign, the *Grand Monarch* himſelf could not ſpeak in terms of better encouragement. Thus do we ſee, that, with a true Tory, the ſafety of the ſtate, and the ſervice of his country, are objects not worth the mentioning. The *glory of his Majeſty's arms* is diſplayed as the only ſtandard of a Britiſh ſoldier.—*Liberty* and *Property*, ye old, tattered, but honourable colours! ye ſhall not be entirely deſerted!—there is ſtill a reſerve for you in the militia of England.

The King, then, being ſo commendably attentive to the proſperity of the *army*, 'tis preſumed that his Majeſty truſts the management of his *civil* affairs entirely to his miniſters: but has the Firſt Lord of the Treaſury done any thing amiſs? He declares himſelf to be but a Clerk of the Council. Have the Secretaries of State, the Secretary of War, the Firſt Lord of the Admiralty, been charged with any miſconduct? Not one of them will acknowledge that he acts of himſelf. They are all the mere tools of the ſame council.

Formerly, my friend, a Miniſter could be impeached and puniſhed for the miſmanagement of his own department; it being *then* allowed, that as the King could do no wrong, no wrong could ever be done, unleſs by his inſtruments, the Miniſters; but *now* the caſe is altered; no Miniſter will confeſs that he acts of himſelf, or that he is reſponſible for any thing. So that if you lodge an accuſation againſt any one man, no redreſs can be obtained; for he is ſure to play againſt you the old-faſhioned game of hunting the ſlipper. When, therefore, you underſtand that our affairs are governed by a *Cabal*, and are not concerted by the free, unbiaſſed opinions of the Members of the Privy Council, your wonder will ceaſe at beholding

holding them fo badly conducted. But what has become, you'll fay, of the grand inqueft of the Nation, that ought to controul or rectify every thing! Alas! it is a *pitiful* Parliament that has approved of every meafure, out of compaffion to an unfortunate Minifter. When you fhall have farther examined the principles of thefe Tories, who have got both the legiflative and executive powers into their management, you will be lefs furprized that no reformation or amendment has yet been effected. Far from confidering himfelf to be only the Steward of the public, a *Tory* Minifter, with unparalleled felf-fufficiency, erects himfelf into a mighty and infallible Ruler of the People, who are fubmiffively to obey him, as the propereft Judge of whatever is requifite for their public happinefs. According to him, whofoever pretends to have an opinion of his own in politics, and to differ from him in his ideas of government, is a factious or rebellious fubject; an enemy to his King and country.

Into the hands of *fuch* men did our good King fall, in his youth; and the confequence has been, that, transferring the patriarchial power of a parent, over his own family, to the government of a free and high-fpirited people,—he has, fince the firft three years of his reign, had a conftant ftruggle between the will of his Cabinet and the oppofite opinions of his Subjects, who as conftantly exercifed their old accuftomed rights of fcrutinizing the meafures judged the moft expedient for the public benefit.

It will fave me much writing, my dear friend, if you will take leifure to read the two volumes of *Junius's Letters*, which I have fent you by the laft *London Trader;* for nothing, that I or any other fcribbler can offer, will give fuch a complete notion
of

of the Politics of this reign. When you have acquired a proper knowledge of thofe Politics, we will then proceed to the rife and progrefs of our American Difpute; which will appear to you as natural as that a fhower fhall fall after a fquall of wind.

I cannot, however, conclude this Letter without replying to your obfervation, "that I muft be un-"grateful, indeed, to the Government that protects "me, no, to wifh fuccefs to its arms in every pur-"fuit."—I acknowledge no gratitude to be due for a protection which is my right. Every member of a community furrenders to Government a *part* of his natural liberty, to be protected in the free exercife of the *reft*; and if the perfons entrufted with the adminiftering that protection, fhould prove either negligent, incapable, or unjuft, I may, agreeable to the law of nature, at my peril refift;—firft, with my pen; and, when opinions are collected, as readily with my fword. The *Revolution* fhews this to be juftifiable doctrine; and I am not yet difpofed to relinquifh my right.—But why fhould I not be a friend to Great Britain, unlefs I wifh profperity to every mad enterprize of its Minifters of State? As their wifdom is not infallible, I may be allowed to diffent from their opinions, and may fhew the love of my country equally clear in wifhing well to any improvement which an individual fhall undertake. Sir James Lowther, for inftance, is employing above four hundred men, in banking out the fea from two thoufand acres of land, at the mouth of the river Dee. As a friend to my country, I muft wifh his embankment to fucceed; for there will be an acquifition of fo many acres of valuable land to the King-without one drop of human blood being laid to his charge. If, on the contrary, his project fhould fail,

fail, the labour of so many people, being lost, is so much money thrown useless into the sea. But we have this comfort left, that these four hundred men are still saved to the State, and may, at any other work, be usefully employed.—Mark the difference, my friend, in our *American* plan.—Many thousands of men have been employed, in an attempt to conquer a Country that we could never keep, and to enslave a people who had never done us harm. We have not only lost that Country, but, in the death of the Soldiers who are slain, as well as in the vain occupation of them who are left, we have lost the useful labour of so many men.—I wish they had been employed in embanking the Goodwin Sands!

August 3d, 1779.

FINIS.

ERRATA.

Page 59, Line 15, for *requites* read requires
——104,——24, for *premiditated* read premeditated
——106,——34, erase *In private Life,*
——115,——23, for *uprn* read upon
——135,—— 9, erase *their*
——138,——16, for *vanty* read vanity
——141,——18, for *devont* read devout
——153,—— 3, for *perodical* read periodical
——169,——12, for *dimunition* read diminution
——235,—— 7, for *perodical* read periodical
——308,—— 9, for *their* read there
——326,—— 6, for *but* read while

www.ingramcontent.com/pod-product-compliance
Lightning Source LLC
Chambersburg PA
CBHW020229240426
43672CB00006B/467